AFFLICTING THE

COMFORTABLE

West Virginia and Appalachia
A series edited by Ronald L. Lewis

Volume 4

Afflicting the Comfortable

JOURNALISM AND POLITICS

IN WEST VIRGINIA

Thomas F. Stafford

WEST VIRGINIA UNIVERSITY PRESS

MORGANTOWN 2005

West Virginia University Press, Morgantown 26506

© 2005 West Virginia University Press

All rights reserved.

First edition 2005 by West Virginia University Press

10 09 08 07 06 05   8 7 6 5 4 3 2 1

ISBN 1-933202-04-1 [cloth]

Library of Congress Cataloguing-in-Publication Data

Afflicting the Comfortable: Journalism and Politics in West Virginia
xx, 332 p.   25 cm.

1. West Virginia—Politics and government—1950–1990. 2. American newspapers—West Virginia History—20th century. 3. Journalism—West Virginia History—20th Century. 4. Journalism—West Virginia History—1950–1990. 5. American newspapers. I. Title. II. Stafford, Thomas F., 1914–1993.
IN PROCESS

Library of Congress Control Number: 2005934484

Jacket design by David Alcorn
Interior design by Than Saffel
Printed in U.S.A. by Thomson-Shore

THIS BOOK IS DEDICATED

to the memory

of W. E. Chilton,

publisher of

The Charleston Gazette,

friend, employer,

and sparring partner,

AND TO

Margaret Wilson Bledsoe Stafford,

my wife of more than fifty years,

my toughest critic,

and staunchest supporter,

with gratitude

for the enrichment brought

to both my life and work.

Contents

PART THREE

PART FOUR

Foreword

BY RONALD L. LEWIS

THE YEAR 1968 WAS A "BRUTE OF A YEAR," Thomas Stafford writes in his memoir, *Afflicting the Comfortable: Journalism and Politics in West Virginia*. During that year, the USS Pueblo was seized by the North Koreans; in Vietnam the Viet Cong launched the Tet Offensive; Martin Luther King, Jr. was assassinated in Memphis and riots broke out in over one hundred cities; Robert Kennedy was assassinated two months later in Los Angeles; President Lyndon Johnson told the world that he would not seek another term; Columbia students seized university buildings to protest the Vietnam War; and antiwar demonstrators were clubbed in the streets by police outside the Democratic National Convention site in Chicago.

1968 was also a "brute of a year" for West Virginia politicians. On February 14 the U.S. Attorney for the Southern District of West Virginia returned indictments charging former Governor William Wallace Barron and five other colleagues for "conspiracy to carry on bribery activities involving state government." The press immediately dubbed them the "Secret Six"; and their indictment, the "St. Valentine's Day Massacre." The indictment charged that during Barron's term as governor, from 1960 to 1964, Barron and his cohorts set up dummy corporations in Ohio and Florida, and then told prospective state vendors that they should pay these corporations to "help" the suppliers to secure state contracts. Once done, the men rigged the state bidding process to reward these suppliers with contracts. All of the payoff money was to be transferred to the Invest Right Corporation, based in Florida, and eventually the six men would divide the money equally amongst themselves.

West Virginians were shocked at the scale of corruption in the Barron administration; many of those involved carried over these corrupt practices into the administration of Barron's successor, Hulett C. Smith, apparently without his knowledge. Between 1965 and 1968 thirteen public officials, along with five of their friends, relatives, and business associates, were convicted and sent to prison on charges of bribery, conspiracy, tax evasion, or falsification of records. Among them were members of Barron's inner circle, including his executive assistant, the state treasurer, the attorney general, commissioner of the Department of Finance and Administration, the liquor control commissioner, the commissioner of the Department of Motor Vehicles, the state road commissioner and his assistant, and the commissioner of the Department of Welfare. Barron himself was convicted of jury tampering and sentenced to five years in prison.

The indictment, trial, and conviction of these men came about through the tenacious efforts of investigative journalist Thomas F. Stafford, and his memoir is largely taken up with his investigation and revelation of this corrupt scheme. Stafford was born in Grafton, West Virginia, in 1914, earned a degree in journalism from West Virginia University in 1936, and then became a reporter for *The Raleigh Register* in Beckley. When the United States entered World War II, he enlisted in the Navy and served as an officer aboard a rescue-and-salvage ship which saw action at the battles of Leyte Gulf and Linhuyan Gulf. By war's end he commanded his own rescue and salvage ship.

After the war, Stafford returned to the *Register* as its editor, and began his long and eventful career as a political and investigative reporter. In 1954, he joined the staff of *The Charleston Gazette* as a political reporter, writer of the "Affairs of State" column, and as associate editor. He resigned from the *Gazette* in 1966, at the advice of his doctor, to take a less stressful position as clerk of the federal district court in Elkins. So many years of investigating and exposing government corruption left him burned out, but "worst of all, I had become cynical and jaded. I had begun to wonder if there was any integrity in government and the business world . . . I had begun to question my own objectivity as a journalist."

No wonder. He had exposed an almost continuous string of corruption cases involving business and state government employees, and nothing seemed to change, only the names and the dates. Barron's Invest Right scandal was only the most egregious abuse of public trust. Most cases involved simple human greed and avarice. The State Road Commission alone kept his typewriter busy on stories about rigged contracts, payoffs, and kickbacks, which had become an established way of doing business. The State Road Commission was not the only source of corruption. Stafford found that nearly every point of exchange between business and government had problems with graft, including pharmaceuticals, automobiles, food, office supplies, and liquor. Nevertheless, seldom was anyone prosecuted; however, U.S. Congressman Robert H. Mollohan paid a heavy price for his greed. While serving as superintendent of the Industrial School for Boys at Pruntytown, Mollohan had accepted twenty thousand dollars to look the other way while a coal operator stripped the land. Mollohan was a candidate for governor in 1956, and the *Gazette*'s revelation of his audacity led to his defeat and the election of his opponent, Cecil Underwood. Stafford believed that the corruption during the administrations of Governor Arch Moore, who served an unprecedented three terms in office (1968–1974, 1984–1988), were just a continuation of the misgovernment of West Virginia which had prevailed for decades. In 1990 Moore was convicted of extortion and sentenced to more than five years in federal prison. Several members of his administration were also convicted and imprisoned.

Finally galvanized into action, the legislature authorized the formation of the Purchasing Practices and Procedures Commission in 1970. During the commission's short history, it brought 107 indictments against thirty-two individuals on charges of bribery and conspiracy involving state purchasing practices. Although the West Virginia Supreme Court of Appeals defanged the commission by removing its enforcement powers, and charges against those indicted were dropped, the momentum had finally swung toward reform. Consequently, politicians took the opportunity to revamp the PPPC, and it evolved into the Commission on Special Investigations. Eventually, an accounting system was implemented to exercise control over state purchasing. Stafford was, therefore, instrumental in fundamentally changing the way the state does business. Stafford had left the *Gazette* by the time these charges took place, but he was pleased that the political fire ignited by his Invest Right investigation had produced tangible reforms. That good government required constant monitoring, however, was subsequently proven by Michael Carey, U.S. attorney for Southern West Virginia. He released a list of cases prosecuted by his office between 1884 and 1990 involving sixty-nine county, state, and federal officials.

The greatest value of *Afflicting the Comfortable*, however, is not as an exposé, but rather as a political history of West Virginia between 1945 and 1993, the year of Stafford's death. Lamentably, there is no standard history of the period, and Stafford was conscious that, as a reporter, he was constructing a historical record.

Print journalists carried an important responsibility, he observed, because radio and television had "turned the newspaper into a chronicle of the day's intelligence . . . the recorder of history at the moment before it becomes history." Protecting the identity of sources was not simply a matter of protecting the press's First Amendment rights, Stafford believed, but to "serve the governed, not the governors," paraphrasing U.S. Supreme Court Justice Hugo Black. If citizens were intimidated into silence and had no check on the misuse of power, democracy itself was threatened.

Good historians link local details into the larger social context, and Stafford does this effortlessly. Corruption in West Virginia, therefore, was not rooted in the flawed character of its people; it was the result of inadequate regulatory and enforcement mechanisms.

The reason corruption was particularly serious during the period from the 1960s through the 1980s was that it was driven into the light by reformers and because so much money was funneled into the state from Washington through the antipoverty programs of the Great Society.

The unprecedented influx of federal funds was accelerated by a powerful state delegation that held strategic positions of power in Congress, Jennings Randolph as chairman of the House Public Works Committee, and Robert C.

Byrd as a member and then chairman of the Senate Appropriations Committee. Awash in money, and without the proper bureaucratic safeguards, corruption seems inevitable.

Mountaineers may always be free, but Stafford shows just how dependent we are on outside economic and political forces beyond our control. Thus, the Appalachian Regional Commission spent large sums of money in West Virginia building infrastructure during the '60s and '70s, and the state's economy boomed.

When Ronald Reagan was elected President in 1980, however, he seriously crippled the ARC by slashing its funding. Just as the federal money was drying up, the state's aging steel and glass industries lost out to cheaper foreign competition and closed; coal mining modernized but employed ever fewer miners. The result was a serious recession during the last decades of the twentieth century. The state had to find a blueprint for self-help, but the problem, Stafford points out, is that the people "wanted more than they could pay for, and their interest was almost exclusively local."

Stafford, the journalist as historian, revels in the details of his story but seeks their broader, and deeper, meaning. He traverses the sometimes shadowy ground between journalism and history in his memoir, almost seamlessly shifting from the first-person present tense of the participant to the third-person past tense of the non-participant observer. The memoir is organized chronologically by gubernatorial administration, but it is much more a survey of government mismanagement in West Virginia. Until historians reconstruct this period of West Virginia history, Stafford's memoir will be required reading for those who would seek to understand these times.

Stafford retired as federal district court clerk in 1984. Throughout his adult life he was deeply involved in the civic affairs of his community and state. In 1989, on the fiftieth anniversary of the founding of the Perley Isaac Reed School of Journalism at West Virginia University, Stafford was presented a special award for his career in journalism and service to the university. The State of West Virginia could have done the same for helping to bring to justice those officials who abused the public trust.

Stafford died in June 1993. It was his wish that *Afflicting the Comfortable* would be published by his alma mater. We are pleased that, through the efforts of his daughter, Margo Stafford, West Virginia University Press can fulfill his wish. We have consciously chosen to regard this well-written memoir as a historical document. As such, *Afflicting the Comfortable* appears here as Stafford wrote it and without editing. It is not only an exciting read, but a significant contribution to West Virginia's political history.

Ronald L. Lewis

West Virginia University

September 2005

Preface

"Government corruption was not invented in the State of West Virginia.
But there are people who contend that West Virginia officials have done
more than their share over the years to develop state-of-the-art techniques in vote theft, contract kickbacks, influence peddling and good
old-fashioned bribery, extortion, fraud, tax evasion and outright stealing."

The New York Times, 1990

"Can anybody govern West Virginia?"

Business Week, 1990

OVER THE YEARS MORE THAN ONE PERSON has urged me to write a book on West
Virginia politics, particularly on my experiences with the Invest Right scandal, one of the most politically unsettling news stories ever to appear in this
state and one with far-reaching ramifications. In the mid-1980s Dr. George
Parkinson, then curator of the West Virginia and Regional History Collection
at West Virginia University, contacted me about putting together my personal
papers and recollections into a kind of memoir, a behind-the-scenes look at
my efforts to track down a story of government corruption that spread further
and deeper than I had originally imagined and that eventually brought down
a governor and other highly placed officials.

Trying to tell this story has not been a pleasant experience. I have had to
relate the actions of people I knew and liked, several of them close friends,
who chose the wrong path in their quest for personal and professional success.
The investigative reporter, contrary to popular belief, is rarely a cold-blooded
bastard. In fact, at the beginning of my career I had no burning commitment
to newspapering. When I graduated from journalism school in the middle of

the Depression, all I wanted was to find a job and earn a living. But publishers bought their help as cheaply as possible, and few of them wanted to bring a college graduate into their newsrooms.

Only Charles Hodel, a crippled orphan who rose through the ranks to ownership of a five-newspaper operation in the two Virginias, was willing to gamble on me. And it wasn't until editor Raiford Watkins, a former Associated Press bureau chief, assigned me to the courthouse beat that I began to understand the meaning of the First Amendment.

A reporter doesn't easily develop the kind of toughness the job demands. Each of us, regardless of his or her position, has a basic human desire to be liked. But this desire unfortunately collides head-on with journalistic commitment and integrity for the reporter who follows the mandate of *The New York Times*, to write "all the news that's fit to print."

Supreme Court Justice Hugo Black said it best when he wrote that the First Amendment gives the press the protection it must have to fulfill its essential role in our democracy. The duty of the press is to serve the governed, not the governors, he advised, and only a free and unrestrained press can expose duplicity and deception in government.

My first lesson in adversarial journalism came when I was directed by editor Watkins to remain in the room during a county board of education meeting until I was dismissed by voice vote at the beginning of the customary executive session. When the time came for my first real test of authority, I timidly asked for a formal vote on my dismissal by the full board. The members acceded to my request, two of them angrily, but I was not only permitted to remain that particular evening but was never again banished from one of their meetings.

It was a heady experience. I felt that I had earned my spurs, or whatever badge a reporter earns when he moves into that small fraternity of journalists who make it their practice to challenge the power structure when the occasion warrants. It was only a small step, but I was on my way. I was sued for libel three times, was a central figure in more grand jury investigations than I care to remember, and suffered the slings and arrows of countless politicians and powerbrokers for a quarter century, but I never altered my course, although the toll it exacted eventually forced me to give up journalism, albeit reluctantly and only after deep soul-searching.

No course in adversarial journalism was taught while I was in school, and those who chose it as a career discipline were few in number. In fact, I found no books on the subject until I discovered *The Autobiography of Lincoln Steffens*, the life story of an Ivy League dilettante who turned to the streets to reveal the agonies of the underprivileged in an explosive series of articles about corruption in America's larger cities. To me it was a mind-boggling book. It impressed me so much that I felt I could never again find satisfaction in any other area of journalism.

Most information reported in the media, aside from weddings, deaths, sports, club events, and the news coming off the "police beat," originates with statements issued by individuals, government officials, business establishments, or press agents looking for favorable publicity for themselves or their clients. This is commonly called the "bread and butter" news that flows through the newsroom in a never-ending stream.

Next is the news behind the handouts, press conferences and carefully orchestrated texts, what's known as "background"—off-the-record comments and non-attributable information. This is where the reporter does his hard-news writing and gives meaning to the First Amendment and its free-press proviso.

There is, finally, a last category of news: the perceptive, investigative, and sometimes abrasive probing for facts, the sort that brings into play all of the hard-won skills and instincts a reporter has had to develop in order to elicit newsworthy data. Few newspapers, particularly in West Virginia, practice this brand of reportage, but in my time I had the good fortune to work for two of them, *The Raleigh Register* and *The Charleston Gazette*. Each in its own way had a passion for delving into official wrongdoing, and for twenty years my principal assignment as a reporter and editor was to chronicle the misdeeds of West Virginia's mighty.

In the performance of his assignment, the journalist has the freedom to go wherever he needs to go in the quest for truth. He has the right and duty to ask an individual for information regardless of whether that individual is a major advertiser or community leader. But, above all, the journalist needs to be guided by a sense of fairness and common decency, and to make accuracy his benchmark. He carries no special charge investing him with the right to destroy respected institutions or personal reputations willfully and without a painstaking search for facts. The journalist can be either a powerful advocate for right or an instrument of wrong, depending on how he handles his assignment.

The sort of journalism I practiced did not generate the kind of interest created by the Watergate investigation some years later. The stage where I plied my craft was not as large; few of the players were national figures. I wrote my largest story in a small Appalachian state some distance from Washington, DC, yet I found that without contact with that center of national power I could never have wrapped up all the loose ends into a tidy, incriminating package.

In the end, it was a far cry from what I had expected as I naively toiled through my courses in journalism and political science as a college student. Sadly, I know that the same kind of events are still being played out in one form or another in the halls of government across America. Nothing really changes but the names and the dates.

Perhaps that's why I put off writing this story for twenty-five years.

Thomas F. Stafford
Bearhunter Mountain
Elkins, West Virginia

Acknowledgments

I WOULD LIKE TO OFFER my thanks to those persons and institutions that helped me assemble the information that went into this book.

I owe a large debt of gratitude to the late *Charleston Gazette* publisher W. E. "Ned" Chilton, who authorized the use of records and files at the *Gazette*, and editor James E. Haught, who pointed me in the right direction when I was trying to locate the information I needed from those files.

I also must thank the historians who helped me along the way, most notably John G. Morgan, author of *West Virginia Governors*, and Otis K. Rice, author of *West Virginia: A History*. I relied heavily on the historical data so ably prepared in earlier years by Drs. Charles H. Ambler and Festus P. Summers; on "West Virginia State and Local Government," a treatise begun by Dr. Carl M. Frashure and completed in 1963 by a West Virginia University Bureau of Government research team of political science professors composed of Claude J. Davis, Eugene R. Elkins, Mavis M. Reeves, William R. Ross, and Albert L. Sturm; and various editions of the *West Virginia Blue Book*, without which no writer could assemble the necessary information for a book of this genre.

Special thanks go to the late Theodore H. White for the delightful passage about West Virginians in his book, *The Making of the President, 1960*. I found him as charming as he discovered the people of this state to be when he interviewed me during the 1960 presidential campaign.

I also utilized the work of those in Washington who prepared the report, "Rivers and Harbors—Flood Control 1962 (Guyandot River Basin, W.Va.)," and of those who prepared the House of Representatives report on "Right-of-Way Acquisition Practices in West Virginia" in 1962.

I am particularly indebted to some very helpful people in the public libraries at Clarksburg, Charleston, and Elkins, as well as at West Virginia University, the West Virginia Division of Culture and History's Archives and History Library, and the United States District Court for Northern West Virginia.

Finally, special thanks go to my wife, Margaret, whose encouragement was so essential during my years of research and writing; to my Pulitzer Prize-winning brother, Charles, for doing a sharp read of the manuscript; to Evelyn Harris, political science professor at the University of Charleston and an expert on government affairs, often recruited as a member of special study groups at the state Capitol, for an exhaustive review of my manuscript; and to my daughter Margo, former associate editor of *Goldenseal* magazine, who toiled uncomplainingly over preparation of the manuscript and who served as editor in trying to give the finished product better continuity and what is hoped to be improved objectivity.

Introduction

*"Wooden-headedness . . . is a factor that plays
a remarkably large role in government."*
Barbara W. Tuchman

IT STARTED OUT like a bad detective novel. I walked out of the bar and down the hall, passing a man who slipped me a large, brown envelope. We spoke cordially but briefly, about nothing of importance; then I went out the door and down the steps to the street on a cool October evening in 1962.

The setting for this little drama was the Charleston Press Club, gone now but at the time one of the most popular and exclusive watering holes in all of West Virginia. The messenger who had handed me the envelope was a high state official, a trusted friend, and a man respected everywhere for his competence and integrity.

It had been one of those days when nothing seemed to go right. All the people I had called in an effort to develop news stories were out of their offices or out of town. When I finally found something I thought I could use for the next day's *Gazette*, it was so mundane that I had difficulty putting the facts on paper with any kind of continuity. Frustrated, and still without a story for the next morning's edition, I had called my wife to tell her I'd be late for dinner. Although this was far from a rare occurrence, she was understandably annoyed with me since she'd planned one of my favorite meals. And then this, my fleeting venture into the world of cloak and dagger, which appeared at the time to be an exercise in futility. It seemed a fitting end to a worthless day.

After taking the envelope back to my office, I opened it to find only a copy of the same report on state purchasing practices that I had received a few days before. I was angry, puzzled—and intrigued. Wondering if perhaps the seeds of a larger story had been somehow buried in the report, I opened it to the title page and found scribbled there three words: "Invest Right Corp." That was all.

As it turned out many months later, I had before me the barest essentials of the most complex and challenging story I would ever write, the progenitor of an escalating series of events that ultimately would send a governor and other state officials to prison and bring down a decades-old political machine.

The printed report I had in my hands had been a year in preparation. It had grown out of a resolution passed by the 1961 legislature, the purpose of which was to bring an end to then-rampant rumors hinting at improprieties in state government purchasing practices, and to prove that all was well in the state Division of Purchases. Millions of dollars worth of contracts, for everything from paint brushes to snowplows, from stationery printing to interstate highway construction, are handled by that one office every year, and the opportunities for thievery and misconduct are limitless.

I had been given this second copy of the report with its cryptic notation only after making several phone calls to various members of the committee responsible for issuing it. No one wanted to talk to me about it, but eventually I hit pay dirt. One individual finally promised to give me something that he said could lead me to actual corrupt practices and to the names of those at the highest levels of government who were responsible.

His promise, however, had not come easily. I had to plead, badger, and cajole before he eventually agreed to meet with me and turn over the allegedly incriminating information. He absolutely refused to see me at his office. He was emphatic about the method of delivery, and he bound me to a promise never to reveal his name or to even hint to anyone about his identity during his lifetime. He had good reason for his insistence on this protection. His name was Julius Singleton, and at the time he was the Speaker of the House of Delegates.

After all that, I still had only the words "Invest Right Corp.," which was little more than I had started with. The actual committee report hinted at the possible existence of a conspiracy to subvert and circumvent establishing purchasing practices, but there was no supporting evidence to buttress this allegation.

In the days between the release of the report to the press and my evening encounter at the Press Club, I had written a column in which I had said:

> *This report, more than a year in preparation, devotes 57 pages to a discussion of state purchasing policies and practices. It is bound well, it reads well and it alludes to possible wrongdoing. But it studiously avoids going any further— either to prove or disprove such wrongdoing. In choosing to be gray rather than black or white, it has succeeded only in making many people suspect— from Governor Barron down to the youngest and least experienced buyer in the division of purchases.*

In carefully nonaccusatory wording, the report said, " . . . the committee believes after reviewing certain files . . . that it appears that favored vendors have among their stock-holders individuals prominent in political life, and that that favoritism may result in a loss to the state." There was no definitive information to give validity to this statement, no listing of names, firms, or products sold.

The report leaned heavily on purchasing embarrassments uncovered by the two Charleston newspapers, the *Gazette* and the *Daily Mail*, during the early days of the Barron administration. It discussed pharmaceuticals, automobiles, food, and office equipment, and quoted from news stories on these subjects. Otherwise, the report was short on facts and developed little on its own. As I said in my column in summary:

> *This is odd indeed. The legislative auditor's office devoted more than a year to investigating purchasing, yet, as the facts bear out, when the final report was written, it was built around information developed by inexperienced*

investigators [reporters] rather than that developed by its own large and well-
paid staff. There is also this to be said. The auditor's office has the full force
of legal authority behind it while the newspapers have only their persuasive
talents and the knowledge their reporters have of the governmental process.

For reasons never made clear, the special committee on purchasing practices adopted the same policy, which some years before had been employed by
a similar investigative body empowered by legislative resolution to look into
wrongdoing in the Highway Department during the administration of Governor Okey L. Patteson.

The published report in that earlier instance was similarly replete with
data unsupported by names, dates, and places. It, too, was a fraud, and not until I took the matter of full disclosure to the highest legislative authority, Senate
President Ralph J. Bean, was I able to examine the privileged version of that
earlier report and publish its contents.

Other such reports, equally important in their purpose, have been released by special legislative committees over the years, and in all too many
cases, these reports also have been lacking in the facts needed to correct the
wrongs their sponsors hoped to address through investigation and exposure.
Government officials at every level too often believe that the public is best
served when it is kept ignorant of the realities of governance.

While driving home that evening I began wondering if the taxpayers were
being treated to yet another act of governmental sleight-of-hand.

The only thing I had going for me after examining the second copy of the
committee report was a gut feeling that I was onto something significant. My
job was to take the hints, allusions, and innuendo sprinkled through the legislative committee's report and turn them into cold, hard, unimpeachable facts.

The next morning I went to the secretary of state's office to ask if any
documents attesting to the existence of an Invest Right Corporation had been
filed. Registration is a requirement of West Virginia corporations and often
is the practice for those created in other states. As I expected, there was no
record of an Invest Right.

I realized then that I was faced with a task of potentially monumental and time-consuming proportions. Somewhere in America there had to be a corporate filing for this mysterious legal creature, but in what state?

I turned first to Delaware, where so many major commercial entities choose to incorporate because of that state's favorable treatment, and made a fast check through the Associated Press office in Dover. In those years the *Gazette* contracted with the AP for the use of its services, in turn giving the AP first rights to any news generated in our circulation area. Unfortunately, nobody at the Capitol in Dover had ever heard of Invest Right.

Next I had to decide which of the remaining forty-eight states I should turn to in seeking an answer. Inquiries like the one I had just made were costly, and while the *Gazette* was generous with its funds for investigative writing, I had nothing concrete to prove that I was onto a worthwhile story.

Perhaps if I had had the benefit of those courses in investigative journalism techniques then being taught at Columbia University, I might had known what my next move should be. But when my former publisher, Charles Hodel, had offered me the opportunity of attending Columbia's special program, an intensive series of lectures by some of the best in American journalism, I had already decided to leave *The Raleigh Register*. My own training in investigative reporting had been primarily on the job. In this particular field of journalism there are few ground rules, and in the early 1960s it was uncharted territory navigated by only a few reporters.

When I started on the Invest Right story, I had premonition and conjecture but no verifiable facts. Going back to the basics, I turned to the standard practice of listing in three separate columns the key elements of my immediate problems: those known, those unclear, and those presumed. In this manner I was able to list as "known" the name "Invest Right Corp." "Unclear" was where the corporation was officially located. "Presumed" was that, because no mention of the corporation's existence appeared in West Virginia records, it was a corporation intended to be hidden from public view and its purpose, as the name implied, was to engage in a massive skimming operation of public funds by unknown persons in state government.

Perhaps I was jumping to conclusions with my assumption of Invest Right's purpose, but I had years before been forced to the cynical conclusion that to be a competent reporter in my chosen specialty of political writing I had to presume guilt until, and unless, innocence could be proven.

Having established this much, the next step was to define the means of accomplishing my investigative goal. To do this, I needed answers to the reporter's initial six questions of "What?" "When?" "Where?" "Who?" "Why?" and "How?" I knew the "What?" I was reasonably confident that I knew the "Why?" What I didn't know was when, where, who, and how, and two years of stubborn digging in three states would occupy many of my off-duty hours before I would finally be able to write my story.

When working on a major assignment I was never afforded the luxury of relief from my regular duties. All the time I was working on the Invest Right piece, I was also responsible for my "Affairs of State" column, my editorial writing, and my straight news and feature writing. I never asked for any special concessions, which is possibly the chief reason why it took me so long to pull the facts together and write the series that would be taglined, at the time of publication, "Brown Means Business."

Development of the story also dragged on for longer than I had expected because of the total refusal of anyone with any knowledge of it to answer my questions. I tried going back to my original source, to previously friendly legislative committee investigators, to Statehouse sources I had found dependable in the past—to everyone, in fact, that I could think of who might be willing to help me without disclosing what I was investigating to the opposition press. But I kept running into the proverbial stone wall. With those three words scribbled at the top of the first page of the legislative committee report, I had obtained almost everything of substance I was ever to learn from official sources in Charleston.

This kind of blanket silence was unusual. The possible existence of corrupt practices in West Virginia government was not. In fact, government corruption was pretty much a case of business-as-usual, standard political practice in the Mountain State, which has a long history of political plunder for personal gain.

Part One

"The state is one of the most mountainous in the country;
sometimes it is called the 'little Switzerland' of America,
and I once heard an irreverent local citizen call it
the 'Afghanistan of the United States.'"

John Gunther on West Virginia for
Inside USA, 1947

Chapter One

DEPRESSION POLITICS

WEST VIRGINIA'S EASTERN BORDER extends nearly to Washington, DC. Its northern border pushes north of Pittsburgh. Its western border goes longitudinally beyond Cleveland. Its southern border is latitudinally south of Richmond. As one wit joked, "It's a great state for the shape it's in." West Virginia, in other words, was and is a hybrid with ties to no particular region. Mapmakers, textbook writers, and congressional committees have never been quite certain how to categorize it geographically. West Virginia is neither northern, southern, nor mid-Atlantic; it is certainly not a Great Lakes state, nor is it Midwestern. It is an American original with all the problems of the original American colonies when they tried to merge their interests, aspirations, and resources into a single federation.

West Virginia's politicians have always been quick to spot an opportunity. It's a time-honored tradition, going directly back to those originally responsible for the state's creation. Since colonial days, the inhabitants of Virginia's mountainous western region had grumbled that the government in Richmond treated their section of the state like a poor stepchild or colonial outpost, sucking out resources and taxes while returning little in the way of financial support. In the midst of the Civil War, western Virginians saw their opportunity and took it—with the blessing of the U.S. Congress. Virginia had seceded from the Union and thrown in her lot with the Confederacy. Western Virginia—where slaveholding was neither popular nor widespread—seceded from Virginia and declared itself loyal to the Union. After the usual internal bickering and horsetrading, Congress—never one to look a gift horse in the mouth and wanting very much to retain access to the railroad lines running through western Virginia to the Ohio River ports—graciously, if unconstitutionally, welcomed West Virginia as the nation's thirty-fifth state.

My great-grandfather's brother was among those gentlemen who hijacked half a state from the Old Dominion and, on behalf of the new state, commandeered any Virginia government monies on deposit in western Virginia banks that they could lay their hands on. Uncle Harmon Sinsel was a farmer, politician, surveyor, and sometime architect who served as one of Harrison County's delegates to the First Constitutional Convention in Wheeling in 1861–'62. Uncle Harmon was also one of the delegates who lobbied hard to preserve "Virginia" as part of the new state's name. He made a stirring speech on the convention floor, calling himself "a loyal son of old Virginia," despite his support of statehood for the western counties, and later seconded the motion proposing that the new state be officially named "West Virginia."

I've never forgiven him for his stance. Other names put forth during the convention included Kanawha, Alleghany, Vandalia, and Augusta. Any of them would have helped give us our own identity, forever distinguishing the new state from the so-called "mother state" of Virginia in the minds of those who hail from elsewhere in the nation, many of whom to this day persist in asking West Virginians, "Do you live near Richmond?"

My own interest in politics, on both the state and national levels, began in college when I took Dr. John F. Sly's political science course at West Virginia University. It was during the Depression era when millions of people were out of work and breadlines stretched for blocks. I still remember that cold, misty day in March 1933 when I took the train from Morgantown to Washington for Franklin D. Roosevelt's first inauguration. Walking from Union Station to the Capitol, I stopped and bought a newspaper. Huge headlines announced that every bank in America had locked its doors a few hours earlier. The outlook was bleak. I wondered, along with much of the rest of the country, what the future held and if the nation was on the brink of collapse.

I found a spot among the thousands of other people waiting to hear the new president's inaugural address. As he would prove over and over through the years, Roosevelt was a masterful speaker with a spellbinding delivery. As he assured his listeners in that now historic address, "This great Nation will en-

dure as it has endured, will revive and will prosper . . . The only thing we have
to fear is fear itself." Our faith and his leadership would restore the world's
first democracy to its former stability. Patience, understanding, and hard work
would set America once again on the road to its intended destiny.

Afterward I watched the inaugural parade, got another glimpse of the new
chief executive in the reviewing stand, treated myself to the movie *42nd Street*
and took the train back to school that evening. I had been a spectator at one
of the great moments in history, but at the time I had no idea what Roosevelt's
inauguration would mean for the country. Nor did the new president. Upon
her arrival at the White House as the new first lady, Eleanor Roosevelt would
remark that the inauguration was "a little terrifying . . . We're in a tremendous
stream, and none of us knows where we're going to land."

As Arthur M. Schlesinger, Jr., wrote some years later in *The Coming of
the New Deal*, the long, difficult road back to national revival began that
very evening. Meeting with members of his cabinet and so-called Brain Trust,
Roosevelt began the formulation of policies which were to alter political, social, and economic conditions in America for the rest of the century. And one
of the staunchest supporters of the president's now-famous New Deal would
be a freshman Democratic congressman from West Virginia, Jennings Randolph, who had been elected on the same ballot as Roosevelt.

In West Virginia, the governor who swept into office along with Roosevelt
in 1932 was former Elkins lawyer-banker Herman Guy Kump, who put together his own version of the Roosevelt Brain Trust. And as a political science
student at West Virginia University, I was privileged to hear firsthand reports
on the governor's reform program when Dr. Sly, my professor, was named
its chairman. Never was I so fascinated by a professor's lectures as when Sly
shared his experiences in Charleston with his upper-division classes.

When Kump moved into the governor's office, he was confronted with
dual concerns, the depressed state of the economy and a revenue problem
exacerbated by the Tax Limitation Amendment that had been ratified on the
same day he was elected governor. From the beginning of the twentieth century until the market crash of '29, West Virginia had depended largely on
property taxation as its main source of income for both state and local govern-

ment. These had been years of almost uninterrupted growth and prosperity for the state, and state government expanded to meet new needs. New state agencies established during these years included the Department of Agriculture, Department of Mines, and Department of Public Safety, all requiring financial support, but revenue creation was not a burdensome task.

Following the nationwide economic collapse, it quickly became clear that changes were needed at both the national and state levels. This need became even more acute as the economic situation continued to worsen. West Virginia's Tax Limitation Amendment was a creature of the Depression. Farmers and businessmen by the thousands were being forced into bankruptcy, and the legislature resorted to cutbacks in property taxation in an attempt to apply the brakes before total disaster resulted.

The effects of the amendment were immediate and broad in scope. Between 1932 and 1934, the amount of revenue received from property taxation plummeted by 40 percent. But while the individual taxpayer had been afforded some relief, the level of government services required remained the same or even increased. The new governor had to venture into uncharted areas of public finance as Roosevelt was doing in Washington. With the doors slammed shut on property as a major source of revenue, Kump and his own brain trust were forced to turn to unpopular sales and excise taxes as a means of restoring West Virginia to fiscal solvency. State government also tightened its belt, reducing the size of the government workforce, cutting the salaries of the remaining workers, trimming services, and adopting centralized purchasing procedures.

One of the earliest management restructuring moves by the new state administration was the dismantling of the magisterial school system, a relic of the agrarian age. Farmers wanted their children at home in the spring and fall to help in the fields, which led to shorter school terms in rural areas than in towns. To provide a balance and guarantee all children the same educational opportunities, the county unit system was written into law and all schools statewide went on a standard nine-and-a-half-month term.

It had been the same with road building. Since 1863 the county courts had determined how and where roads were to be built. A patchwork of roads—

some leading nowhere and others leading to farms belonging to people with political clout—had been the result. With Kump's advocacy, the Highway Department took over administration of the entire road system, a major step toward planned development.

Kump's sweeping and, in some respects, harsh measures paid dividends. By the time he left office in 1937, West Virginia was again in the black, one of the most fiscally sound states in the country. But the governor paid a price for his crisis management. He was never again elected to public office, although he twice ran for the U.S. Senate. Neither time was he even able to get past the party primaries.

KUMP'S SUCCESSOR, Homer Adams Holt, state attorney general at the time of the 1936 election, ran the state pretty much as Kump had before him. He advocated the permanent adoption of the consumers' sales tax (previously a temporary excise), feuded with teachers, and split with the United Mine Workers (UMW) over a Southern West Virginia work stoppage that idled 2,500 miners.

By and large Governor Holt, a former Washington and Lee University law professor and Fayetteville attorney, clung to conservative traditions, a philosophical posture that he retained for the remainder of his political life. After leaving the governor's office, he served as general counsel for one of the nation's largest chemical companies, returned to Charleston as a senior partner in one of the largest corporate law firms in the state, and in 1956 broke with the Democratic Party in order to support Republican Cecil Underwood's campaign for governor.

Holt joined Kump in putting together a political organization that had all the power and perks of New York's Tammany Hall. The influx of federal relief funds for everything from road repairs to park development, the jobs growing out of the newly sanctioned public liquor monopoly, and the state's takeover of road and welfare management created an irresistible pool of patronage to be exploited. Together with State Democratic Chairman Robert G. Kelly, Kump and Holt assembled what became known as the Statehouse Machine.

They ran into a certain amount of resistance along the way. One of the leaders of the opposition was then-U.S. Senator Matthew Mansfield Neely, former mayor of Fairmont and clerk of the West Virginia House of Delegates. Neely had won his first congressional seat in 1913, the seat vacated by John W. Davis when he was appointed U.S. solicitor general. Neely won three consecutive terms in Congress before being elected to the U.S. Senate. He lost his Senate seat in 1928 to Republican firebrand Henry D. Hatfield, a former governor, but was returned to Washington two years later by the largest vote ever cast up to that time.

Neely was a man of massive ego and ambition, and by right of party seniority he chose to challenge Kump and Holt when they sought to extend their control of the Statehouse into the next administration. A populist Democrat, Neely formed an alliance with the UMW, which had risen in influence during the Roosevelt years. With his powers of persuasion and charisma on the hustings, Neely was a formidable adversary capable of posing a serious threat to the Kump-Holt organization.

With the gubernatorial election of 1940 approaching, Kump and Holt tapped their associate, R. Carl Andrews of Charleston, as heir apparent. Andrews, successor to Robert Kelly as state Democratic Party chairman, had the same conservative bent as his sponsors, something Neely and the labor leadership were unwilling to accept. As the deadline for filing for office approached, Neely held forth in the press, declaring that he could name at least thirty Democrats more qualified for governor than Andrews. At the last moment, Neely himself filed for the governor's race, shocking his supporters.

Neely's decision to enter the race for governor was disappointing to his family as well as to his supporters, as his daughter, Corinne, confided to me later at a Young Democratic Convention in Huntington. By choosing to run for governor, Neely gave up his seniority in the U.S. Senate which would have made him one of the most powerful members of Congress in a matter of years. The general belief at the time was that Neely's backers in the labor movement pressured him into giving up his Senate seat in order to make the run for governor, since Neely was far likelier to beat the Kump-Holt machine's anointed successor than any other candidate the labor leadership could field.

One of the Democrats Neely had earlier mentioned to the press as having gubernatorial potential, Criminal Court Judge Harley M. Kilgore of Beckley, filed to run for Neely's Senate seat. During a late-hour conference in Charleston, one of those insisting that Kilgore be given the nod was Raleigh County Prosecuting Attorney Warren A. Thornhill, who had been active in the Neely-Labor faction for years. In the background, offering his own support and advice, was Congressman Joe L. Smith of Beckley.

Neely's power play, the grist for newspaper headlines for weeks, destroyed the Kump-Holt hold over the Democratic Party. Kump, who lost to Kilgore in the Senate primary that year, returned to Elkins. Holt packed his bags and went to New York as general counsel for Union Carbide Corporation. Andrews, after a term as Charleston's mayor a few years later, became chief lobbyist for the West Virginia Coal Association.

Neely's first year as governor was marked by such successes as the legislature's passage of permanent registration of voters, nonpartisan county boards of education, and a teachers' retirement fund. But he never fully settled into his new position, seemingly unable to give the governorship the attention it required. He then made one of the biggest mistakes of his public career, filing for the 1942 Senate race halfway through his term as governor. He whipped Kump in the primary but lost in the general election to the Republican candidate, Charleston lawyer Chapman Revercomb.

Neely was an anomaly without parallel in West Virginia politics, a man with serious weaknesses as well as remarkable strengths. He lacked the ability to sense the direction of the prevailing political winds when personal ambition was at stake. Had he been more alert to shifting trends, more aware of voters' expectations, he never would have challenged Henry Hatfield in 1928 or Chapman Revercomb in 1943.

Neely remained a powerful presence on the public stage after his 1928 defeat, as he proved two years later when he won his Senate seat by a startling margin. His problem in the '28 campaign was facing a Republican opponent in Republican times, a man who had the same charm and appeal as Neely himself. Hatfield had been the "man of the people" before Neely developed his own star quality, and Hatfield was running on the same ticket as that popular World War I figure Herbert Hoover. Neely's problem in 1943 was his failure to keep faith with his constituents, not once but twice in only four

years. The voters who had elected him governor only two years earlier were
understandably disgruntled to find that he wanted to quit in midterm—when
the country was fighting a world war—and they punished Neely by choosing
his opponent, Chapman Revercomb, as their senator.

NEELY'S ELECTION as governor was a benchmark in West Virginia politics. That
election brought an end to the almost viselike grip business and industry had
held on the electoral process for decades. The neoconservative element in the
Democratic Party led by Kump and Holt was relegated to a backseat. A different type of leadership took center stage, its makeup fashioned by Neely who
drew in such labor leaders as UMW President John L. Lewis and a coterie of
oldtimers from the county courthouses. Neely had been methodically assembling this faction since he was first elected to Congress before World War I.
With the election of Roosevelt to the presidency in 1932, he was able to bring
the last phalanx, organized labor, into the ranks.

The struggle of workers in West Virginia to organize had begun in the
nineteenth century. They had made some gains by the early 1900s but their
ranks were decimated during the mine wars. Where, for instance, the UMW
had been able to increase its membership to almost fifty thousand by World
War I, membership in the whole of the State Labor Federation, of which the
UMW was an affiliate, had shrunk to only three thousand by the time FDR
took office. But in a matter of weeks after Roosevelt's inauguration, conditions began to improve. Labor's right to bargain collectively was written into
law in the first hundred days of the New Deal, and the infamous Yellow Dog
contracts, used by owners to demand commitments from their employees not
to organize, were abolished.

Neely, who had worked tirelessly with organized labor while in Washington to improve workers' bargaining rights, called in his IOUs, and as union
membership increased in the coalfields, steel mills, and other parts of this
highly industrialized state, his political influence expanded along with it. By
the time he filed for governor, it was a foregone conclusion that he would win.
And while in office he continued to consolidate his power by putting together
a political organization that would keep him the number-one powerbroker in

state politics until 1956 (except for that foolish move in '43, when he tried to bequeath his leadership position to Robert H. Mollohan).

FOR ME, the years of the Kump and Holt administrations were spent learning my craft in the classroom and on the job, gaining some experience in the trenches. Thanks to World War II, I spent most of Neely's term as governor in trenches of a different sort.

By the time Governor Holt left office, I had enjoyed the distinction of being offered a ride while hitchhiking back to college by the wife of Governor Kump, who was traveling in the official limousine driven by a state police officer. I had courted Senator Neely's daughter Corinne on and off for several years. I had discussed international relations with an Austrian prince in the informal surroundings of my fraternity house. I had ventured into the exciting world of journalism knowing practically nothing about my profession. And I was paid accordingly—$2.50 a day for as many hours as my boss told me to work, in that era before the passage of a wage and hour law.

I had also bungled my first assignment as a political reporter, an interview with Governor Holt as he disembarked from a two-passenger biplane at Sessler Field in Beckley. My editor, Raiford Watkins, had told me to question him about the closed-shop issue that had caused a mine strike in the nearby coalfields.

I was too awed by the fact that I was interviewing the governor as he stepped off an airplane to conduct a decent interview. The questions I asked were inane and nonproductive. Watkins later moved into the breach. A former Associated Press bureau chief in Charleston, he called Holt and learned precisely why he had come to Beckley.

Then he gave me hell.

It was while my editor was acquainting me in no uncertain terms with the journalistic facts of life that I came to realize that a college diploma did little more than give me the skills to write obituaries. I knew I was years away from attempting any major reporting. But by the time Watkins finished his tirade, I thought I was light-years away from ever taking on anything resembling the Invest Right challenge.

Chapter Two

A New Battlefront

THE GOVERNOR WHO FOLLOWED Matthew Neely into office in 1944, Clarence "Fats" Meadows, was an uncomplicated man but an agile practitioner of the political arts. A native of Beckley, he was charming and facile, a raconteur with more tales to tell than an old vaudeville comedian. And in a small and unpretentious office next to Meadows's was Okey Patteson, the governor's executive assistant, the first to hold such a position in state history. While Patteson enjoyed none of the perks and privileges of an elected official, during this and the next two administrations he would prove to be one of the most influential men in the West Virginia power structure.

West Virginia came out of World War II hard-muscled and bursting with energy, ready to begin reshaping itself for a new period of peace and prosperity. For Governor Meadows it was a rather tranquil administration. For the thousands of young men coming home from the battlefront it was a period of restlessness as they tried to readjust to civilian life and to conditions they no longer accepted on faith. They had seen a bombed-out London, a Manila in rubble, the devastation of Berlin and Dresden, ruined and wasted towns and countryside worldwide.

Peace had been achieved, but West Virginia's sons returned to find reminders of battlefield destruction disfiguring the homefront. Timberlands had been overcut, farmlands overgrazed, oilfields pumped nearly dry, and miles of once verdant hillsides scarred by strip-mining. West Virginia had contributed her young men and her vast resources to the war effort, and the state had been left the poorer for it.

After spending much of the war in the South Pacific, I returned to work at *The Raleigh Register.* A few months later, my publisher, Charles Hodel, called me at home on a Sunday. Never one to waste time during office hours on the minutiae of management, he asked me to meet him that afternoon at the office. A few minutes after my arrival, he asked if I would like to become editor. This had been my fondest dream since college, and I accepted without even asking about salary or fringe benefits.

As we discussed my new responsibilities—among them that I would have full control of editorial policy—I imagined that I had been offered the job because of my years of dedication as a reporter or my naval experience during the war, rising from enlisted man to ship's command. But Hodel had a way of pricking your vanity with a few words.

"One of the reasons I chose you as editor," he mentioned casually, "was that you used such good judgment in choosing a wife. Margaret Bledsoe is a fine young woman." I settled quickly but not easily into my new position. After four years in military service, my writing was rusty. I had to struggle many hours at home patching together editorials and columns. One of my most acute concerns, and the subject of much of my writing at the time, was the condition of the land in the mountains around Beckley.

The myth of superabundance had almost wrecked much of the country in the years before I was born, until the idea of land reclamation began to be promoted during Theodore Roosevelt's presidency. The Civilian Conservation Corps and Soil Conservation Service restored some sanity to land management during Franklin Roosevelt's years in the White House. But there were still holes in the environmental fabric. The most glaring abuse in Southern West Virginia was strip-mining. It might be excused during a world war. In peacetime it was a shameful example of the plunder-for-profit attitude which only a generation before had clogged streams, caused flooding, destroyed wildlife, and bankrupted farmers. But under the law, there was no way to stop it.

The only weapon I had at my disposal was the editorial. Some people said I was wrong to criticize the coal operators, that they were simply trying to make a living and were providing jobs for others. My response was that they were removing coal that should be left untouched until another war came along or until coal in deeper seams became so scarce that surface mining was the only alternative.

On one occasion, when stripping was begun on the edge of Babcock State Park in neighboring Fayette County and coal trucks were using park roads to deliver their loads to the railroad, my editorial opinion was directed at the State Conservation Commission. This was too much for easygoing Governor Meadows.

Through his conservation commissioner, former weekly newspaper editor Jack Shipman, he put a stop to further use of the park roads. The editorial had been simply a harassing tactic on my part, but it focused attention on the disdain the strippers had for land management efforts. Their goal was profit, pure and simple, and the arrogance and callousness they displayed in its pursuit was boundless.

Coal stripping never stopped during my years in newspapering. Criticism of the practice came from most editors around the state, yet all it did was persuade the legislature to apply a few modest restraints. It did, however, help give coal strippers the social acceptability of slumlords.

Some deep-mine companies also moved into the stripping business, but they seemed to make at least some effort at reclamation. I'm reminded particularly of Raleigh Coal and Coke Company and the New River Company. R. J. Burmeister, president of Raleigh Coal, called one day and offered to take me on a tour of the reclaimed portions of his company's holdings. Ebersole Gaines, New River's president, held a press viewing of his company's reclaimed lands. There may have been other coal lands we never saw that remained unreclaimed, but Raleigh Coal and the New River Company were at least establishing a precedent.

In all honesty, I may not have been entirely objective in my assessment of Raleigh Coal's efforts. The company's president, Ray Burmeister, was my wife's uncle by marriage, a man I liked and respected personally. But I prided myself on never pulling my punches editorially, which led to more than one uncomfortable family gathering over the years.

Governor Meadows was never one to take a firm stand on the wise use of the natural environment. One factor contributing to this reticence may have been Meadows's own ventures into oil and gas speculation while he was in office; his attitude was more that of the developer than the conservationist. One example of his indifference to land use was his position—or lack thereof—on strip-mining at Grandview State Park, near Beckley, which boasts one of the most beautiful vistas in all of West Virginia. Meadows chose to do nothing about the impending threat to the park, leaving it for his successor to wrestle with later on.

Despite his refusal to address the problem of strip-mining, Meadows had his share of concerns to deal with while in office, beginning with a demand from state teachers for a pay raise. He resisted them briefly, then suggested a "stop gap" increase until he could "judiciously study the problem." The pay issue was defused to a degree by a legislative study sanctioned in 1945 and completed a year later. Prepared by Dr. George D. Strayer of Ohio, it became known as the Strayer Report and remained a mission statement in education for a decade.

Among the highlights of the report considered at a special legislative session were the recommendation that the position of state school superintendent become an appointive rather than elective office, and the observation that West Virginia had neither the population nor the economic resources to support more than one university. The appointive-superintendent amendment was placed before the voters at the next election and was defeated, but a dozen years later R. Virgil Rohrbough of Grafton—coincidentally, my sister's husband—became the last elected and first appointed state school superintendent. And in 1961, the legislature would choose to ignore the Strayer Report's recommendations and allow Marshall to shed its college status for that of university.

At the 1947 session of the legislature the teachers were granted a significant pay raise, and the sheriff's fee system, a scandalous perk dating back to the nineteenth century, was abolished. The toughest foe the sheriffs faced during this controversy was *Gazette* editor Frank A. Knight, a former member of the House of Delegates. Knight recruited support from newspapers all across the state to help eliminate the practice of allowing county sheriffs to grow rich off the "beans and cornbread" diet they fed the prisoners in their jails.

Labor unrest was a problem for Meadows throughout his term. Major strikes broke out in 1946 at the International Nickel plant in Huntington and at the Wheeling Electric Beech Bottom plant. Then in the spring of 1947 another strike erupted at the sprawling DuPont chemical plant in Belle, a few miles upriver from Charleston. Tempers rose to such a pitch that picket lines flared up around the Capitol and the Governor's Mansion. After days of fighting at plant gates and in conference rooms, the DuPont walkout ended, and Meadows emerged as he had from earlier strikes with his reputation as a mediator untarnished and even, perhaps, enhanced.

ROAD IMPROVEMENT was another thorny problem during Meadows's years in office, one which had never been adequately addressed since the state's formation. In fact, as far back as 1784, George Washington had touched on the subject in a letter to Benjamin Harrison, then governor of Virginia, urging the construction of a road across Virginia to the Ohio River.

But matters other than roads seemed to take priority in the Statehouse. When roads were built, they were usually financed with private capital or an infusion of federal money. Upon achieving statehood, West Virginia turned its attention first to the development of railroads and navigable rivers. Road building, what there was of it, continued to follow the same system used by Virginia since the eighteenth century. An elected road supervisor was responsible for the condition of the roads in each precinct, and he accomplished the work by pressing able-bodied men into road repair work two days each year.

If a man was unwilling to perform the service, he was required to pay $1.25 in lieu of each day's work. Unfortunately, many road supervisors adopted the practice of sweeping the local bars and saloons for replacements and putting those unfortunates to work on the roads, sober or not.

Stubborn adherence to this system, coupled with the problems of topography, led to a lack of decent roads, one of the major reasons why West Virginia trailed neighboring states in economic development. In this, the most mountainous of the eastern states, the cost of building each mile of road is substantially higher than in any other state in the country. For well into the twentieth century, if traffic wasn't moved by rail or water, it barely moved at all.

The first step by state government to undertake responsibility for the road system came in 1897 when an inspector of highways was appointed. It was a report by this official in 1908 to Governor William Dawson concerning the poor condition of the roads that led to the appointment of a commissioner of public roads.

The next important actions were ratification of the optimistically titled Good Roads Amendment in 1920 and assumption by the state of limited control of the road system the following year. Under the terms of the amendment, the legislature was empowered to issue bonds on a revolving basis up to an aggregate total of $50 million for the building of paved roads between counties.

Still, West Virginia, even in those years, lagged behind most of the other states, and when Meadows took office, he found that road building had become a need of compelling proportions. From his office windows he could see one of the very few four-lane thoroughfares in all of West Virginia, Charleston's Kanawha Boulevard. Statewide, there was a tortuous, mountainous network of poorly maintained roads, which in many cases still followed the paths of the original Indian trails.

Among the major actions of the Meadows administration was advocacy of a bond issue for improving roads within counties, known as the Farm-to-Market Amendment, and support of planning for the West Virginia Turnpike. This turnpike, the most costly and ambitious road construction project undertaken in the state up to that time, was envisioned as the forerunner of a privately financed highway system that in time would extend northward to the Ohio River and link up with the Ohio Turnpike then being built across the Buckeye State.

As planned and built, the West Virginia Turnpike ran from Charleston to Princeton. Extensions north and south came some years later with the construction of I-77 from Cleveland to Columbia, South Carolina, as part of the interstate system authorized by Congress in 1956.

West Virginia's first governor, Arthur Boreman, called for a system of free schools, toll roads, and highway improvements in his inaugural message. Eighty years later Meadows was still wrestling with similar problems, and he is remembered as a chief executive who kept the books balanced, put out brush fires at plant gates, and began the planning efforts for programs that would be implemented by future governors.

After leaving office early in 1949 he returned to the practice of law, opening an office in Charleston. He also held an interest in three radio stations. After a few years he moved to Fort Lauderdale, Florida, where he continued the practice of law and the refinement of his golf game. He died at the age of fifty-seven while visiting his father-in-law at Clifton Forge, Virginia.

One of the shrewdest decisions Meadows made as governor was the appointment of Patteson as his executive assistant, a decision which allowed the governor time for travel and his frequent golf matches. Patteson took up the reins with such skill and composure that before Meadows left office his assistant had become known around the state as the "governor-without-portfolio."

A less conspicuous but also influential presence during the Meadows years was former Congressman Joe L. Smith, who had chosen to retire from the House of Representatives in 1944. Meadows's fellow Beckleyan and campaign manager during his run for the governor's office, Smith, like Patteson, was usually on hand for the big decisions of the Meadows administration.

These were the years when Southern West Virginia enjoyed an unprecedented degree of political influence. Both the state's governor and just-retired but still powerful congressman were from Beckley. The congressman's successor, Dr. E. H. Hedrick, and U.S. Senator Harley M. Kilgore were also from Beckley. The governor's highly capable assistant, Patteson, was from nearby Mount Hope, in Fayette County. All were Democrats.

When West Virginia first became a state, the Democrats' long control of the political process came to an end. West of the mountains, there was a natural hostility toward the Democratic leadership in Richmond, which for decades had done little to address the interests of the citizens of the Trans-Allegheny. The West Virginia electorate switched its support to the Republican Party—the party of Lincoln—until 1870. Democratic traditions remained strong, however, and again asserted themselves with that year's elections, a condition which lasted for a quarter century. Around the beginning of the twentieth century, the mood in the country and the state began changing again. The Republicans regained the hearts of the voters in 1896 and remained in almost total control of the elective machinery until FDR's landslide in 1932.

The rare Democratic exceptions during this time were Governor John J. Cornwell's election in 1916, Joe L. Smith's election to the U.S. House of Representatives, and Neely's election to the House and later Senate. Neely was first elected to Congress in 1912 and served either in the House or Senate almost continuously until he stepped aside in 1940 to seek the governorship. Smith was first elected to the House in 1928 and remained there until his retirement in 1944. Neely and Smith developed a friendship while serving together in Congress, and it remained strong for the duration of their public careers.

In background they were as alike as hound dogs. Both were literally born in a log cabin, Neely in Doddridge County, Smith in Raleigh County. Neely had been mayor of Fairmont, Smith mayor of Beckley. Both were Democrats elected to Congress during Republican landslides. But in demeanor they were as different as night and day. Smith was quiet, a listener rather than a talker—a rarity for a politician and a fact he called attention to late in life when he remarked that he had never made a speech on the House floor or on a campaign platform. Neely was a grandstander, an orator in the tradition of William Jennings Bryan. In their political craftsmanship they were artists. Both were accomplished tacticians who understood their constituencies from top to bottom and were on a first-name basis with all the old pols in their precincts.

Neely and Smith were a major force in the election of Clarence Meadows as West Virginia's twenty-second governor. With the departure of Kump and Holt, the two moved to center state and remained powerbrokers in their party throughout the turbulent postwar years.

But a new and different type of political personality would appear in the wings during Meadows's term as governor: Robert Carlyle Byrd of Crab Orchard in Raleigh County. Smith would be on hand when Byrd faced the biggest test of his political career, his bid for a seat in Congress, armed only with a $300 loan and a fiddle.

Chapter 3

Editorial Influence

THE ELECTION OF OKEY PATTESON as Meadows's successor was a given and allowed the governor's office to continue the development and implementation of policies already in place.

Patteson, who had been successful in the sale of motor cars and real estate in Mount Hope, had learned his political craft in the precincts and as sheriff of Fayette County. The move to Charleston as the first executive assistant to the governor in the state's history gave him on-the-job training and positioned him to run for the highest office in state government.

As Meadows's assistant, Patteson occupied an office next to the governor's and worked closely with him on a daily basis, conferring with Meadows on all the matters that flowed across the chief executive's desk. Patteson did his job well and seldom irritated people, no small accomplishment in and of itself. He had warmth, and was skillful in his handling of sensitive issues. He made himself indispensable. And sitting where he did, he was able to build a power base that spanned the entire state. When election time rolled around, it was a foregone conclusion that the party and its powerbrokers would elevate him to the number-one position.

Times were good in West Virginia when Patteson moved into the governor's office in early 1949. The postwar boom had not yet spent itself, and the state treasury was overflowing with surpluses. No governor in decades had enjoyed such prospects as Patteson did on the day of his inauguration.

I had become directly acquainted with his political style and personal magnetism in the late days of the 1948 general election campaign. As editor of the *Register*, I was attending a buffet luncheon Patteson was hosting for a group of business and professional people at the Black Knight Country Club in Beckley. As the guests departed afterward, I stood talking with one of Patteson's people when, with a rather neat maneuver, Patteson himself and his aides suddenly surrounded me.

Patteson said quietly, "Tom, let's talk."

We sat down in a corner of the ballroom as the waiters cleared the tables, and for the next half hour Patteson outlined his platform. He spoke of wanting to become the "road-buildingest governor in history," of wanting to strength-en public-school education, of other improvements he wanted to make in state services. Finally, he looked me straight in the eye and said, "I've got to have your endorsement if I'm to be elected."

Although I knew he was fueling my vanity, I was realistic enough to rec-ognize that there was some logic in what he said. Outside of Charleston, no one area of the state had more political clout in those years than Beckley. Patteson and Governor Homer Holt, Neely's predecessor, were both from Fayette County. Current Governor Meadows, U.S. Senator Harley Kilgore, and Congressman E. H. Hedrick were all from Beckley. As a consequence of the goodwill and influence dispensed from their offices, much of the strength of the majority political party was centered in the circulation territory of the *Register*, a newspaper with a loose affiliation to the Democratic persuasion and a prime endorsement prize.

Like Patteson, his two primary opponents had solicited the *Register*'s support. Also like Patteson, former House Speaker and attorney James K. Thomas of Charleston had accepted with grace my explanation that our news-paper did not take partisan stands in the primaries. Former judge and po-litical boss R. D. Bailey of Pineville was another matter. In his role as reign-ing sovereign of neighboring Wyoming County, it was difficult for Bailey to comprehend that the prerogatives he considered his due did not extend into Raleigh County and the offices of the Democratic paper he read every day. I would have firsthand experience with his exercise of those prerogatives some years later during a libel suit.

Patteson's approach was as pleasant and charming the second time around as it had been during the primary. "I've been reading the *Register* since I was a little boy," he said, "and I've come to think of it as my hometown paper. You can understand what I mean, Tom, when I say I need your support in my campaign for governor. To be perfectly frank, it would be a political embarrassment if I had to admit around the state that I couldn't get the endorsement of my own town's paper."

I liked him. I liked his straightforward approach. But an editor doesn't bargain away his newspaper's influence based solely on charm, wit, and an engaging personality. So, struggling mightily against my inherent desire to please and be a nice guy, I decided it was time to lift our discussion out of the marketplace of politics and into what I preferred to think of as the realm of public service.

"*Register* endorsement will come at a price," I said in the unsure voice of an editor who had never before found himself in the role of powerbroker.

"What's the price?" he asked, not blinking an eye.

For several months I had been campaigning against the surface mining of coal just below the overlook at Grandview State Park. The mountain across the New River had already been stripped, and Charleston Coal Company was now in the process of moving its equipment to the mountainside of the park itself. There was no alternative short of outright purchase of the mineral rights to prevent mining within the park, and the mine reclamation laws then on the books were so replete with avoidance clauses that once the coal was removed there was no way to force the company to repair the damage it had caused.

In my stories and editorials I had also been seeking the reopening of a wing of Pinecrest Sanitarium, a tuberculosis treatment center on the outskirts of Beckley. It had been closed during World War II and all efforts to persuade Governor Meadows to find the money to reopen it had failed. In those years tuberculosis was a highly contagious disease, and there was a need for the beds at the hospital if the state would provide the funding.

I explained all of this to Patteson while we sat in the Black Knight ballroom and found him to be a sympathetic listener. He readily agreed that both problems should be addressed and said that in two weeks, when he would be returning to Beckley for a rally at the Memorial Building, he would publicly commit himself to taking corrective action if elected governor.

He was as good as his word. On the Saturday night of the rally, he had a copy of his speech delivered to my office detailing the promises he had made. Within six months after he took office as West Virginia's twenty-third governor, Pinecrest was returned to full operation and enough additional acreage had been purchased at Grandview to place it forever beyond the reach of surface mining, expanding the fifty-one-acre park to 878 acres.

Was this trade-off of newspaper endorsement an ethical exercise? It would be an interesting question for a journalism school discussion, but at the time that I made the deal I was more interested in my publisher's reaction than a classroom ethics course.

Back at the office that afternoon, Hodel's response was unequivocal. "You did well," he said after I told him what had happened. I went to my office, scanned that day's edition of the paper, went home, and became violently ill. Although my publisher had okayed my first big test of editorial privilege, my stomach was not as accommodating.

WEST VIRGINIA'S FISCAL FUTURE appeared promising when Patteson went before the legislature to deliver his first message as governor. In the context of this outlook, he urged passage of enabling legislation for the $50 million farm-to-market road program which had been approved at the polls the previous fall, and, under authority of an act passed two years earlier, appointed the West Virginia Turnpike Commission.

Another achievement during his first year in office was the passage of legislation he had advocated to establish the West Virginia University medical school.

New storm clouds were forming on the horizon, however, and a year after Patteson took office the Korean War broke out. The governor went to Charleston's National Guard Armory to deliver a farewell message to the departing troops. Throughout his term he agonized over the loss of young West Virginians to yet another war, in this case a no-win "police action," continuing the state's tradition of answering the call to arms at a greater-per-capita ratio than any other state in the nation.

Storm clouds of another sort formed during his second year in office when he had to make the hard decisions on the new medical school, a bonus for World War II veterans, and fire-boss legislation, which were all then before the legislature. Site selection for the medical school was an issue forced on him by a legislature unwilling to make the choice itself.

Financing for the veterans' bonus was another hot potato tossed to him by faint-hearted lawmakers. And the fire-boss bill put him squarely in conflict with the mine workers who had helped elect him. Patteson solved the bonus problem by calling a hundred or so bankers together at the Statehouse to hear his plan for selling bonds on the open market, with state investment funds added as a purchasing incentive.

They bought it.

He broke with the mine-workers union when he chose to support the fire-boss legislation that would require a fire inspector at the end of each shift. And on the medical school location he turned to friends, educators, and experts in the medical field for guidance. I was among those whose opinion he sought on the issue.

One day Dr. Doff Daniel, a Beckley physician, came to me with a message. "The governor wants you to take a position one way or the other on the location of the medical school," he said. "He looks on the *Register* as his hometown paper, and he wants to know where you stand."

I was startled to hear from Patteson in this manner, but Daniel smiled and explained, "I was in his office yesterday, and he thought this was the better way to contact you." At the time Daniel was my wife's physician, as well as a long-time friend of her family.

"Tell the governor," I replied, "that I'm gathering information on how other states are handling the matter of medical school location, and I'll be ready to say where we stand in two weeks." I had almost finished pulling together the data I needed, but I still wanted a few days more to study it and write a series of articles before I stated the *Register*'s political opinion.

To the consternation of my boss at the time, Charlie Hodel, and my boss-to-be three years later, Frank Knight, when I finally wrote the editorial I was firmly in favor of a campus location. Building the medical school anywhere other than Morgantown, I felt, would erode the overall quality of education at WVU and would lead to a needless and expensive duplication of facilities and academic talent. Hodel wanted the school built at Beckley; Knight wanted it in Charleston. As it turned out, I was the only editor in southern West Virginia to favor Morgantown.

The medical school was built in Morgantown. The governor apparently had the ammunition he needed.

ANOTHER CONTENTIOUS QUESTION during much of Patteson's term was the West Virginia Turnpike issue. The bondholders and the Turnpike Commission, citing long-term traffic studies, supported the construction of only a two-lane highway, with creeper lanes in the more mountainous sections. Patteson demanded that the road be built to four-lane standards, and he drew support for his position from several newspapers, the most vocal of them *The Charleston Gazette*.

Believing that anything was an improvement over what was then a tortuous, two-hour-plus drive from Beckley to Charleston, the *Register* fell in behind the bondholders, whose concept would reduce driving time to one hour. The battle was joined in federal court, and the eighty-eight-mile turnpike was finally completed from Charleston to Princeton in 1954 to the standards wanted by the bondholders. The cost was $133 million.

Blessed throughout his term with a tax structure that produced annual surpluses, Patteson was able to support construction of a parking garage and a third office building for state government. He also had the good fortune to preside at the dedication ceremonies following the completion of the state's second office building, the $4 million structure on the corner of what was then Washington and Duffy Streets.

But like his predecessor Meadows, Patteson too found himself squarely in the middle of a prolonged coal strike, this one at the Elk River Coal and Lumber Company in Clay County. An estimated five hundred miners joined in the picketing, and as the strike wore on, gunshots echoed across the hills, reminiscent of the mine wars earlier in the century. During the strike two cars carrying workers were overturned, two bridges were dynamited, and a power station was blown up.

The ongoing violence forced Patteson to adopt a sterner-than-normal posture with his State Police Superintendent, W. E. Burchett, and finally, near the end of his term, the violence subsided. During the worst of the trouble, Patteson issued a proclamation authorizing Burchett to seek assistance from the Clay County sheriff's office to help maintain order.

Another problem for Patteson as his four years in office drew to a close was sharp and protracted criticism from the *Gazette* regarding road-building practices. Alluding in its news columns to building costs that were higher than usual, the newspaper charged that more than a few contracts for maintenance and new construction gave indications of violating accepted bidding procedures. The news stories led to a legislative investigation, but nothing came of the findings.

Patteson was embittered by this criticism, pointing out that while he was in office, 2,931 miles of secondary roads were built, 502 miles were reconditioned, 831 miles were rehabilitated after flood damage, 313 new bridges were constructed, and 314 bridges were rehabilitated.

The turnpike was not completed until Patteson's term was over, but upon leaving office he continued his commitment to the state's first major multiple-lane highway by becoming general manager of the Turnpike Commission. His original four-lane vision would finally be realized more than thirty years later at an additional cost of $784 million.

As Meadows had done before him, Patteson began looking around late in his term for a bright and personable successor. The governor chose Attorney General William C. Marland as his heir apparent and campaigned tirelessly on his behalf. On election day he saw this youngest of chief executives in West Virginia's history deliver his inaugural address as the state's twenty-fourth governor.

Patteson's political patronage that election year was not extended to another promising young man in the Democratic Party, who had served two terms in the House of Delegates and was then serving a term in the State Senate. When he decided to make his first bid for the U.S. House of Representatives, Robert C. Byrd was operating a mom-and-pop grocery store at Sophia, in Raleigh County. His early career also included stints as a trash collector, gas station attendant, welder, and meat butcher. Along the way, he had also joined the Ku Klux Klan.

Byrd's Klan connection had been revealed by his primary election opponent in the Senate race. During the 1952 general election, the *Gazette* published a letter Byrd had written in 1946, the year he had first sought a seat in the state legislature. In the letter, he wrote, "The Klan is needed today as never before and I am anxious to see its rebirth here in West Virginia and in every state in the nation." It was the beginning of one of the longest political careers in all of West Virginia's history.

Despite leaving the office of governor a more respected man than when he had first been elected to it, Okey Patteson never again ran for public office. After serving as turnpike general manager, he returned to his real estate business, but soon was offered the position of president of the Raleigh County Bank in Beckley. He remained there, a successful banker, until his eyesight began to fail. He died in a Beckley hospital on July 4, 1989, at the age of ninety.

One of Patteson's most humbling experiences occurred during a hunting trip in 1932, when an accident cost him both of his legs. He had himself fitted with prosthetic limbs below the knee but afterward always walked a little awkwardly. Although in constant pain, he never made excuses for his condition, and used his position as a public figure to promote advancements in the care and treatment of the handicapped.

MISCELLANY ∘ "WHASS GOIN' ON?"

ON THE LAST EVENING of my first week as a newspaper reporter, I received a call from the police station. "Somebody's been killed by a train down at the railroad station," my informant said.

I told editor Watkins where I was going, and that somehow I'd get back in time to write the story before the midnight deadline.

The body had by this time been taken to a nearby funeral home, where gathered for the purposes of their respective callings were the county sheriff, city police chief, and county coroner.

The victim was dead. That's for sure. Being young, and with a young man's curiosity—and stomach—I looked at him. The train had not been kind.

The big question at the moment was the victim's identity. Nobody knew who he was. Finally, somebody said, "Why, that's Ernie Smith," and after another look at the body the others agreed. Being new in town I had no idea who Ernie Smith was. I asked for some background information on him and was told that he was one of Beckley's most notable and affable drunks.

The discussion of Ernie continued, and in time Ernie achieved new stature, evolving into a respected and beloved member of the community. Had it been election day and had Ernie been running, he could easily have been elected mayor.

But suddenly the conversation stumbled to a halt as Ernie himself staggered into the funeral home and asked, "Whass goin' on? Who's dead?"

With the victim thus unidentified, I rushed back to the office and wrote my story. It was a straight-out, colorless account of a train victim's death.

Afterward, I told Watkins about Ernie and what had happened at the funeral home. My editor looked at me indulgently, as a father might an errant son, and asked, "Why didn't you write the story you're telling me now?"

It's a little late, Mr. Watkins, sir, but I finally have.

Chapter 4

A Byrd's Eye View

THE PUBLIC DISCLOSURE of Byrd's membership in the Ku Klux Klan during his younger years was considered a heaven-sent gift by the political establishment in West Virginia. When this morsel of intriguing news appeared in the press, Byrd was little more than one of a number of rising stars on the political horizon. But the very fact that his star was in ascendance had the powerbrokers more worried than they had been since the troublesome days of the 1920s. In Byrd they saw a friend of the workingman and, hence, a threat to the status quo. His youthful error in judgment gave them the opening they needed, the ammunition to halt his advance before he became too much of a threat to their stranglehold on state politics.

At the *Gazette*, where policy had been pro-business ever since W. E. Chilton had divided his time between publishing the newspaper and serving in the U.S. Senate in the early 1900s, the business view was gospel. And Patteson had consistently demonstrated his support of business interests and philosophy during his term as governor. The big guns were out and pointing in Byrd's direction.

This young man from the coalfields had become almost a legend among working people in only a few short years. As a member of the House of Delegates and later as a state senator, Byrd had never lost a race. He had pledged his faith to the Democratic Party, his wife, and the Baptist Church, and had no other special loyalties. He simply had a passion to serve his people, and rank-and-file voters reacted favorably when he came to call and ask for their votes. Among the party's powerbrokers, this set off loud alarms.

The breaking of the story about his Klan connection had all the signs of a staged affair. Patteson met with Byrd at his office in the evening and the *Ga-*

zette ran the story the next morning in an edition that circulated through all the counties where Byrd was running for Congress. It was a severe blow. Byrd had been labeled an unacceptable candidate by the party's titular head, and all future campaign funding from the Democratic Party had been withdrawn. For a man of lesser drive and determination, it would have marked the end of his public career. But as time and events would prove, Byrd was not a man of ordinary caliber.

I called him the morning the story appeared in the *Gazette* and asked for a statement for that afternoon's *Register.* He appeared at the office a couple of hours later with his written statement in hand. "You'll have to sign it, Bob," I told him. This request for his signature, standard newspaper policy, clearly angered Byrd, but he had no choice. He signed his name at the bottom of the page. Our story appeared that afternoon, a story saying that his decision to join the Klan was due to youthful folly, a mistake Byrd now regretted and would continue to regret for the rest of his life.

An evening or so later I visited him at his home in Sophia. Our friendship had grown since I had first interviewed him at the end of a counter at Posey Rhodes's Carolina Supermarket in Crab Orchard where he was working as a butcher. That was in 1946 when Byrd first ran for a seat in the House of Delegates. He was then an unknown in Beckley political circles but was the leader in a field of thirteen candidates. Our editor, Randolph Norton, wanted to find out more about him.

That interview, the first Byrd ever gave, produced no startling revelations. He came on a little strong in his desire to please a newsman, but a piece of campaign literature he gave me was a bit different from the standard fare passed out by most candidates. And his campaign slogan was catchy: "Byrd by name. Byrd by nature. Let's send Byrd to the legislature." He used the same jingle in later campaigns, and this, along with his mountain charm, his talent with a fiddle, and speeches heavily laced with references from his Baptist upbringing, won over audiences everywhere he spoke.

My trip to Sophia shortly after the story on his Klan affiliation appeared was to make sure he understood that the *Register* was not planning to forsake

him. After his visit to my office to drop off his statement, I had discussed it
with my publisher.

Hodel's reaction was a smile and the comment, "You'd be surprised if
you knew some of the men who joined the Klan back in the 1920s." A few
great men had made the same mistake, he said, reminding me of President
Roosevelt's nomination of Hugo Black, one of the finest justices ever to serve
on the Supreme Court, in the early New Deal years, and Black's admission
that he had once been a member of the Klan.

Byrd and I talked for about an hour—in his spartanly furnished apartment above the store—about his hopes and dreams for the poor and workers
of West Virginia. He also commented, somewhat bitterly, about the withdraw-
al of party funding, calling it a ploy by Democrats in the power bloc to force
him out of politics. As I left, he clenched his fist and struck the porch railing
as he said, "They're not going to win this race."

Byrd's discipline and will to win paid off in the end. He told me that evening that he was strapped for funds, that his grocery store had been drained
of every cent possible to finance the race, and his only recourse was a door-
to-door begging campaign among friends and church members for enough
money to keep his name alive as a viable candidate. Byrd learned a valuable
lesson during that political campaign. The road he had chosen to travel was
a lonely one. If he was to travel it for any distance he would have to build his
own political base within the majority party, and he would have to nurture
that base with tender loving care. He followed this course throughout his
public career, answering all requests for help with a promptness seldom seen
in Washington, visiting the precincts as often as possible, and periodically
submitting his "Byrd's Eye View," a report on sensitive issues of national concern, to newspapers around the state for use as they saw fit.

Byrd's manner was that of a tense and driven man, especially in his relations with staff. He was known all over Capitol Hill as difficult to work for, even
on nights before holidays. Twice I recruited public relations aides for him, and
neither one lasted more than a year. The office pace was frenetically busy, and
Byrd had a notable turnover of personnel. But he never asked more of his staff

than he was willing to give himself. He consistently maintained a long after-hours schedule, at home as well as in the office, a reflection of the work ethic he learned during a hard-scrabble youth in the coalfields.

HE WAS BORN CORNELIUS CALVIN SALE, JR., on November 20, 1917, in North Wilkesboro, North Carolina. After his mother died in the influenza epidemic of 1918, his father, a furniture maker, shipped the ten-month-old boy to a sister in Stotesbury, West Virginia. The child was given the new name of Robert Carlyle Byrd, and had no idea that he had been adopted until he was sixteen years old.

Byrd's childhood in the coalfields was one of extreme poverty. For years he didn't attend Sunday school because he had no socks. He helped to supplement the family income by gathering scraps from neighbors to feed his father's hogs. He picked up coal along the railroad tracks to heat the miner's shack where they lived.

Byrd doesn't remember ever being kissed by his mother. The only toy he ever had as a child was a small pedal car. Not until he was married did he live in a house with running water. And even after marriage to his high school sweetheart, Erma Ora James, their first refrigerator was an orange crate hung out a window for winter storage of perishable foods.

In his first race for the House of Delegates, he moved around the county by hitching rides with friends. The fiddle he had learned to play some years before proved to be a campaign asset. With such mountain tunes as "Goin' Up Cripple Creek," he won over his audiences and started building a constituency that has never been equaled by any other political figure in the state's history.

His rise through the political hierarchy was never easy. His acceptance outside what in West Virginia is described as "crick and holler" country was replete with embarrassing incidents. In the early 1950s I invited Byrd to address the Beckley Rotary Club. By then he had served in both houses of the state legislature and was in his second term in the U.S. House of Representatives. He had attended Concord College, Morris Harvey College, and Marshall College in his pursuit of a degree. He was a man with an impressive list of credits, committed to bettering himself and his state.

But all too many of the merchant-banker-coal-operator crowd, the movers and shakers of Beckley society—more than a few of whom had started out in circumstances similar to Byrd's—looked upon their congressman as "that boob" or "the butcher boy from Crab Orchard." As soon as word got out that I had invited him to address a regular meeting, I began receiving snide remarks and complaints. Some of the members thought I was soiling the club's elite image by extending an invitation to Congressman Byrd.

He couldn't help noticing the coolness displayed by the members as he sat and chatted with them during dinner. Their rudeness was embarrassing to both me and, I'm sure, the guest speaker. But the chilly atmosphere began to melt rapidly a few minutes into his speech.

After introducing Byrd I positioned myself so I could watch the crowd's reaction, and I almost laughed out loud as the determined resistance in the room gradually lessened, turning first to interest and then to acceptance. As he spoke, Byrd drew the names of various members into his remarks, a trademark tactic. His subject matter had been well researched.

Within fifteen minutes Byrd had won over a roomful of hostile Beckley businessmen, and in that fifteen minutes I realized that he was unstoppable. I was certain then that he could win whatever contest he chose to enter.

But he was forced to struggle every step of the way. Byrd often had more trouble getting an introduction at Democratic campaign gatherings than he did winning elections.

"I remember one meeting where they made me feel particularly unwelcome," he recalled later. "I felt in those days that those of us who weren't lawyers were looked down upon. I don't know what gave me the impression . . . but anyway, the gentleman who introduced me was a lawyer. He introduced me as a fiddle player and butcher running for Congress. So when I stood up to speak, I said this fellow who didn't want to introduce me had said I played the fiddle and worked in a butcher shop, and he didn't mean it as a compliment. I said Thomas Jefferson played the fiddle, so why shouldn't I? And William Shakespeare worked in his father's butcher shop, so what's wrong with that?"

Then Byrd, who had already distinguished himself as a student at three West Virginia colleges, made a promise to his audience. "If it's the last thing I ever do, I'm going to get myself a law degree."

And he did. Byrd spent ten years of his after-hours time studying for a law degree at George Washington University and American University while serving in the House and Senate. He graduated cum laude in 1963 at the age of forty-five.

BYRD WENT TO CONGRESS as a conservative. He railed against welfare cheaters and opposed major civil-rights legislation. He was a hawk during the Vietnam War and denounced student protestors. But by the time his fellow senator from West Virginia, Jennings Randolph, an old-time New Dealer, nominated him for Senate whip at the Democratic caucus in 1971, Byrd had developed into a moderate, having by then voted for open housing, gun control, and the extension of the Voting Rights Act of 1965.

During the early 1960s Byrd had joined his southern colleagues in filibustering against civil rights, once holding the floor for twenty-one hours and reading into the record news reports of black men raping white women. "Men are not created equal today," he said, "and they were not created equal in 1776, when the Declaration of Independence was written. Men and races differ in appearance, ways, physical powers, mental capacity, creativity, and vision."

He expressed the same contempt for anti-war protestors who opposed the Vietnam War, describing them as "hypo-critical, self-centered, selfish, long-haired, know-it-all students and pseudo-intellectuals" who wanted to "encourage Hanoi and help kill American boys."

This, I thought at the time, was not the Bob Byrd who had taught a Bible class at the Crab Orchard Baptist Church. This was not the Byrd I had heard speak on the American promise at homespun political gatherings high in the Southern West Virginia mountains. This was not the Byrd I had talked with for hours in his office or at my home about old-fashioned virtues.

This was a frustrated and angry Byrd, a man frustrated that his hidebound southern associates were moving too slowly on civil rights legislation and angry at himself for having thrown in his lot with them in his effort to gain a foothold on the Senate leadership ladder, a foothold that was necessary if he was to be able to make a difference to the people of his state. I was critical of his political stance in editorials and in my column, and for many years afterward his letters were no longer signed "Bob." They were signed "Robert" in his precise penmanship.

His change in philosophy, as a man more concerned with civil liberty and related matters, was a subject of frequent discussion in the capital press. His explanation for the shift was that the issues and circumstances had changed more than his own position. A longtime "Byrd-watcher" had another view: "He realizes where the tide is going, and he will drift with it to compile a public record that is more defensible and acceptable."

Today Byrd is characterized as a little right of center. This is where he wants to be, for in his opinion the American people stand ideologically at about the same place. His positions through the years on major issues, some of them the most sensitive in all of history, had astounding voter acceptance. He served three terms in the House of Representatives, representing Raleigh, Boone, Kanawha, and Logan counties, before making his first bid for the U.S. Senate. When he won his senatorial seat, he became the first West Virginian ever to serve in both houses of the state legislature and U.S. Congress.

His win record thereafter in his Senate campaigns was so impressive that in 1976 he ran unopposed in both the primary and general elections. Even in his only difficult race, the 1982 election when his opponent was Republican Congressman Cleveland K. Benedict, of Lewisburg, Byrd captured 69 percent of the vote. First elected to the U.S. Senate in 1958, Byrd has served longer in that august body than anyone else in this state's history, a testament to his constituents' support of his public service.

WHILE BYRD WAS ALWAYS a popular political figure with West Virginia's rank-and-file voters, he was generally ignored around Washington by the media and political powerbrokers until he took on Edward M. Kennedy for the position of Democratic whip in 1971. His defeat of an incumbent and nationally prominent personality was portrayed by news writers as an overnight coup, but actually it was years in the making. In his four years as secretary of the Senate Democratic Conference, a previously low-grade job, Byrd had functioned as Majority Leader Mike Mansfield's right-hand man, performing the routine chores that had never interested Kennedy. While Byrd's better-known colleagues were off enjoying the Washington social scene in the evenings, Byrd was hard at work on all the prosaic but necessary business of the Senate, learning the intricacies of the Senate rules in the office of the parliamentarian. This thankless work paid off handsomely. "Now," as was later stated in The Atlantic, "he knows those rules better than any of his peers, and can make the rules do whatever is needed by him, his friends, or his party."

Byrd succeeded Mansfield as majority leader, the highest position in the Senate, served as minority leader while the Republicans were in control during part of the Reagan administration, and later returned to the majority leader's post. He stepped down from that position in 1988 to become chairman of the powerful Senate Appropriations Committee. Years ago, when I asked him about his ultimate ambition, he told me that it was to be chairman of appropriations, not realizing at the time that he would rise even farther in the Senate or that he would be considered for a seat on the U.S. Supreme Court during the Nixon administration.

After Byrd resigned as majority leader and took over the chairmanship of the Senate Appropriations Committee, he was determined to see that West Virginia got a share of the federal funding for everything from military-hardware development to space exploration, which had been going for so long to such states as Texas, California, Virginia, and Connecticut. West Virginia had been at or near the bottom of the allocations list for decades.

Byrd was criticized by his fellow members of Congress and in the media for his actions, but he was successful in bringing the FBI's fingerprint identification center to Clarksburg, a new $80 million federal building to Charleston, a $30 million federal building to Beckley, funds to complete Corridor G from Williamson to Charleston by way of Logan, funding to build a long-awaited section of Corridor H from Buckhannon to Elkins (as well as additional funding to continue construction of the road to the Virginia border), and $60 million for a federal prison near the Raleigh County airport that would house more than 1,500 inmates and employ over three hundred people.

There were more federally funded projects, both large and small. In the 1990s Bob Byrd became a one-man economic development authority for West

Virginia, singlehandedly bringing more new jobs to the state than the governor's development office was able to do with a large workforce.

This man who came from a childhood of poverty and hardship, who struggled with intense determination through the American political process with very little help except for the unwavering faith of his constituency, excelled at everything he undertook along the way. And he eventually was granted the recognition he had earned. The *Gazette*, which had tried to force him out of politics in 1952, selected Byrd as the outstanding West Virginian of 1974 and 1977. The newspaper had never chosen anyone for this honor more than once. A *U.S. News & World Report* poll of American leaders entitled "Who Runs America" rated him the most influential person in the United States in 1979. In 1988, when Byrd stepped down as majority leader, one of his earlier foes, Senator Ted Kennedy, expressed the opinion of many of his congressional colleagues when he delivered this tribute:

"I have discovered a lot about political life in the twenty-five years I have served in the Senate. But the two most important lessons I have learned can be summed up very quickly—it is difficult to challenge an incumbent president, but it is impossible to challenge Bob Byrd.

"Genius is the capacity for taking infinite pains—and to some extent that is the secret of Bob Byrd's genius. Probably no senator since 1789 has had a greater mastery of the complexities, and the possibilities, of the Senate rules than Bob Byrd. Again and again under his leadership that mastery has enable him to cool the hottest passions, resolve the angriest gridlock, and permit the Senate to work its will. Above all is his commitment to the people of West Virginia and the public interest of the nation."

Chapter 5

A MAN FOR ANOTHER SEASON

WILLIAM CASEY MARLAND broke the mold when he became West Virginia's twenty-fourth governor on January 19, 1953.

From the outset of his term he let it be known that he had no intention of acting as waterboy for the land barons and industrial giants who had dominated state politics for nearly a century. He had already warned during the campaign, "I am for change." In his inaugural message he cautioned that government had grown "without proper planning and . . . become more cumbersome that it should be." He further emphasized his philosophical leanings by having as his guest at the inauguration a towering and powerful figure in organized labor, UMW President John L. Lewis.

Marland threw down the gauntlet shortly after the inauguration. In his first address to the legislature he asked for passage of a severance tax on natural resources. The West Virginia congressional delegation, the state's teachers, and organized labor were in favor of this effort to reinforce fiscal solvency, but the business lobbies screamed foul and the battle of the year was joined. Marland's sponsors in his almost meteoric rise to the governorship had apparently neglected to examine their candidate's early life before bestowing their blessings on his ambitions. Marland had been a coal miner. In his wallet on inauguration day he carried his union card.

Born in Illinois, Marland had moved to West Virginia with his family at the age of seven. His father was superintendent of the vast mining operation at Glen Rogers, where young Bill Marland went to work first as a slate picker and later as weigh boss. During World War II, Marland served on a cruiser with the famed Task Force 58, which won more battles in the Pacific than any other fleet of ships. Later he commanded his own ship, a landing craft which ran troops and supplies ashore at Leyte Gulf and Luzon. Before he reached his mid-twenties, Bill Marland had seen more of the raw side of life than practically any of his predecessors.

He earned his law degree from West Virginia University, where he was a hardworking and accomplished student, serving as president of the student board of editors of the *Law Quarterly* and earning membership in the prestigious Order of the Coif. After leaving law school, he was appointed law clerk to U.S. District Judge Ben Moore; the next year he was named assistant attorney general. When Ira Partlow resigned in 1949, Marland was appointed attorney general. A year later he was elected to fill the last two years of the Partlow term. His final move, with the sponsorship of Governor Patteson, was into the governor's office.

Early in the tempestuous battle over the severance tax, Marland invited me to the Governor's Mansion in Charleston for lunch. The *Register* had come out firmly behind him in a series of editorials, and he wanted to talk to one of the few editors in the state who was in his corner. There weren't many of us. With the *Gazette* as their chief spokesman, the business lobby was creating a furor and thrashing the governor and his programs with the help of their pet legislators.

It wasn't the first time Marland and I had talked about matters of mutual interest. During his campaign for governor, he had come by my office before the primary to discuss his platform, and late in the general election he had dropped by our house in the Beckley suburbs, hoping for *Register* endorsement. It was obvious that he had been briefed by Patteson. He spent some time explaining what he hoped to accomplish as governor and expressed the belief that he had a better grasp of state affairs than his Republican opponent, former U.S. Senator Rush D. Holt of Weston.

I suppose by this time I had become seasoned as an editor. Because of a longstanding policy of abstaining from partisan endorsements in the primaries, I had avoided having to choose between Marland, raised in neighboring Wyoming County, and a fellow Beckleyan, Congressman E. H. Hedrick. But now it was time to either fish or cut bait, as the saying goes in the mountains, and I made my newspaper's decision undisturbed in body or spirit. Shortly afterward I left with my wife for a family dinner at the Black Knight Country Club, the same establishment where Patteson and I had reached an understanding four years earlier.

The trade-off with Marland? A road from Glen Daniel in Raleigh County across Skin Poplar Gap to Boone and Logan counties. This road, if built, would greatly improve access between three major coal-producing counties and would ultimately lessen the cost of travel and transportation.

Toward the end of his term as governor Marland mentioned one day in his office that the Skin Poplar Gap road was being built. By that time I was living in Charleston and working for the *Gazette*. "It's been difficult and expensive," he added, "but I want you to know I keep my word."

ON THE DAY that I had lunch with the governor early in his term, I brought my brother with me at Marland's insistence. Charley was then an Associated Press staffer in Huntington, and we had intended to get together for a day at the legislature. "Bring him along," the governor said. "One more Stafford won't ruin my digestion."

Marland was visibly on edge during lunch. And the severance tax was not his only concern. "I inherited a lot of problems when I took office," he told us. Departmental empire-building and overlapping responsibilities had grown during the twenty years of one-party rule in the Statehouse. "I've got to make some changes, and they won't be popular with the people who have been running things in the past."

We talked about the severance tax, a piece of legislation that would be used to finance the medical school, pump new life into public-school education, and put the Highway Department on a pay-as-you-go basis. We also talked about several state parks the governor wanted to build, particularly one at Blackwater Falls in Tucker County. "Tucker was prosperous and booming in the past," he mused. "The lumbermen came in and stripped it of timber. Then the coal operators dug out the best coal. Nothing much is left, and we have to help those people."

Later, as I drove back to Beckley, I found myself thinking about the young man Charley had introduced me to at the Capitol before we went to the Mansion for lunch. A first-term member of the House of Delegates and a Republican, he was brash and caustic in his comments regarding the Democratic governor. He and Charley had been fraternity brothers at WVU.

I had no idea at the time that both of them were destined for bigger things. Charley, as a member of the Washington press corps, would be accorded American journalism's highest honor, a Pulitzer for investigative writing. His former fraternity brother would go on to Congress and later earn the distinction of becoming the first governor in West Virginia history to be elected to three four-year terms. His name was Arch Moore.

THE *GAZETTE*, whose policy on the severance tax was being guided in large measure by an outside editorial board composed of a banker, a businessman, a mid-level state official, and the chief lobbyist for the coal industry, was the most strident of the state papers in its opposition. So effective had the criticism become late in the session that Marland went to the legislature with a special message.

"When our coal is gone," the governor said, "there will be nothing to which our people can turn for their livelihood . . . I say to you, let's use this suitable source of revenue because whether we like it or not, West Virginia's hills will be stripped, the bowels of the earth will be mined, and the refuse strewn across the valleys and our mountains in the form of burning slate dumps."

But those slate dumps and stripped hillsides weren't visible from the Capitol, and the legislature had been too long beholden to the coffers of commercial enterprise in this mineral-rich state. In a House of Delegates vote which stopped all future action on the measure, the severance tax was killed. Marland and his supporters were so soundly defeated that the tax would not be considered again as a possible source of revenue for the next three decades.

Marland had one of the best minds of all the governors I have known, but occasionally he could be stubborn and foolish. He might have fared better had he not awarded a wine account to his then-retired father and ordered road improvements to his Dutch Ridge farm. He had none of the hill-country charm and political savvy of his predecessor. He was a man of vision and passion, but he lacked a certain understanding and the well-honed political instincts he needed to achieve his goals.

During Marland's first year in office, the legislature tried to infringe on his authority by adopting a budget padded with self-serving and nonexistent anticipatory revenue. Its validity was so questionable that the Board of Public Works refused to increase revenue estimates, a constitutional requirement before the budget could go into effect, and the governor had to call the lawmakers back into special session to correct these inequities. The session lasted one day.

There were already clouds on the economic horizon when Marland took office. Not enough tax revenue was coming in to meet the state's needs, and the governor was forced to order a 5 percent across-the-board reduction in spending to keep the state out of bankruptcy. In his second year in office he caused more conflict by firing two members of the Turnpike Commission as well as one member of the State Board of Education and the WVU Board of Governors. The Supreme Court moved into the fray. In a single decision, it validated the turnpike firings but overruled the governor on the two board firings.

Many of the governor's appointments to state positions ran into resistance in the Senate, which had consent authority. The atmosphere became so tense that on one occasion the Senate leadership was unable to explain, after a closed-door session, why it refused to approve a Northern Panhandle appointee to a minor advisory board. When questioned about it, one embarrassed senator responded, "We don't know. We had to be against somebody, and he had a funny name."

One of Marland's appointees who generated headlines was W. W. Barron, the governor's new liquor commissioner. Barron didn't last long. He lost his job in a sweep that also took off the public payroll Joe F. Burdette, chairman of the Board of Control. Both men had remarkable recuperative powers, however. Barron would return a few years later as attorney general and Burdette as secretary of state, both elective positions.

Midway through his term Marland again tried to raise taxes. Advising the legislature that surpluses were now history, and that any thoughts of financing capital improvements were an absurdity without new sources of revenue, he asked for increased taxation. He got little of what he sought.

But Marland was a determined man. At a special session in May 1955, called by the governor for the purpose of dealing with state school aid, he won a major battle, one that had previously been fought by both Meadows and Patteson without success. The legislature passed a law compelling the counties to increase their assessed valuations or lose a portion of their state aid.

This form of taxation had been neglected since passage of the Tax Limitation Amendment in 1932, and some counties, cities, and school districts were in desperate financial shape. On a graduated scale, the new act provided that all such property would be assessed in 1956 at no less than 35 percent of appraised value, with the amount growing 5 percent per year until a ceiling of 50 percent was reached in 1959.

The legislature also approved formation of two commissions on education, one to examine the public schools and the other to look into higher education with the idea of creating one rather than two policy-making bodies. The most important outcome of these studies would be the creation of the Board of Regents, authorized to oversee state colleges and universities.

In that same year, Marland retained the Cambridge, Massachusetts, consulting firm of Arthur D. Little, Inc., to help him find methods of attracting new industry to West Virginia. Jobs were disappearing in the coalfields as mining became more mechanized. The postwar industrial stimulus was fading. Unemployment had become a problem for the first time since the Great Depression.

Adopting a concept recommended by the Massachusetts consultants, Marland began touring the country in search of new industry for West Virginia. In a speech at the Harvard Club in New York City, where he began his tour, he enumerated the state's assets, describing West Virginia as "amply blessed" with such resources as coal, timber, oil and gas, and a dependable labor force. "I am here," the governor told his luncheon guests, "as a representative of two million West Virginians who want nothing more than the opportunity to show you that our state may be a profitable location for one of your operations."

Marland was greeted with courtesy by the business, industrial, and financial representatives present, but one of them expressed an opinion I would hear repeated often in other cities the governor's entourage visited in search of new business. "Why are you trying to pirate away our industry?" this textile manufacturer asked. "We're having trouble holding on to what we have now."

In spite of this attitude and the fact that every other state in the country was in the marketplace hustling for new business and promoting its best qualities, approximately seventy new industries employing almost fifty thousand workers moved to West Virginia during Marland's term, among them the $216 million Kaiser Aluminum and Chemical Corporation plant in Ravenswood.

A constant problem for Marland throughout his years as governor was the legislature's distrust of his actions and motives. Early in his term, he had legislation introduced calling for expansion of the state park system with revenue bonds. The bill moved through the Senate and House with barely a negative vote cast. But on most issues, the legislature seemed suspicious of Marland and his intentions, even to the point of trying to reorganize the Highway Department by passing a bill creating a ten-member oversight commission. The governor vetoed this ill-conceived effort to seize control, reasoning that committee management would so dilute responsibility that it would have a counterproductive effect on road building.

The legislative effort to reorganize the Highway Department, however, led to a decision by Marland that would benefit the state for the next decade or more: his appointment of Burl A. Sawyers as road commissioner. Sawyers developed his own reorganization plan which clarified and strengthened the layers of authority within the department, formed a new Personnel Division and created a centralized accounting system.

SAWYERS ALSO ADOPTED a proposal the *Gazette* had suggested editorially as a means of making the West Virginia Turnpike a road to somewhere rather than the "road to nowhere" it had been labeled by the national press. One day after I had moved to Charleston, I was leafing through the *Congressional Quarterly*, a Washington information service, and discovered that some three thousand miles of the forty-three-thousand-mile interstate highway system had yet to be allocated to the states. Locating a map of the interstates and their projected development, I found that an area southward from the Great Lakes to Florida had been ignored in the original planning.

On the map, I sketched a route from Cleveland by way of Charleston, West Virginia; through Charlotte, North Carolina; to Columbia, South Carolina, where Interstate 25 would provide a link with Interstate 95 to the east. It made sense. But this proposal was hardly new. Running generally along U.S. 21, it was simply an updating of an old Lakes-to-Florida dream that I had first heard about as a young reporter covering a Beckley Chamber of Commerce dinner before World War II.

I put the idea on paper as an editorial, passed it to Harry Hoffmann, who by this time had succeeded the late Frank Knight as editor, and we were off and running. Sawyers read the editorial, liked the idea, and started building support for the proposition by calling together delegations from Parkersburg, Charleston, Beckley, Princeton, and Bluefield to discuss it at a meeting in the House of Delegates chamber. With Marland's backing, Sawyers also contacted highway commissioners in other states.

Meanwhile, I sent copies of the editorial to newspapers in Cleveland, Akron, Charlotte, and Columbia and began talking to candidates for office whenever they dropped by the *Gazette*. They were fair game. Candidates frequently launch political campaigns with a single-minded focus on winning the election, and only begin looking around for programs or platforms after they discover that public office is more service than sinecure. In their desperation for inspiration, they become easy prey for a newsman with a promotional scheme in mind.

During the year when Marland's term was winding down, the Lakes-to-Florida superhighway became a major campaign issue. But while Democrats and Republicans alike endorsed it, this was the year the Democrats would be thrown out of the Statehouse by Republican Cecil Underwood, and Underwood would be the one to take the idea to Washington where it would find a receptive ear in the Eisenhower administration.

THE BRUISES AND SCARS from Marland's first legislative battle never quite disappeared. They remained with him throughout his term as governor and in his last message to the legislature, delivered on January 9, 1957, when he asserted that conditions remained basically unchanged from the day when he first took office. He expressed satisfaction in having been able to obtain legislative approval for the new state parks and for the funds he needed to launch the industrial development program; in serving as the state's chief executive when the federal government chose Greenbank as the site for what was then the largest radio astronomy observatory in the world; and in having been able to raise teachers' salaries and pave roads while keeping the budget balanced. "It has been both fascinating and educational, an experience that will be the highlight of my life," he concluded.

Never was a remark more tragically prescient. Disillusioned, disappointed and depressed after the severance tax defeat, Marland had begun drinking, and as the years wore on, his bouts with the bottle became more serious. By the time he left office, rumors about his problem were spreading everywhere across the state; around Charleston it was a common cocktail hour topic. The image of the golden boy—intelligent, good-looking, an outstanding student of law and political prodigy—was sadly tarnished.

Much of Marland's last year in office was occupied by his effort to position himself to run for the U.S. Senate. When Senator Kilgore died in February 1956, the governor appointed his tax commissioner, William R. Laird III, to fill the remainder of Kilgore's term. But it would be a frustrating and difficult campaign for Marland. Little was left of Governor Kump's New Deal coalition, which had peaked with the election of Holt in 1936. By the time Marland entered the governor's office, its effectiveness in the political arena was virtually nonexistent.

Sensing the shift in the political winds, Senator Neely and former Congressman Joe L. Smith began looking for a means to maintain their own influence. They agreed to endorse Neely's protégé, first district Congressman Robert H. Mollohan, as the Democratic candidate for governor in the '56 election and installed Smith's younger son, Hulett, as Mollohan's campaign manager. This job would position the younger Smith for his own run in the gubernatorial election four years later and perhaps establish a new political dynasty in southern West Virginia. It would also guarantee Neely and Smith another eight years of influence.

This maneuver was shortsighted. In effect, it would have shifted the governorship from its power base in southern West Virginia to the northern part of the state for a single term. For four successive administrations, the governor's office had been occupied by a candidate from the southern center of Democratic strength: Fayette, Raleigh, and Wyoming counties. To shift it away from that center for one term and expect it to shift back essentially on demand four years later was unrealistic and politically reckless.

The Democratic Party was further splintered when Marland's mentor and sponsor, Patteson, decided to join big coal's effort to place Senate Clerk J. Howard Myers in the governor's chair, the man who had been left at the starting block in 1952. And when Patteson signed on as Myers's campaign manager, he let it be known in no uncertain terms that he was abandoning his former protégé, Governor Marland.

Patteson's public break with Marland was a mistake, one which would have serious consequences for the Democratic Party. "My association and contact with [Marland]," Patteson announced, "led me to believe that he was honest, trustworthy, highly efficient, and strictly sober . . . Now I realize my faith was misplaced." Patteson failed to take into account the many accomplishments of Marland's term and the loyal constituency Marland still had within the party, a constituency that Patteson only alienated with his comments.

Patteson apparently had lost his touch, as I began to discover when Knight, editor of the *Gazette*, assigned me to write press releases for candidate Myers as a favor to Patteson. I found the campaign poorly organized and underfunded, and it ultimately collapsed, along with Patteson's power base, after a hundred thousand dollars in promised donations from a group of southern coal operators failed to materialize. In the primary, Myers came in third in a five-man race.

The entire 1956 Democratic campaign was a classic political bungle from start to finish. In the same election, Marland first endorsed his former tax commissioner, Milton J. Ferguson, for governor, but in a last minute bid to prop up his own campaign for the Senate, he switched his support to the Neely-Smith candidate, Robert Mollohan. Mollohan's campaign, however, lacked focus from the very start, and a ghost from his past would throw it into complete disarray. The public disclosure of his dealings with a Northern West Virginia coal company, which had been allowed to strip coal on state land belonging to the Industrial School for Boys in Pruntytown while he was serving as superintendent of the school, severely damaged his chances. Mollohan was beaten in the general election by House Minority Leader Cecil Underwood, and Marland lost his Senate race to former Senator Chapman Revercomb. Two other Republican winners that year were my sister's husband, R. Virgil Rohrbough, who was elected state superintendent of schools, and my brother Charley's former fraternity brother, Arch Moore, who took over Mollohan's seat in the U.S. House of Representatives.

AFTER HIS DEFEAT, Marland went into the practice of law in downtown Charleston. He said he hoped to establish an industrial-development consulting service, but this venture wasn't particularly successful. Politics was still in his blood, and when both U.S. Senate seats opened up in 1958, Marland signed on as a candidate. One opening was for the regular term while the other was for the unexpired term of Neely, the aging political patriarch who had died on January 18.

Marland chose to run for the short term because it offered more seniority. He lost in the primary. An old New Deal warrior and former congressman, Jennings Randolph, came out of airline management to win the seat. Randolph would serve in the Senate as a committed and respected liberal until his retirement in 1986. Robert C. Byrd, then a congressman, ran for the full-term seat and, like Randolph, won easily, turning old-timer Chapman Revercomb out of office. Randolph, Governor Underwood's appointee to finish out Senator Neely's unexpired term, turned out Jack Hoblitzell, the former Republican state chairman.

Marland left Charleston within a year after the election, going to work for West Kentucky Coal Corporation. His life from then on was a downward spiral, due primarily to his inability to give up alcohol. The pride of the WVU law school and former governor of West Virginia eventually wound up driving a taxicab in Chicago.

Marland finally conquered his drinking problem and returned to West Virginia in 1965 as an associate director of James F. Edwards Enterprises, a company committed mainly to the training and racing of horses. "I haven't had a drink in four years," he told friends. But his return to the state where he had shown so much promise would be of short duration. He died of cancer six months later.

Funeral services for Marland were held in Barrington, Illinois, where he then had his home. Among those in attendance at the service in the Barrington Methodist Church were Governor Hulett Smith and Senators Randolph and Byrd. In keeping with Marland's wishes, his remains were cremated and the ashes scattered over his Dutch Ridge farm in West Virginia from Smith's private plane by state pilot Edsel France.

Bill Marland's story was a real-life tragedy. He struggled mightily to return the political process to what he believed it should be, government by the people. But as even some of his critics acknowledged, he was a man for another season, a governor out of step with his own times.

Chapter 6

POLITICAL SHAKE-UP

THE 1956 ELECTION YEAR was a politically exciting time in West Virginia. Democrats turned testy while Republicans shouted with glee when Cecil Harland Underwood was elected as the state's twenty-fifth governor. Such behavior was understandable. Underwood was the first Republican in twenty-four years to be elected to the state's highest office.

Opinions as to why this surprising event occurred, in the face of an over-whelmingly Democratic voter registration, varied widely. The presence of incumbent President Dwight D. Eisenhower, also a Republican, on the same ballot was certainly an advantage for Underwood.

Many credited Underwood's low-key charm and charisma as well as his unblemished background as the primary factors in his election. Others said voters simply rebelled against the quality of the candidates offered by a party that had controlled the West Virginia electoral process for so long.

The average voter could identify with Underwood. He had started life as a farmer's son and had worked his way through college to earn a degree in education, eventually becoming vice president of a small Christian college. He had been the legislature's most vocal advocate of budgetary restraint for a dozen years when he entered the race for governor.

By contrast, his opponent, U.S. Representative Robert H. Mollohan, had gotten his hands soiled in a coal-mining venture. While serving as head of the Industrial School for Boys at Pruntytown, where his responsibility was the rehabilitation of wayward youths, Mollohan had personally benefited when a private coal company began strip-mining operations on school lands.

In his analysis of this election four years later, WVU political science professor William R. Ross wondered "whether the Republicans won the election in West Virginia in 1956 or whether the Democrats simply lost it . . . "

Regardless of who won and who lost, the '56 election was a political classic. Mollohan, as personable as Underwood, was a U.S. Congressman with the power and influence of the Statehouse machine behind him. He was also labor's choice in this heavily unionized state.

Underwood, on the other hand, was relatively unknown. His only claim to fame was several years of service as minority leader in the House of Delegates. But after the business community lost its chosen candidate, Howard Myers, in the primary, it swung behind Underwood with all of its force and power. Even one of its most respected spokesmen, former Democratic Governor Holt, then a senior partner in one of the state's largest corporate law firms, publicly endorsed the young legislator.

The Republican leadership planned its strategy well. Waiting for the best possible moment to strike out at Mollohan in the closing days of the campaign, it took its best shot, the Boys' School strip-mine deal, to the *Gazette*, a newspaper of independent Democratic allegiance, rather than to the staunchly Republican *Daily Mail*.

The *Gazette* broke the story with big, bold headlines, quoting Republican State Chairman Jack Hoblitzell who claimed to have documented proof that Underwood's opponent had received more than twenty thousand dollars in exchange for his "influence" in helping Grafton Coal Company obtain stripping rights on state-owned land. Hoblitzell produced three checks as a basis for his charge, and pointed out that Mollohan had been superintendent of the school when they were written.

Mollohan denied the charges, but the *Gazette* did a follow-up stringer on his relationship to Grafton Coal during his tenure at the school. By election morning even the UMW's leadership had grown red-faced as a result of Mollohan's eventual admission that he had been an officer of Grafton Coal. In 1950s labor circles, the UMW had been found guilty of the worst of hypocrisies, endorsing a former coal company executive.

Underwood's victory was decisive. He outpaced Mollohan by 63,381 votes, and by winning office at the age of thirty-four he bested Marland's record as the youngest governor in the state's history.

UNDERWOOD WAS INAUGURATED on January 14, 1957. Snow had fallen the night before and it was cold and brisk as he took the oath of office before a gathering of well-wishers in front of the Capitol. With nature so uncooperative, the affair was less festive than his fellow Republicans had hoped it would be after waiting on the sidelines for a quarter century.

In his inaugural address, Underwood held out the olive branch to the Democrats who had been elected with him, saying, "I have been heartened beyond measure by the statesmanlike attitude and declarations of those of both parties who are to serve with me in the legislative, executive and judicial branches of state government." But in almost the next breath he gave political harmony a kick in the teeth. Every state official holding office by virtue of executive appointment was directed to resign. Underwood chose not to follow standard procedure by sitting down with them and reviewing their records. Most were Democrats, appointed by Democrats, and he wanted them gone.

The only Republicans elected to major state offices that year had been Underwood and the new state school superintendent, Rohrbough, who had defeated an aging W. W. Trent. The legislature remained lopsidedly Democratic, as did the rest of the budget-writing Board of Public Works—the secretary of state, auditor, treasurer, attorney general, and agriculture commissioner.

Six minutes after midnight on inauguration day, the oath of office had been administered to Underwood at the Kanawha Hotel in what was described by the *Daily Mail* as a secret ceremony. "My purpose," Underwood said, "is to prevent any more resignations and lame duck appointments." Rumors had been rampant in Republican circles that Senator Neely, then eighty-two, might resign and let Marland name a Democratic successor. At the same time, the governor of a few minutes issued orders to suspend all state contracts for liquor, road equipment, and tires, a decision he was to regret over the next several months.

The blustery winter weather that greeted him on inauguration day continued for some weeks, and the governor's precipitate effort to take charge resulted in a wave of embarrassing incidents. Road Commission firings left him shorthanded, with inexperienced crews to clear the highways after heavy snowfalls. Equipment breakdowns went unrepaired for lack of spare parts. Service in state liquor stores slowed almost to a crawl as untrained workers took over their new jobs. Some popular brands of spirits disappeared from the shelves for several months, depriving state coffers of the lucrative tax on liquor.

In his first message to the legislature, Underwood once again promoted bipartisanship. "The electorate," he said, "has made it amply clear that it regards lawmaking as a duty which must be carried out in an atmosphere of impartiality, independence, and absolute consecration to the public good." But no governor in years had had to face the kind of uphill battle Underwood did when he took office. He may have been as dedicated to the spirit of cooperation as he claimed in his public utterances, but his supporters preferred power to harmony. They had helped elect the first Republican governor in two decades, and they were ready for their payoff, in the form of jobs, favors, and control.

In the words of Bill Veek, one of baseball's most colorful figures, they were telling Underwood, "I do not think winning is the most important thing. I think winning is the only thing."

UNDERWOOD'S "ATMOSPHERE OF IMPARTIALITY" died an early death. The legislative leadership introduced a bill to extend the merit system to most state employees, a move which would have locked thousands of Democrats into their jobs. When Underwood took office, only a token number under the federal civil-service umbrella were in the merit program. The governor's reaction was fast and historically shrewd.

In a veto message, he recalled a "striking parallel" when in 1916 a "Republican legislature, motivated by the same fears and purposes as this legislature, enacted legislation which . . . was designed to freeze job holders in office. The governor-elect at this time was a Democrat, the late Honorable John J.

Cornwell. Governor Cornwell was forced to serve out the entire term of office saddled with some of the most inhibitive restrictions ever imposed on a chief executive." Underwood's veto remained unchallenged. Not until the Barron, Smith, and Moore administrations of the following decade would the civil-service proposal find a receptive ear in the Statehouse.

Although the pitched battle between the governor and the legislature continued throughout the session, Underwood was successful in gaining passage of most of his first-year program. He was granted authorization to reorganize the Road Commission, set up a Mental Health Department, establish the Department of Finance and Administration, and form a bipartisan commission on property equalization and reevaluation.

Underwood often said before and after becoming governor that the chief executive had little influence on state affairs, that he was a creature of the legislature. Having been both governor and legislator as well as a political science student and author of a master's thesis entitled "The Legislative Process in West Virginia," Underwood was more qualified than most of his peers to make this assessment.

Constitutionally, as Underwood said in his treatise, the legislature determines basic governmental policy, decides on the public services to be offered, and appropriates the money for these services. The right and authority exist, in other words, for the legislature to assume general supervision over the operation of the executive branch, including the power of the Senate to pass upon appointments of the governor to many essential state positions.

Underwood was given a quick lesson in the legislature's control over the appointive process when, at a special session in the summer of 1957, he sent to the Senate approximately one hundred appointments for review and action. The majority Democrats summarily postponed consideration until early in the following year.

This move was made only to harass the governor, as some of the senators admitted quietly, but it had the unintended effect of disrupting the orderly function of government administration. Underwood became so furious that he summoned his department heads into a meeting in the Senate chamber where he condemned the action as frustrating and demoralizing to his administration. He charged that the Democrats were trying to cripple normal operations and added bitterly, "Government by threats, reprisals, blackmail, and intimidation has no place in this Republican administration. We are going to give West Virginia a sound and honest administration even if we must drag the Senate shouting and obstructing all the way."

The delay on appointment review, together with the civil-service bill, had been an orchestrated ploy on the part of the Democrats, born out of their own disunity and disharmony. But it was only part of a calculated effort to so destabilize the new administration that the Democrats would have no trouble winning back the governor's office in 1960. The party leadership, badly splintered by the 1956 elections, had begun its campaign to regain control of the Statehouse with a meeting at the Daniel Boone Hotel shortly after Underwood took office. Some of those present at the second meeting, however, were more interested in shaping coming events for personal gain than in solidifying the Democratic alliance.

Underwood was better positioned tactically than he might have imagined. Divisiveness was a real problem in Democratic circles. Although approximately one million West Virginians were eligible to vote and 62 percent were registered Democrats, those whose influence was greatest were disinclined to rally 'round the flag.

Down the road they saw an opportunity to take control of the party machinery. Those who supported the gubernatorial aspirations of potential candidates like Senate President Ralph Bean, House Speaker William Flannery, Treasurer Orel Skeen and, Attorney General W. W. Barron were beginning to cut private deals. There were also quiet meetings in Clarksburg and Huntington, but they had little beneficial effect on the party's interests as a whole.

Partisan politics was not all that caused the static in the Capitol atmosphere during Underwood's first year in office. Unemployment, most of it in the coal industry, was spreading across the state. Felt most acutely in the largest mining areas, it also began to reach into the textile and glass industries as foreign competition made its first inroads on the American market.

Underwood tried to create jobs for the unemployed with a $10 million road-maintenance program. He bloodied his nose with this effort when he had the road to his father's farm at Joseph Mills repaired at the taxpayers' expense. He and his road commissioner, Patrick C. Graney, were further criticized for the lack of quality in the repair work on 2,400 miles of secondary roads.

IN MID-NOVEMBER 1957, the academic community hosted a pre-legislative conference at The Greenbrier, one of the world's finest resorts. Planned by the WVU Bureau of Government Research and bankrolled by the Ford Foundation, the conference was held to explore problems relating to renewable natural resources, taxation, finance, public-school education, and highway development. It had been more than a decade since such a conference had taken place in America; the last one had been held in Washington state in the 1940s.

In attendance were 85 percent of the legislature, the governor, members of the State Supreme Court, the Board of Public Works, and the state's congressional delegation. WVU President Irvin Stewart opened the conference with a plea for a nonpartisan attack on the state's growing economic ills. "The problems to be discussed here are persistent and difficult," Stewart said. "Their solution is important to a sound future for West Virginia. Delay in finding solutions will be costly to the state and postpone their effectiveness to the point where they will be of no help to many people now living."

Another headliner on the program was Tax Commissioner John A. Field, who stressed the importance of property reappraisal to the fiscal stability of the counties, municipalities, and school districts.

Two months later the legislature convened in regular session. Among the proposals offered by the governor were two that had been on the agenda at the Greenbrier conference, the "incentive plan" for public-school education and the "backbone" superhighway-building program.

The incentive plan, as outlined by State Superintendent of Schools Rohrbough, proposed a broad range of educational programs to improve the public-school system. Each county would assess its resources and needs and develop a program of improvements. Implementation of these improvements would be funded equally by the counties and the state.

The road program, as sketched out by Road Commissioner Graney, was based on a system of limited access roads that would merge into the proposed interstate highway network, making West Virginia accessible by four-lane roads to the rest of the nation for the first time in history.

These recommendations were practical and affordable. But they were proposed by a governor who during all his years as a legislator had opposed new taxation. He had been one of the few members of the House of Delegates to consistently vote against the annual budget.

Underwood tried with his next legislative message to justify his position. After proposing $52 million in new taxes, he quoted English statesman Edmund Burke: "Mere parsimony is not economy . . . Expense, and great expense, may be an essential part of true economy."

The governor asked for $37 million for the expressway system and $15 million for the incentive school plan. "The problems facing West Virginia are staggering," he warned. "As in the past, it would be easier at this session to let them ride . . . to find that there was not sufficient agreement on an education solution to take any action; to fear that we have not adequate resources for such a highway program."

Some influential members of the legislature admitted privately that Underwood's program made sense, but there was an election down the road and they were unwilling to jeopardize their chances of reelection. Instead of $52 million in new taxes, the lawmakers approved a shade over $9 million, which included $5 million for the statewide property reappraisal.

AFTER THE LEGISLATURE WENT HOME, Underwood and his staff turned their attention to the critical state of unemployment. Five months later, the governor called the legislature into special session to consider an extension of unemployment benefits for an additional twelve weeks. This was approved.

He also involved himself in the off-year election that fall, but his candidates and his party were crushingly defeated. The Democrats were so successful at the polls that by the time the lawmakers met the next January, a common witticism around the chambers was that the few remaining Republicans could have caucused in a phone booth. The big winner in the mid-term election was Congressman Smith's son, Hulett, then chairman of the state Democratic Party, who more than anyone was credited with restoring vigor to his party.

The chronic problem of joblessness claimed most of Underwood's attention in the third year of his term. "We are still faced with basic unemployment of fifty thousand West Virginia workers, most of them displaced by the coal industry," he told the legislature. "In the past eighteen months, more than forty-two thousand have exhausted their regular unemployment benefits."

After his address, the legislature once more granted relief, but not much. The governor was given authority to set up an Economic Development Agency and was awarded $9 million in new revenue for road improvements. As a means of emphasizing the economic situation, Underwood toured the hardest-hit sections of the state, as did Congressman John M. Slack. And U.S. Senator Randolph gave added emphasis to the problem by convening a senatorial subcommittee for a series of hearings on unemployment in Southern West Virginia.

In 1959 Underwood traveled to the Soviet Union under the sponsorship of the Institute on International Education. The trip was billed as a goodwill tour, and upon his return home Underwood reported that he had been impressed with the friendly nature of the Russian people. America, he added, "spends too much time trying to contain communism instead of selling Americanism."

Throughout his term, Underwood was criticized for traveling too much, although he made many of his trips as a kind of supersalesman for the state. On other junkets, he was openly critical of fellow politicians, both in West Virginia and in other states. During a Southern Governors' Conference at Sea Island, Georgia, governor after governor excused himself from the program to go to the pressroom for special conferences on a racial disturbance taking place in Little Rock, Arkansas. This was one of the first big racial outbursts in the South after the U.S. Supreme Court handed down its decision on school desegregation. These offstage news briefings became so disruptive that the governors almost lost touch with the formal agenda, as did the reporters present. On the last day, Underwood was publicly critical of such actions, observing that his fellow governors had been there to address problems common to their states and administrations, not to release hourly comments on racial problems in Arkansas.

On a trip to another Southern Governors' Conference, this one in Asheville, North Carolina, Underwood met with his fellow executives on matters of mutual administrative concern. It was an eye-opening session for some of us in the press section. In some states, school administration was still a magisterial district responsibility and road planning was controlled largely at the county level. These systems had been discarded in West Virginia as no longer practical back during the Depression. And tax reform, which West Virginia had been moving into with its property-reappraisal program, was also more a dream than a reality in much of the South.

While at Asheville, Underwood spoke to his fellow governors on the "doctrine of strict accountability." In his state, he explained, the Board of Public Works had absolute budgetary authority, regulated the expenditure of monies and released all funds appropriated by the legislature. Further, he said, it had become a custom to chip away at executive authority by shifting it away from the governor and into the hands of "countless" advisory boards. As a result, executive authority had become so diluted and diffused that hardly anyone could be held clearly accountable for inefficiency or wrongdoing.

At the opening of the legislative session in 1960, Underwood recommended improvements to highways and state parks as a means of providing jobs for the unemployed, still a thorny issue. According to the governor, the Parks Division of the Conservation Commission could easily spend $19 million on new and improved parks alone, but because of the resistance he had encountered previously from the legislature, he was asking for only $8 million in new taxes for both roads and parks.

In his legislative message he said, "The fate of this program—indeed, the fate of West Virginia—is now in your hands. It is solely your responsibility, an obligation for which you will be held accountable." The legislature responded with $4.4 million in repair monies, most of it for park improvements.

THE GOVERNOR SPENT MUCH of his last year in office campaigning for his chosen successor, his public institutions commissioner, Harold E. Neely, who was
running against party regular Chapman Revercomb. Underwood also spent
time on his own campaign for the U.S. Senate. Neely and Underwood both
won the primary runoff but lost in the general election, Neely to Attorney
General Barron, and Underwood to the incumbent, Randolph.

Underwood adopted vintage Republican tactics in his campaign for the
Senate, which consisted primarily of criticism of the Democrats in general and of his opponent in particular. One of his most scathing criticisms of
Randolph was made at an Appalachian Governors' Conference in Annapolis,
Maryland, where he charged that the senator was responsible for the loss of
between $40 million and $45 million in interstate highway money intended
for West Virginia.

The Democratic-controlled legislature had already unwittingly set a
snare for Underwood with the creation of a Crime Commission at the close
of its budgetary session in February. After hearing rumors of lax control of
organized crime in some parts of the state and of possible payoffs to high state
officials, the leadership decided to look into the allegations with Senate and
House members serving as the investigative body.

Among the first witnesses summoned were several former State Police
officers who had either been dismissed or had moved into other lines of work.
Early testimony was so sensational that Underwood reacted with a shocking
show of force. His historian called the incident a "dramatic moment," but
at the time it seemed more "banana republic" democracy than high drama.
On the second day of the legislative hearings, the governor stormed into the
hearing room unannounced and, in a statement lasting about two minutes,
accused the legislators of exceeding their mandate. "You have become a commission of character assassination," he charged. Accompanying the governor,
in full dress uniform, were State Police Superintendent Hazen Fair and Adjutant General William E. Blake of the West Virginia National Guard.

There in a Capitol hearing room stood a distraught governor, flanked on
either side by the implied threat of armed reprisal. Underwood had, in other

words, brought with him the top officers of the state militia and the civilian constabulary. It was not, perhaps, the wisest action by a sitting governor who was even then campaigning for a U.S. Senate seat.

The crime investigation ultimately turned out to be a costly, headline-seeking witch-hunt. At a series of hearings in Charleston and elsewhere, Underwood and his administration were accused of all manner of wrongdoing, but in the end the legislature was proved the wrongdoer. Two years later, the commission was declared unconstitutional by the State Supreme Court. The only real outcome of this farce was a diminished respect for both the governor and the legislative leadership.

A more positive note was sounded in the last year of Underwood's term when he unveiled a plan for the gasification of coal through the use of nuclear energy. In a report to the people of the state, he asserted, "The world, the U.S., and West Virginia are on the threshold of a new age—the nuclear age, the missile age—bringing in new challenges and new opportunities. For this new age we must plan." This concept, coming soon after the Soviets had shot Sputnik into space, found an attentive audience, but it would not be enough to win Underwood the election less than a month away. Randolph beat him easily.

In his farewell address to the legislature, Governor Underwood cautioned, "For ten years technological change has been stripping the flesh of West Virginia to the bone . . . Within this economic catastrophe a resilient economy will be born. We must see and understand what West Virginia is today. Also, we must have a vision of what it can be tomorrow."

DESPITE THE UNRELENTING PROBLEMS Underwood had encountered while trying to deal with a Democratic legislature, he ran for governor against Hulett Smith in the 1964 general election but lost. Four years later he ran again but was beaten in the primary by Arch Moore. And in 1976 he made a third attempt to return to the office he had won in 1956. This time his opponent was Jay Rockefeller, and Underwood's defeat was crushing. He lost by a margin of almost two to one, the worst defeat for a gubernatorial candidate in state history up to that time.

Underwood was never without prestigious employment after he left the governor's office. He went first to Island Creek Coal Company as a vice president, later became vice president of Monsanto Chemical Corporation, was president of Princess Coals, then served as president of Bethany College. He resigned from three of those positions to make another of his runs for governor, but after losing to Rockefeller, he became active in the development of new uses for coal.

In 1996 Underwood again ran for governor, this time defeating his Democratic opponent, Charlotte Pritt, and thus becoming, at the age of seventy-four, the state's oldest as well as youngest governor.

MISCELLANY ° THE GUNS OF STATE

FEW AMERICAN NEWSPAPERS are subjected to the threat of military might because of their editorial expressions under the First Amendment. At least not in the mid-twentieth century.

Except the *Gazette*.

One afternoon we heard unusual rumblings outside the newspaper's Hale Street offices. Looking out a window we were stunned to find an Army tank sitting in the parking lot across the street, turning its gun toward the editorial office. A moment later, Adjutant General William E. Blake climbed out of the turret and walked across the street with a big grin on his face. Hoffmann and I recalled that in the morning edition we had been mildly critical of the West Virginia National Guard.

Screwing our courage to the sticking point, we walked out the door and, in the middle of Hale Street, shook hands with Blake.

Hoffmann negotiated a truce in the best of hill-country tradition, and shortly afterward, the three of us, with Executive Editor Dallas Higbee in tow, adjourned to the Press Club. We proceeded to get ourselves gently sloshed, enjoyed a fine meal, and the crisis of the moment was averted.

If only Washington could understand how easy it is to solve problems of state over the dinner table.

Chapter 7

"One Brief, Shining Moment"

During the 1960 election year, West Virginia moved into the national political spotlight when John F. Kennedy and Hubert H. Humphrey squared off against each other in a bid for the Democratic presidential nomination.

A prelude to this confrontation had been staged four years earlier in the smelly old stockyards amphitheater on Chicago's south side. As Theodore H. White noted in his book, *America in Search of Itself*, "Elections are important; they give Americans not only their chief sense of participating in their government, but, more importantly, a sense of control." Control is what politics is all about, and in 1956 the American people took control of their presidential elections for the first time in a half century.

Before the mid-1950s, the party bosses had run the national conventions from the back rooms. The elected delegates' endorsement of the bosses' nominees for president and vice president was little more than a formality. In 1956, however, a politically shrewd and hard-drinking womanizer from Tennessee, U.S. Senator Estes Kefauver, whom I once had the opportunity of observing in action at Charleston's Daniel Boone Hotel, changed the system by turning to the primaries as his gateway to power. It was a novel concept at the time, but political conventions have never been the same. Although still a shallow and meaningless extravaganza, conventions are now held mainly to officially anoint the candidate who has won the most delegates in the state primaries.

The 1956 national convention was a benchmark not only for the American political process but for the state of West Virginia as well. Several major figures in the state Democratic Party made their final appearance as party leaders there, most prominently Governor Marland, Congressman Robert

Mollohan, and Senator Neely, the delegation chairman. Neely, very frail at the time, would die before the next mid-term election. It could be said that Marland's and Mollohan's careers were part of the debris washed away in the coming landslide.

The outcome of the '56 Democratic Convention was, of course, foreordained. The presidential nominee was to be the intellectual and patrician Adlai Stevenson, a former Illinois governor and one of the all-time best-qualified nominees the Democrats ever placed at the head of their ticket. But moments after the traditionally orchestrated nomination of this great man, Stevenson walked to the rostrum and announced that he would not be choosing a running mate, that the next day's balloting for vice president would be an open contest. At that moment we witnessed both hail and farewell—hail to the people's convention of the future and farewell to the boss-controlled carnival of the past.

All night long the vice-presidential hopefuls campaigned furiously. I attended a Humphrey rally at 4:00 a.m. By the next afternoon the only viable candidates were Humphrey, Tennessee's Kefauver, and a young senator from Massachusetts by the name of Kennedy. In a wild two-hour series of ballotings, Humphrey faded fast, and it was a fight to the finish between Kefauver and Kennedy, with delegate trade-offs coming so swiftly that I had trouble keeping up with what was going on even in the West Virginia delegation.

Kefauver's cross-country campaigning during the primaries finally paid off. He scooted past Kennedy to win the vice-presidential nomination. Kennedy lost that contest but gained national recognition, and his star began its meteoric ascent.

The final phase of the 1956 campaign dwindled into a dreary political exercise. Eisenhower was the incumbent and he was running against Stevenson for the second time in four years. The outcome was a foregone conclusion. Only this time the defeat was more crushing and demeaning to the gentleman from Illinois.

FOUR YEARS LATER Humphrey and Kennedy faced off again, this time for the presidential nomination, and by then the only path to the presidency was through the primaries. Their battleground would be Wisconsin, one of the cleanest states politically, and West Virginia, one of the most corrupt.

Humphrey, who had expected Wisconsin to have built-in advantages for him since it bordered his native Minnesota, nevertheless lost there to Kennedy, and West Virginia was his last best hope for the 1960 nomination. Kennedy had a different problem. Raised a Catholic, he was handicapped by the myth that a member of his faith was not an acceptable tenant of the White House. Kennedy had tried to dodge this issue through much of the campaign, but across the country it had garnered so much attention that for the first time since 1928, when New York Governor Al Smith ran against Herbert Hoover, religion and the presidency had become a matter of national debate.

Although Kennedy won Wisconsin by 56 percent, he carried only six out of the ten districts, and his winning margin came from predominantly Catholic precincts. Humphrey carried those precincts that were primarily Protestant. Wisconsin failed to give Kennedy the decisive victory he needed, and winning in West Virginia became crucial to his effort to prove that his religion was not a bar to the country's highest office. Although it was a sparsely populated state that sent non-committed delegates to the convention, it was 95 percent Protestant. If a Catholic was to make his stand on the religious question anywhere, West Virginia was the best possible proving ground.

Kennedy was not a complete unknown inside the state when he filed to run in the primary. He had visited West Virginia as a senator with his wife, Jackie, and as early as 1956 had begun setting up his organization in the state, headed by Robert P. McDonough, a Parkersburg printing-plant owner. But theology was never mentioned in early planning for Kennedy's West Virginia campaign. Harry Hoffmann and I had met with Ted Sorenson, one of the brightest of Kennedy's bright young men, when he came to Charleston on a fact-finding trip before the campaign was officially launched. Sorenson's chief interest at that time was in voter profile, and his questions were more cultural than religious, more attuned to economics than politics. He had no need to question us about religious demographics. Kennedy and his staff were already aware, as we were not, that West Virginia at that time had fewer people affiliated with organized faiths than other states.

When Kennedy showed up after midnight on February 6, 1960, in Secretary of State Joe Burdette's office to file for the primary, he seemed eager to confront the most sensitive issue of his campaign. He told the press that he was there to answer Humphrey's challenge. "I was delighted to oblige," he commented.

Both candidates had prepared themselves thoroughly. I had a chance to look at the Humphrey campaign book; Hoffmann, the Kennedy book. Each one had a profile of every county, right down to the identities of the local political leaders and the most pressing local issues.

THE CONFRONTATION between Kennedy and Humphrey in the Mountain State would become the stuff of political legend.

Kennedy, the young, handsome, Harvard-educated son of a multimillionaire, had served as staff assistant to his father when the elder Kennedy was named U.S. ambassador to Britain. He was a war hero and PT boat commander who had been wounded during his exploits in the South Pacific. He had written a bestselling book, *Profiles in Courage*, and had been awarded the highest of all journalistic honors for it, the Pulitzer Prize.

Humphrey, an affable Midwesterner with an impish grin, had grown up during the Depression years. The son of a small-town pharmacist, he had trained in the same profession, earning a Phi Beta Kappa key along the way. From youth to manhood his life had been a struggle. At one point in his early years, he worked several jobs simultaneously to pay off a political-campaign debt, with his wife, Muriel, pitching in to help meet the expenses of everyday living.

Kennedy, whose grandfather had been mayor of Boston, came from a background of wealth, privilege, and political power in the Bay State. Humphrey had to fight his way alone and underfunded through the precincts to the mayorship of Milwaukee and ultimately the U.S. Senate, honing his political skills along the way. Both men were of liberal Democratic sentiment, although Humphrey leaned farther left than his opponent.

I had the rare opportunity before either candidate filed in the West Virginia primary to interview them both. They were as opposite in conviction and commitment as Ronald Reagan and Walter Mondale. These taped interviews, which I transcribed for more thorough study, helped me decide which would be my personal choice in the coming election. Humphrey was far and away my favorite, an opinion for which I was chided at the *Gazette*.

Everybody, from publisher Chilton and editor Hoffmann to nearly every staff member, had lined up behind Kennedy. Our newsroom, in fact, was turned into an unofficial public-relations center for him when the national press corps began showing up in Charleston.

In my first interview with Humphrey at the Beckley Hotel, I found him personable, forthright, and informed, a politician of uncommon honesty. Kennedy was different. Although he was known for the charm he could exert, it was not in evidence during my interview with him at the Kanawha Hotel in Charleston. Instead, he came across as cold and aloof and his answers seemed scripted and calculated. Kennedy appeared to be looking toward the White House with every answer. Humphrey looked to his conscience.

Perhaps my assessment of Humphrey was also influenced to some degree by an encounter I had with him shortly after the interview in Beckley. I was walking out of the Glass House restaurant on the West Virginia Turnpike with my daughter when we ran into Senator Humphrey on his way in.

He immediately said, "Why, Tom, how are you?" and stopped to chat. I introduced my daughter, expecting him to murmur something polite but vague, then continue with his conversation. My daughter was already accustomed to, if tired of, being ignored by politicians who wanted to hold what she considered to be long, boring conversations with her father.

But the senator bent down, shook my daughter's small hand, and, looking her in the eye, asked her several questions, listening to her answers with every evidence of genuine interest. It may have been nothing more than a shameless ploy to win the support of a doting father who happened to cover politics for an influential newspaper. But the senator won another supporter that day, one already able to spot insincerity and weary of political posturing despite her tender years. Unfortunately for Humphrey, she was far too young to vote.

THE GURUS OF JOURNALISM from Washington and New York—James Reston, Joseph Alsop, and others—descended on West Virginia to get their own personal reading on coalfields politics and the Kennedy-Humphrey campaign. One of them, Theodore White, took the time to try to understand who the voters were and what motivated them as individuals. In his book, *The Making of the President, 1960,* White, whom I respected as one of the finest reporters of my generation, said of West Virginians:

> *"These are handsome people and, beyond doubt, the best mannered and most courteous in the nation. These are people who teach their children to say 'sir' and 'thank you' to their elders; they speak in soft and gentle tones; their relations with their Negroes are the best of any state with any significant Negro population, north or south. The Negroes, being treated with respect and good manners, reciprocate with a bearing of good manners and respect. Whether on a West Virginia bus or in a crowded West Virginia store, men and women are well-behaved and friendly.*
>
> *Moreover, these are brave people—no state of the union contributed more heavily to the armed forces of the United States in proportion to population than did this state of mountain men; nor did any state suffer more casualties in proportion to population. That they should live as they do is a scar and shame on American life, an indictment of the national political system."*

WHEN KENNEDY AND HUMPHREY moved into West Virginia for the final phase of the primary campaign, Humphrey was clearly in the lead. Late in 1959 the Lou Harris polling organization had found a 70–30 margin for Kennedy among Mountain State voters, but after the Wisconsin primary this lead had eroded to a 40–60 split in favor of Humphrey. "What happened?" Kennedy asked. Harris replied, "No one in West Virginia knew you were a Catholic in December. Now they know."

Kennedy, his friends, brothers, and sisters campaigned on his war experiences; Humphrey had none. They brought Franklin D. Roosevelt Jr. into the state to talk about his own father's record as architect of the New Deal. They implied that Humphrey was simply a stalking horse for Adlai Stevenson, Senator Stuart Symington, or Lyndon Johnson.

Still, the question of religion remained the major stumbling block of Kennedy's campaign. The nature of the issue made it impossible for Humphrey, the most tolerant of men, to run in favor of tolerance. His hands were tied. Only Kennedy could campaign on this point, and gradually this handicap on the Humphrey campaign turned the tide in Kennedy's favor. "I refuse," Kennedy said time and again, "to believe that I was denied the right to be president on the day I was baptized." The voters listened.

Two weeks before the election, Humphrey's margin had dropped to 55–45; by the Saturday before the Tuesday primary it had declined to 45–42. It was a bleak day for the Humphrey campaign. They left Charleston early that morning in a cold, drizzling rain for an upstate bus tour through Clay, Gassaway, Sutton, Weston, and Clarksburg. By the time the bus reached Sutton, Humphrey and his staff discovered that Kennedy money was being spread around everywhere. On the Braxton County courthouse grounds, I asked a troubled Humphrey aide what was bothering him. "They're buying the election," he replied glumly. Humphrey himself told me that he had no chance of competing with Kennedy's spending. His own campaign was broke.

As later investigations by West Virginia Institute of Technology Professor Richard K. Bradford and others determined, the Kennedy camp was spending heavily at the precinct level.

But I knew during the primary, from inquiries I had made among various contacts, that votes were being bought in Kennedy's name in Charleston's tenderloin district, the area bounded roughly by Summers Street, the New York Central Railroad tracks, and the Elk and Kanawha rivers.

Following the primary, more stories started filtering out of Washington and New York to the effect that, in their effort to win, the Kennedys had invoked the standard South Boston win-at-any-cost strategy in counties like Logan, Mingo, and McDowell.

Perhaps West Virginia's reputation for freewheeling political corruption figured into the Kennedy campaign's choice of the state as a proving ground.

Here they had a better opportunity than in other states of buying the win they badly needed.

But Harry Hoffmann, unwilling to believe any rumors, no matter how credible the source, went to bat for the Kennedy reputation to, as he explained it, "set the record straight." And he refused to change his mind.

Months later Esther Lederer, better known as advice columnist Ann Landers, came to Charleston to speak at the Municipal Auditorium. Afterward Chilton hosted a late-evening supper for her at the Press Club. When she asked Hoffmann if there had been vote-buying in the Kennedy-Humphrey primary, he said no. She simply smiled and mentioned that she had been a longtime Humphrey friend.

It took the outspoken Chilton to settle the issue in his own blunt fashion when he told Neal R. Pearce, who was researching his book *The Border South States*, that Kennedy "bought a landslide, not an election." While the Kennedy campaign officially reported spending one hundred thousand dollars in West Virginia, Pearce commented:

> *There is no question that Kennedy had outspent Humphrey many times over—his expenditures were over $250,000 compared to the Minnesotan's meager $30,000. A lot of the Kennedy money was judiciously used with county factions, and there is little doubt that some of it ended up in "bought" votes in the classic West Virginia manner.*

Other writers have since placed the amount spent by Kennedy at a much higher figure. Whatever the actual amount, in the end money provided the winning edge. By the time the voters started going to the polls, it was all over but the shouting, although no one was willing to predict the outcome, least of all Kennedy. Believing that he had lost in West Virginia, on election day he boarded his family plane with Jackie and flew home to Washington. As he admitted afterward, he didn't want to face the press that night as a loser.

When by 10:00 p.m. the returns from across the state showed a Kennedy sweep, calls went out for him to return to Charleston. He hurriedly pulled himself together, and he and Jackie arrived back in the capital city early the next morning for a press conference in the Kanawha Hotel. In the meantime, his brother and campaign manager, Robert, had gone to the Humphrey headquarters to pay a courtesy call, where red-eyed supporters stood around silent and disconsolate. With tears in his eyes, a quiet and dejected Humphrey sat waiting for the press to set up their cameras. "I have a brief statement to make," he said. "I am no longer a candidate for the Democratic presidential nomination."

At Kennedy headquarters, the scene was noisy and jubilant. When the winner walked in, smiling and cheerful, he was asked, "What are you going to do now, Jack?"

"I have to study up on the problems of Maryland tonight," he said. "I'm campaigning there tomorrow." But before reboarding his plane for the trip back to Washington, he examined the returns from around the state. Coming finally to those for McDowell County, he shook his head with a pleased smile on his face. "That Sid Christie," he remarked. "He said we'd win there and even told me how many votes he could deliver to me."

Christie and his family had long controlled politics in McDowell, that most southern of West Virginia counties. While they ran a clean organization by coalfield standards, they expected results. They were as good as their word in the Kennedy-Humphrey primary, and Kennedy paid his debt handsomely. Despite some resistance in Congress, he was successful in naming Christie, a county judge, to the federal district court bench. Sidney Christie became a judge for both the northern and southern districts and served capably until his death some ten years later.

AT THE DEMOCRATIC NATIONAL CONVENTION, an event highlighted by the arrival of Kennedy in an American Airlines plane emblazoned "Flagship West Virginia," he was nominated on the first ballot. Afterward, Arthur Edson of the Associated Press rhapsodized:

> *If our political disputes are ever remembered as our battlefields are*
> *now, West Virginia will become a national shrine. For it was in West Virginia's*

beautiful mountains, in its thriving cities, in its impoverished
coalfields that the decisive battle was fought that gave John F. Kennedy
the Democratic presidential nomination.

The following campaign between Kennedy and Richard M. Nixon was bitter and vigorously fought. But Kennedy's wit and charm, his great style and his ability to expound extemporaneously on the issues—and that South Boston win-at-any-cost strategy—carried the day. He won the presidency by approximately one vote per precinct across the country.

On the Saturday before the general election, Robert Kennedy touched down at the Huntington, West Virginia, airport for a short press conference with a scattering of newsmen and interested supporters. Afterward, while waiting for his staff to reboard, he and I chatted briefly.

"We love West Virginia and what it has done for us," he told me. "If we win on Tuesday—and right now we're not sure—we won't forget you."

A prophetic statement. West Virginia was never so remembered by Washington as it was during the next three years.

John F. Kennedy had never seen the degree of poverty that he found in West Virginia. He had grown up cushioned by wealth. And arriving in the mountains for his first tour of the precincts fresh from vacationing in the sun and luxury of Jamaica's Montego Bay, he found the experience emotionally shattering.

He could scarcely bring himself to believe that citizens of the United States were forced to live as they did in the coalfields. "Imagine," he said to one of his assistants one night. "Just imagine kids who never drink milk." Kennedy's exposure to the misery he found in West Virginia affected him profoundly, and after taking office he set to work to ease the suffering.

AT THE END OF WORLD WAR II more than 115,000 miners were needed to mine coal, but by the time Kennedy traveled to West Virginia in search of votes, mechanization had reduced the workforce to only forty-three thousand. The effects of this loss of jobs were felt in every sector of the economy. Approximately one-tenth of the population was destitute.

As his first official act as president, Kennedy issued an executive order doubling and improving surplus commodity allotments for poverty-stricken families in West Virginia and other states. A short time later, with less fanfare, he appointed a special task force in West Virginia to determine the state's most critical needs. Among those named to this body were his former state campaign chairman McDonough, editor Harry Hoffmann, and State Road Commissioner Burl Sawyers. This group's discussions, combined with efforts in Washington and at the Statehouse in Charleston, led to some of the more notable accomplishments of the Kennedy years in the White House.

Thanks to Kennedy, the food stamp program, which later was adopted nationwide, was first authorized as a pilot venture in McDowell, Logan, and Mingo counties. The sale of the Naval Ordnance Plant in South Charleston to FMC Corporation was approved, which meant 1,800 new jobs for the Kanawha Valley. A public-works program was begun in West Virginia, which gave employment to fifty thousand jobless people. The Area Redevelopment Administration program was sanctioned by Congress, which led to the opening of woodworking plants in Braxton and Mingo counties and the retraining of thousands of chronically unemployed people. Private industry was encouraged to build such plants as North American Aviation in Princeton and Lockheed Aircraft in Clarksburg. Research into the possibility of making gasoline from coal was set in motion with the opening of a pilot plant in Marshall County.

Tariff Commission changes were approved, granting relief to the West Virginia flat-glass industry. Grants amounting to $24 million were authorized for the development of Canaan Valley, Twin Falls, Pipestem, and Hawks Nest state parks. New defense spending was channeled into the state, moving it up from last place to forty-second among the states in the awarding of government contracts. And the construction of Interstate 79, from the Pennsylvania border to Charleston, was approved.

The Kennedy years made an indelible mark on West Virginia. In 1960, the state was nearly flat on its back economically. In the next three years, unemployment fell from 105,000 to forty-four thousand, and migration out of the state was arrested. Manufacturing payrolls grew by eleven thousand, and manufacturing investment increased by $146 million.

The Interstate 79 project, an ingenious one, was the brainchild of Road Commissioner Sawyers. He scrapped plans for building Interstate 64 by way of Gauley Bridge and Rainelle, a highway engineer's nightmare, and rerouted it down the already constructed West Virginia Turnpike to Beckley. With the mileage saved, supplemented by additional, still-unassigned interstate mileage that Governor Barron was able to wangle out of the Kennedy administration, Sawyers had the means to build Interstate 79. Sawyers also joined with U.S. Representative John Slack to get authorization for what in the beginning was called the "Industrial Road," the vital link between Interstate 79 near Sutton with Interstates 64 and 77 at Beckley.

So much federal money was available during these years that Governor Barron set up a branch of his office at the Congressional Hotel on Capitol Hill in Washington, with Paul Crabtree in charge, to help facilitate the flow of every possible federal dollar into the state. The governor's efforts were further aided by the state's two senators: Jennings Randolph, chairman of the Senate Public Works Committee, and Robert C. Byrd, a powerful member of the Senate Appropriations Committee. There was only one problem, as expressed by Sawyers and Welfare Commissioner W. Bernard Smith. West Virginia simply did not have the tax revenue available to match the vast sums of money the Kennedy administration was willing to funnel into the state.

Kennedy's continuing commitment to West Virginia was illustrated by a quiet, behind-the-scenes incident on the state's hundredth birthday. On June 20, 1963, the president flew to Charleston to deliver the keynote address highlighting the day-long celebration. Because of the heavy downpour of rain that greeted him upon his arrival, he spoke for only about two minutes to the huge crowd jamming the Capitol grounds. In the privacy of the governor's office following the ceremony, and unknown to the crowds outside, Kennedy pledged the federal government's share of funding for four new state parks.

BUT THE KENNEDY ADMINISTRATION's efforts to help West Virginia occasionally misfired. One example was the effort in the early 1960s to develop support for the Justice flood control dam and reservoir in Southern West Virginia, a project carrying a $60 million price tag.

Since 1929, water management studies had been conducted periodically along the Guyandot River, which starts high in the mountains near Beckley and meanders through coal-rich country to Huntington where it empties into the Ohio River. Normally the Guyandot is a placid stream, except on those rare occasions when rain falls in abnormally high quantities. In heavy rain the Guyandot grows mean, flooding Logan, Pineville, and other towns along its banks. But until 1962 none of the studies conducted indicated that a flood-control project would be cost effective.

The 1962 Justice proposal study was weak on facts, which was brought to my attention by the general counsel for the Norfolk & Western Railway, J. M. B. Lewis of Roanoke, Virginia, when he stopped by my office. "We can't get our side of the story told," Lewis complained.

He had asked the U.S. Army Corps of Engineers, the Department of the Interior, and the Bureau of the Budget to assist him in arranging for a public hearing in Wyoming County, but everywhere his request was stonewalled. "We need a forum," he explained, "and we hope you'll give it to us." In other words, as sometimes happens when all else fails, he had turned to a newspaper for help in getting his story to the public.

It was quite a story. The Justice dam and reservoir, if built as designed, would have forever prevented the removal of 57,250,000 tons of prime metallurgical coal, more than $3 million worth of natural gas and almost $2 million worth of timber—in 1960s values. When translated into a marketable product, the coal alone had a value at the mine entrance of better than $118 million, and the mining of it would have generated $179 million in wages for coal miners. Also, $26 million in federal taxes and substantial amounts in state and local taxes would have poured into government coffers during the mining effort.

As I dug into the story, I learned that the dam project was so narrowly cost-effective that, had the Lewis information been presented as testimony at a public hearing, the project would have gone down in flames as too costly to build. Somewhere along the way a conspiracy of silence had taken hold, and this important data was being suppressed by a bureaucracy of public servants who either were being directed by their bosses to ignore it or were playing a political game of their own with unknown parties.

These were the Kennedy years when West Virginia enjoyed favored-state status. Suddenly a dam on the Guyandot, which had not been justifiable for thirty-three years, became a living, breathing boondoggle in a matter of months. I devoted several of my "Affairs of State" columns to the subject, but without Senator Randolph the issue never would have received the public airing it deserved. Randolph called a hearing of the Senate Subcommittee on Public Works at the Capitol in Washington, and the full story was placed on record by spokesmen for the Norfolk & Western, the UMW, Georgia-Pacific Corporation, Consolidated Coal Company, Hope Natural Gas Company, and United Producing Company. Witnesses testifying on behalf of the government continued to maintain that the loss of coal and gas would be negligible.

A few weeks later, Randolph's administrative assistant, Jim Harris, came to see me and asked if moving the dam site a few miles downstream would be an acceptable solution.

"Will the move allow access to the coal and gas properties?" I asked.

"Yes," he replied.

The project was examined all the way to the White House, but finally the location was changed and other alterations made. Several years later, when the dam was completed and dedicated, it was named for R. D. Bailey of Pineville, who in the past had been one of the most powerful Democratic political bosses in Southern West Virginia. Bailey had also been the attorney for one of the plaintiffs in my very first libel suit.

Four members of West Virginia's congressional delegation, who were interested in improved water management, endorsed the project at the hearing held by Randolph: Senator Byrd and Congressmen Ken Hechler, Elizabeth Kee, and John Slack. Had they originally been privy to the whole of the information presented at the hearing, the alternative site could have been settled on earlier without all the frustration, publicity, wasted time, and expense to the taxpayers that went into documenting the injustices in the original Justice proposal. As it was, well-intentioned people were unnecessarily embarrassed by a rigid bureaucracy and a pack of deal-makers along the Guyandot.

PRESIDENT KENNEDY'S GENEROSITY to West Virginia, the state he called his second love, came to a sudden and tragic end five months after his speech at the centennial celebration. But the elevation of Lyndon Johnson to the presidency had little negative impact on the momentum and direction of federal funding. In fact, among the earliest of several programs proposed by Kennedy and pushed through Congress by Johnson after he took office was the creation of the Appalachian Regional Commission, which over the years has funneled federal funding into the building of many miles of four-lane highways, the construction of scores of water and sewage systems, and the enrichment of public health facilities.

Johnson was also responsible for the Civil Rights Act of 1964 and, under his Great Society banner, an expanded anti-poverty program, mass-transit funding, Medicaid for the poor, aid to elementary and secondary schools, expanded housing opportunities for low-income families, college loans and scholarships, and national foundations for the arts and humanities. While West Virginia was never the personal crusade for President Johnson that it seemed to be for Kennedy, Johnson's commitment to promoting a broad range of programs to improve life for countless Americans at every economic level brought needed help and hope to the people of this state.

But while charity and compassion seemed to be watchwords in Washington in the early 1960s, they were given short shrift in Charleston. As the Roman satirist Juvenal observed, "Avarice increases with the increasing pile of gold."

MISCELLANY ⋄ "THE CHILDREN'S HOUR"

SOME YEARS AGO, while we were visiting my brother's family in the Washington suburbs, Charley and I thought that our offspring would enjoy a visit to the White House. I made arrangements through Senator Byrd's office for our two daughters and a schoolmate of my niece to take the tour.

Thanks to Byrd, the girls were given one of the special VIP tours and came home hours later chattering about the experience. Being young, however, and less than impressed with politics and adults in general, they had been uninterested in waiting a few minutes to have their picture taken with President Johnson in the Oval Office. The photo had been suggested by an alert White House aide who had struck up a conversation with the girls and discovered that two of them were daughters of newspapermen. When the girls related the story afterward, they mentioned that the aide looked rather stunned when they thanked him politely but informed him that they "didn't have time."

Several years earlier I had been among a group of West Virginians who checked in at the main gate to see President Kennedy. Also in the entourage were Governor Barron and Commerce Commissioner Hulett Smith.

I hadn't gone through the normal clearance procedures that the others in the group had, and during lunch I told them I wasn't on the official list to see the president. They assured me all the way to the gate that I wouldn't have any trouble making it into the Oval Office for a briefing on the Appalachian Regional Commission legislation which Kennedy was expected to endorse. "We'll vouch for you," one of them said.

At the White House entrance the Secret Service officer on duty said, "Mr. Stafford, step aside, please." He had gotten word that we had been discussing my situation at the gate.

The others filed into the president's office. I remained in the lobby talking to members of the press I had known on the campaign trail, among them Bill Lawrence of the *New York Times*. While I was there, Kennedy's press secretary, Pierre Salinger, gave a briefing that I found interesting, but which held little to offer the *Gazette* readership. Eventually the Secret Service officer invited me to a special event in the Rose Garden. "I'm sure you'll enjoy it," he said.

It was a grand affair. The president, Mrs. Kennedy, and other dignitaries were in attendance, and the garden was lovely on that early summer day. The ceremony was being held in tribute to one of the world's great men, Winston Churchill, who was being awarded honorary American citizenship. During these festivities I couldn't help but recall that my own state had made Churchill an honorary West Virginian the previous March. And that I had played a minor role in it. Delegate J. F. "Free" Bedell of Charleston had come to me only moments before the opening of the House session and said, "Tom, I need a resolution. Would you write it for me?"

"What about?" I asked.

"I think West Virginia should make Winston Churchill an honorary citizen," he replied.

I rushed into the pressroom, pounded it out on an ancient typewriter and gave it to Bedell just before the session started. The resolution sailed through the House and Senate, and in a few days the former British prime minister became an honorary citizen of the state of West Virginia.

Months afterward Bedell handed me a letter from Churchill thanking the legislator for the honor bestowed upon him. "This is yours," Bedell said. "You wrote the resolution." As I stood in the Rose Garden on that beautiful summer day, I was reminded that West Virginia is not always a follower. Sometimes it leads the way, if only in the making of grand gestures.

But I never got the grand tour that would later be given to my daughter. Other than the Rose Garden, the only other special area of the White House I was ever invited into was the cabinet room where Kennedy's commerce secretary, Luther H. Hodges, briefed the press on the president's endorsement of the Appalachian Regional Commission—despite the fact that the governor of West Virginia was willing to vouch for me.

Part Two

"Put not your faith in princes."

Niccolo Machiavelli

Chapter 8

He Never Used the Broom

WEST VIRGINIA'S TWENTY-SIXTH GOVERNOR, William Wallace Barron, elected to office in 1960 on the same ballot as Kennedy, used to tell the story about walking out of church as a boy while his father was delivering a sermon.

"Why did you do that?" Dr. Fred Barron asked his son later.

"The sermon wasn't very interesting," young Barron replied.

This was one of the few recorded moments in Governor Barron's past when he openly exercised independence of spirit. Today he is remembered as a master compromiser, a man who believed that it is better to bend to the demands of reality than break under the burden of principle.

Barron was an able student of the political craft as traditionally practiced in West Virginia. He discovered early in his career that it takes longer to change many minds than to change a few, and from then on, conference-room bargaining and assembly-room accommodation became his favorite tools of statecraft.

As majority whip in the House of Delegates during the Patteson administration, as chairman of the Liquor Control Commission during Marland's term in office, and as attorney general during the Underwood years, Barron was well positioned to study the strengths and weaknesses of his predecessors and to hone his own skills for a future political run.

From Governor Underwood, Barron learned not to provoke legislative passions in quest of the high ground. From Governor Marland he learned not to try to change fiscal policies deeply rooted in the past. And from Governor Patteson he learned how to turn patience and low-key persuasion into political virtues.

He learned well. During his four years as governor, West Virginia experienced its greatest period of prosperity. Its citizens had more money, spent more money, and saved more money than at any other time in state history.

Barron's interest in politics began in his youth and led to his first state job in the Workmen's Compensation Department following his graduation from Washington and Lee University. He later received his law degree from WVU and followed that with a Dale Carnegie public speaking course. He paid his dues, as the saying goes, as a Democratic precinct worker in Elkins. As a youngster he transported voters to the polls and performed other menial chores, eventually working his way up to precinct captain. His first elective office was that of mayor of Elkins, and he modestly distinguished himself by organizing a cleanup of the streets around town. To emphasize his commitment to the project, Mayor Barron himself pushed a broom as one of the volunteer sweepers.

After serving for two terms in the House of Delegates, Barron's first big test of the precincts came when he filed for attorney general as a relative unknown. By then, Governor Marland had both appointed him liquor commission chairman and fired him from that position, an encumbrance Barron managed to overcome with skillful campaigning and his own secret weapon—his wife, Opal Marie Wilcox Barron. Out along the campaign trail, Opal's smile, wit, and innate charm warmed the hearts of voters as much as Barron himself. Thanks in large part to Opal, he won the primary with a 2,317-vote edge over his opponent, former State Treasurer William H. Ansel Jr.

Barron had a brilliant and handsome opponent in the general election, Charleston attorney and city council president John A. Field Jr. But the statewide Democratic majority gave Barron the advantage. Field was appointed tax commissioner by then-Governor Underwood and later resigned to accept an appointment to the federal bench. Ironically, it was from this position that Field would some years later sentence Barron to prison.

Barron's talent for accommodation became evident about the same time that rumors of his gubernatorial ambitions began surfacing. The attorney general, as the state's legal advisor, prepares written opinions for state and local officials. In this capacity his duty is to advise them on how the law reads and relates to their actions, not on how it can be bent to suit the whims of a particular public official. But more than a few department heads mentioned that when they went to Attorney General Barron for legal opinions relating to problems in their departments, Barron would ask how they wanted the opinion written, apparently hoping to curry favor and build friendships with an eye to his political future.

And when compared to the work ethic of his predecessors, attorneys general such as Ira Partlow and John Fox, the output of the office under Barron was as lacking in quantity as quality. An examination of the number of opinions written tells the story. Barron and his staff were more committed to positioning him for the governor's race than to carrying out their constitutional duties.

BY THE TIME HE LAUNCHED his campaign for governor, Barron had managed to round up most of organized labor's support, as well as the ragtag elements of the old Statehouse gang from the pre-Underwood years. His campaign theme was the cleanup of West Virginia's roads and byways, and he talked cleanup all the way to election day.

"I'll take up a broom on inauguration day," he told his audiences, "and start sweeping down Capitol Street in the hope that this will start a statewide drive for a cleaner, more beautiful state."

As the May primary neared, Barron appeared from polls and courthouse gossip to be the clear and certain winner—until one of his opponents, Orel Skeen, made a startling accusation. Skeen claimed that Barron had offered him sixty-five thousand dollars to stay out of the race for governor and further, that he had a tape recording of their conversation to prove it.

Skeen was a decent man. He had made a name for himself as a stern but fair warden at the state penitentiary in Moundsville. It was from this springboard that Skeen, a self-styled "rural rustic," had run for and been elected state treasurer. As treasurer, he served competently and eventually, like Barron, decided to make a run for the governor's office.

I had been traveling with Skeen on one of his campaign swings when he said he might have something of interest to me as an investigative writer. I had heard through the grapevine that Skeen and Barron had talked, and that Skeen might want to use the conversation as a campaign bargaining chip. A few days later, the tape of their conversation was handed to me at Charleston's Ruffner Hotel. I took it back to the office, put it on one of the *Gazette*'s tape recorders, and immediately found it to be badly flawed. The quality of the recording was very poor. I was forced to go to the most electronically sophisticated equipment in town, at WCHS, to try to unravel the essence of Skeen's and Barron's meeting.

Over a period of two hours, a technician played and replayed the tape while I tried to decipher it. Never have I heard such profanity as poured out of this tape, most of it from Barron. Eventually I was able to determine that, while sitting on a couch in Skeen's living room, Barron had offered his opponent sixty-five thousand dollars to remain on the sidelines rather than run.

The rest is now a footnote in the history of West Virginia politics. The story of that taped conversation was reported in the *Gazette*. Barron denied the accusation. He even brought a slander suit against Skeen, but came to terms with him after the election and dropped the suit.

Meanwhile, Hulett Smith, another Democratic contender for the office of governor, tried to distance himself from the Barron-Skeen affair, hoping to garner support from voters disgruntled by his primary opponents' actions. Back at Barron's headquarters, as a couple of his strategists told me after the primary, everybody was ready to throw in the towel. They were nearly out of funds, and the Skeen affair was hurting their campaign. All Smith needed to do at that point was come up with a few thousand dollars more for an advertising blitz and precinct seed money and the Barron campaign would have been finished. But Smith never seized the opportunity.

As it happened, the week after the primary, my wife and I ran into Smith in Washington. Over dinner, he complained that his campaign expenses had amounted to a shade over forty thousand dollars—a high figure for a 1960s gubernatorial primary race—most of which had come from his family's deep pockets.

A few months later, during Thanksgiving dinner at our mutual brother-in-law's home, Smith remarked that he could have won the election if another story like the Barron-Skeen exposé had been published. Never one to sacrifice accuracy on the altar of family harmony, I replied that money had actually been the deciding factor. With Smith's wealthy parents and in-laws sitting there, I added, "If you had spent a few thousand dollars more, you rather than Wally Barron might be the governor-elect today." As I recall, my wife's foot made painful contact with my shin under the table.

The gubernatorial race in the general election was unexciting and anticlimactic. Barron's Republican opponent, Harold E. Neely of Hinton, appeared uninformed about the intricacies of governmental management, although he had served as both commissioner of public institutions and insurance commissioner. This fact was embarrassingly evident whenever he and Barron were questioned on *Meet the Press* platforms across the state. Neely's judgment and political savvy were also called into question after he chose, against the best possible advice, to use on statewide radio the whole of the mostly unintelligible Barron-Skeen tape.

Throughout the general election campaign, Barron continued talking cleanup in the manner of hotdogs and Mom's apple pie, and kept Opal by his side every step of the way. He and Opal made a good team; she was friendly and outgoing while he was a bit shy. By nature an impeccably tidy man, he left the impression wherever he campaigned that he was organized and on top of things. It was a no-contest election. Barron won by a wide margin.

The year 1960 was a banner one for Democrats in West Virginia. Kennedy won the presidency, attracting to the polls the biggest percentage of voters since William Howard Taft defeated William Jennings Bryan in 1908. Statewide, Barron made a better showing than Kennedy, beating Republican Neely by more than sixty-six thousand votes. The Democrats had come home again after four years in the hinterlands. Barron was in the right place at the right time and took advantage of every opportunity that presented itself.

IN 1954 GOVERNOR MARLAND had appointed a citizens' commission to analyze West Virginia's tax structure. This commission made no specific recommendations, but its efforts generated several years of dialogue on weaknesses in the revenue system. The legislature created another tax study commission

in 1959 to avoid having to pass any of the taxes proposed by Governor Underwood. Among the recommendations of this body were a personal income tax
and an increase in the consumers' sales tax.

Enactment of the recommended sales and income taxes was not a foregone
conclusion for incoming Governor Barron, and after taking office he moved
quickly on these measures. From the moment of his election Barron was busy
lining up support for his programs. He never even took the time on inauguration day to push the broom down Capitol Street as he had promised during his
campaign. He spent most of his days oiling the wheels of his organization to
ensure a smooth ride for the next four years. The highlight of this effort was a
meeting in the House of Delegates chamber attended by labor, business, and
political leaders, among them former Governors Holt and Patteson.

What Barron said to this group was characteristic of the private as well
as the public man: "You are showing West Virginia and the outside world that
labor, management, and other segments of our society can work together as
responsible citizens."

That Barron was a man of uncommonly persuasive powers quickly became evident. He was not only able to gain approval from the legislature for a
boost in the sales tax but managed to push through the enactment of the controversial state income tax, a measure neither of his immediate predecessors
had been able to get past a first reading. During the same legislative session he
also won approval for the creation of a Commerce Department and sweeping
changes in the Department of Natural Resources.

For the remainder of Barron's term the thorny subject of tax increases
was only a minor issue for his administration. Each year he felt compelled to
ask for an extension of the penny increase in the state sales tax for unemployment relief, but this was all. The income tax produced more revenue than had
been anticipated, and during his term the effects of the statewide property-
reappraisal program approved in 1958 began coming on line, which lessened
the fiscal burden for the school districts, counties, and municipalities.

BARRON HAD SEEN his two most recent predecessors stumble on basic policy
implementation, and he chose the "reasoning technique" espoused by Lyndon

Johnson as a more certain path to success. He was as much a proponent of the separation-of-powers doctrine as any former occupant of the governor's office, but he believed that when separation threatened a deadlock, the powers of both the executive and legislative branches should be brought together in a search for workable solutions.

Barron's staff from the attorney general's office formed the nucleus of a disciplined management team. The night before the inauguration, the new governor went through the same post-midnight oath-taking ceremony instituted by his predecessor, Underwood. At the ceremony, Barron's successor as attorney general, C. Donald Robertson, mentioned to me that Barron was moving nearly his entire staff from the attorney general's office to the governor's office. In fact, the governor had already assigned each staffer a particular task, right down to dealing with individual members of the press. Among those who transferred with him from the east to the west side of the Capitol were his first assistant, Curtis B. Trent, who would fill the same position in the governor's office; Fred H. Caplan, who went on to the Public Service Commission and later the State Supreme Court; and Virginia Mae Brown, who transferred to the Insurance Commission. Mrs. Brown later was shifted to the Public Service Commission where she was tapped as a presidential appointee to the Interstate Commerce Commission.

In the weeks following the inauguration, the new governor also tapped his recent primary opponent, Hulett Smith, to head the newly created Commerce Department. Fairmont attorney C. Howard Hardesty was appointed tax commissioner. Hardesty turned the appointment into a stepping stone to a vice presidency of West Virginia's biggest coal producer, Consolidation Coal Company, while Smith found the promotion of industry an advantage during his second run for the governorship four years later. Two old pols were also brought into the Barron fold, Clarence C. Elmore, who moved from an administrative position in the Liquor Commission to the chairmanship, and Burl A. Sawyers, who returned to management of the State Road Commission, the same position he had held under Governor Marland.

These were shrewd appointments on Barron's part. Sawyers attracted the splintered elements of the old Marland faction, Elmore came with a powerful

Democratic block from the southern coalfields, and Smith brought with him the remnants of the Mollohan-Neely organization. It was already understood in party circles that Smith would be the frontrunner for governor in 1964. Thus, Barron was putting together the foundations of a strong power base from which he could exercise a large measure of control over state politics through his newly fabricated Statehouse machine for at least the next eight years.

THERE WAS AMPLE EVIDENCE after his first appearance before the normally hostile legislature that Barron's advance preparations were already paying dividends. Within a few weeks he had won remarkable support for everything of importance he had asked for. Besides the tax measures and the creation of the new Commerce Department, the governor was granted approval for a pay raise for teachers, liberalization of unemployment and workmen's compensation benefits, and formation of a Human Rights Commission. The legislature also granted university status to Marshall College in a backroom trade-off with supporters of liquor-by-the-drink in bars and restaurants.

Five months after taking office Barron recalled the legislature to Charleston for a special session to consider a work-and-training program for the unemployed. "We cannot forever expect coal to be the hub of our economy," he said. "Today it is a main spoke, to be sure, but we must add the spokes of chemistry, steel, glass, timber, and agriculture."

Through contacts he had made during the recent election campaign, the governor turned to the Kennedy administration for help in further strengthening his public-works program. At an unheralded meeting in early summer at Mont Chateau State Park near Morgantown, Barron sat down with Abraham Ribicoff, one of Kennedy's most talented cabinet members, and hammered together a work-and-training program that was unique for its time. It was designed to shift welfare recipients from the dole to gainful employment by training them in the skills necessary to hold a job.

Barron's petition for worker relief was granted by the legislature, and with the assistance of the Kennedy administration he set up a plan for aid to the unemployed, which became a national model and was later written into federal law. Through this program, Barron and his staff made it possible for fathers on welfare to go to work in roadside cleanup and maintenance jobs around city halls and county courthouses. In time, the more ambitious were shifted into training programs where they could sharpen old skills or develop new ones. Thousands eventually moved off the relief rolls into jobs in mines and factories.

Barron's commitment to cleanup, the linchpin of his campaign platform, never lessened throughout his years in office. As director of his official cleanup program the governor appointed his longtime friend and former law partner, Bonn Brown. To emphasize the progress of the work, Barron had a billboard placed in front of the Statehouse, with lightbulbs for each county. As the counties met particular standards, their bulbs lit up. By the time all of the lights were glowing, West Virginia's roadsides were cleaner than they had been at any time in the state's history, or were ever likely to be again. The old junk cars had been removed, the trash dumps full of everything from old refrigerators to used tires had been cleared away, and tons of roadside litter had been cleaned up. The highways sparkled from Harpers Ferry to Huntington, from Wheeling to Welch.

This work, while only cosmetic, had a stimulating effect on state pride, reinforced when the program won national recognition. The effort was primarily showmanship on Barron's part, but unlike many campaign platforms, it actually had positive results.

SHORTLY AFTER BARRON TOOK OFFICE I had lunch with Dr. Harold "Hap" Shultz, a scientist of international reputation, at the Union Carbide Technical Center in South Charleston. That meeting led to the surprising discovery that Barron was a man with a willingness to take chances, a visionary as well as a coldly practical politician.

My meeting with Shultz resulted from a conversation the scientist had had with Ned Chilton about the new Greater Kanawha Valley Foundation. The foundation's mission was to encourage Charlestonians to bequeath a portion of their acquired or inherited wealth to community enrichment, and Shultz had indicated an interest in helping the fledgling organization gain a foothold in the community. Chilton made a lunch date with him on my behalf, explaining that as foundation secretary I could better discuss its aims and goals.

During the luncheon, we were quickly sidetracked by another Shultz concern. He complained that he had tried on several occasions to contact Barron but had been given the usual "he's in conference" brush-off every time he phoned the governor's office. Shultz, a German-American with access to the great and powerful around the world, was unaccustomed to such rebuffs. I told him that I was certain no slight had been intended and that I would see if I could do anything to help. In the first frenzied days of any administration, phone calls flood the governor's office. Most of them are from people who voted for the winning candidate or contributed to his campaign, and many of the callers want immediate action on anything from an appointment to some commission to repairs on the road in front of their homes to a rebuke for the teacher who disciplined their child.

An hour or so later I called the governor and explained about Shultz's difficulty and why he was trying to contact him. Barron exclaimed, "My God, we'll arrange a meeting this week," and told me to be at the meeting with him.

The information Shultz had been trying to pass along to the governor was staggering in its implications. Dr. Edward Teller, the Hungarian-born physicist who was in large part responsible for the development of the hydrogen bomb, had been in touch with Shultz about a federal program known in scientific circles as Project Plowshare. Teller maintained that methods could easily be found to safeguard the environment against pollution from underground atomic explosions, and Project Plowshare was designed to explore peaceful uses for atomic explosives.

Experiments so far had been conducted out in the west, but Teller felt that the time had come to begin testing in the east, preferably in West Virginia because of its relative remoteness from major metropolitan areas. He was primarily interested in exploring his thesis that controlled nuclear explosions could be used to gain freer access to the deeper reserves of oil and natural gas, and to use the explosions as lightning-fast earthmovers in the construction of flood-control dams and similar projects.

Teller's credentials were impeccable. In 1941 he teamed up with Enrico Fermi in the classic experiment to produce the first nuclear chain reaction. Two years later he was recruited by Dr. J. Robert Oppenheimer for the top-secret atomic weapons project at Los Alamos. Believing that thermonuclear hydrogen fusion was the wave of the future, at the end of the war Teller turned to the creation of the hydrogen bomb.

When all of this was laid out before Barron, the governor expressed interest in the project. He decided to appoint experts to work with Shultz, wanting both to explore the practicalities of the project and to examine its dangers to West Virginia's environment. Within weeks the committee began its work. I was assigned the role of the governor's personal monitor on the project. Because of the alarms such a project could set off all over the state—fears of atomic bombs exploding in the mountains—Barron asked me to take notes at every meeting, including one to be arranged with Teller in California, and to make a full report to the press at the conclusion of the study.

This assignment, readily approved by Chilton and Hoffmann, caused me unexpected headaches. It wasn't long before the Statehouse press corps heard rumors of high-level secret meetings somewhere in the recesses of officialdom, and that a *Gazette* associate editor was somehow involved. Various reporters buttonholed me, demanding to know what was going on and lambasting me for what they assumed to be a violation of my First Amendment obligations. I could only advise patience, assuring them that in due time they would learn everything.

After a few months of some of the most intensive research I have ever been a party to, this committee completed its work and submitted a report to the governor. He in turn called a press conference and released the committee's findings. If ever a headline was a dud, this was it. Project Plowshare, the study concluded, might have possibilities at some unspecified future date, but it was not economically feasible at the present time.

Was the Project Plowshare study worth the time, effort, and money put into it? The committee of geologists, engineers, and scientists involved thought so, if only for its scholarly research. If at some point in the future oil and gas become scarce enough to justify their recovery through the use of nuclear explosives, or if it becomes more practical to build dams with nuclear explosions than with conventional earthmoving techniques, the Plowshare concept will be available.

And where are the copies of the Shultz-Teller study? The original is probably buried somewhere among Barron's papers at Glenville State College. My own copy is gathering dust at the former Columbia Gas headquarters office in Charleston. I gave it to one of Columbia's top executives years ago.

The civil rights issue, which in those years was creating such turmoil in a number of southern states, had so far been a less volatile subject in West Virginia. Thanks to Governor Marland, ours had been one of the first states to endorse the spirit and legal purpose of *Brown v. Board of Education* seven years before. In 1962 Governor Barron issued a directive banning racial discrimination in hiring on the part of the state. He also appointed Mildred Bateman director of the state's mental health department, the first black person as well as the first woman named to a high position in state government. But West Virginia's commitment to equality was put to a test at the world-renowned Greenbrier Hotel while Barron was playing host to the Southern Governors' Conference. In attendance at the conference were such nationally-known supporters of segregation as Alabama's Governor George Wallace and Arkansas Governor Orval Faubus.

Interest stirred among the members of the national and state press who were there to cover the Governors' Conference when they learned that a caravan of more than a hundred civil-rights activists was en route to White Sulphur Springs with plans to stage a march through the spacious public rooms of the historic old hotel. The press corps was on hand for what they expected to be a volatile encounter when Barron and hotel manager Truman Wright met the demonstrators at the front gates of the resort. Standing back to back while some of the activists sang and shouted, Barron and Wright talked to the leaders.

Finally Barron asked them to designate a committee to accompany him to his suite to discuss their grievances. Still expecting fireworks, members of the press followed along a little to the rear as the group moved across the grounds of the hotel. But the press corps was left to wait in the hallway outside Barron's suite while he conferred with the demonstrators. Barron's well-known skills at negotiation and compromise managed to defuse the situation. Afterward, he explained to the press that the leaders had agreed to end their demonstration in exchange for the governor's promise to meet with them a few days later at his office in Charleston to discuss their complaints in depth.

The next day the Southern Governors' Conference moved to block several resolutions drafted by Wallace. Two months after his meeting with the civil-rights leaders, Barron issued an executive order prohibiting discrimination in the hiring of state employees and requiring the insertion of a clause prohibiting such discrimination in all state contracts.

MISCELLANY ° "ASK A STUPID QUESTION . . ."

WHEN BARRON SENT his blue-ribbon committee to California to meet with Teller on the intricacies of his Plowshare Project, I found myself sitting beside Teller at lunch. The seating arrangement was purely happenstance.

In one minute's worth of conversation, Teller had exhausted my entire store of knowledge of the subject, whereupon I suggested he talk with other members of our group. Unfortunately, Shultz had been unable to make the trip to California, so within thirty minutes Teller had bled us dry of our collective wisdom and left our entire group reeling. We were all so intellectually and emotionally drained by this encounter that when one of the scientists at the Lawrence Livermore Laboratory suggested we restore our equilibrium with a visit to a nearby winery, we embraced the idea wholeheartedly.

The winery was owned by the Concannon family, one of the most notable names in California wine country. The aging founder himself took us on a tour of the property. After he had shown us the casks he had brought around the Horn as a young man in the late 1800s and had told us about the grapevines he had nursed all the way from France, I asked, "Why isn't your wine sold in West Virginia?"

"We have all the market we can handle," he replied with a smile.

"What market is that?" I pressed.

"The Army, the Navy, the Marine Corps, and the Catholic Church."

Chapter 9

"RUN IT UP THE FLAGPOLE"

GOVERNOR BARRON ENJOYED one distinct advantage not afforded any of his predecessors. West Virginia celebrated its hundredth birthday during his administration. During the centennial year of 1963 Barron made numerous public appearances around the state, attending a hundred celebrations, according to his staff.

President Kennedy and Vice President Johnson were among the honored guests at two of these events which helped make the year a resounding success. West Virginia marked its centennial with taste, fanfare, and aplomb, and Barron was the genial host of the year-long festivities.

New programs celebrating West Virginia's history and heritage were launched in conjunction with the centennial. An old river scow, anchored at Charleston's levee, was converted into a classic showboat and christened the *Rhododendron*, complete with actors in period costume performing old-fashioned melodramas for the passengers' entertainment. The Cass Scenic Railroad offered visitors the chance to ride an old steam locomotive up an abandoned logging spur through one of the wildest and most pristine areas of the state.

It became so popular that the state made it a permanent summer attraction and eventually began restoring the old logging town of Cass. The first National Youth Science Camp, which would become an annual event, was held at Green Bank's radio astronomy center. At the New York World's Fair of 1963-64, hand-blown glassmaking demonstrations made West Virginia's one of the most popular pavilions. Visitors could watch a vase, goblet, or figurine being fashioned by some of the state's best glassblowers, then purchase that or a similar item in the pavilion's gift shop.

BARRON'S INTEREST IN PROMOTING new ideas as part of the state's centennial helped breathe life into the arts-and-crafts movement, which was a faltering cottage industry when he took office. All over West Virginia there were men and women who were still creating beautiful furniture, toys, jewelry, musical instruments, quilts, ceramics, and baskets by hand, the cultural legacy of their pioneer ancestors. But such craftspeople were a dying breed. There was little or no marketplace for their creations, and a unique part of the state's heritage stood in imminent danger of being lost.

From time to time the subject would be raised, but government support for a crafts revival went no further than lip service. The outlook changed, however, when Barron and Kennedy came into office in the same election. Both wanted desperately to end the poverty that gripped their constituencies, and both were looking for solutions to this dilemma.

Casting about one day for a subject for my column—the bane of all columnists' existence—I decided to write about this problem. The further I got into the subject, the better I liked it. As the final paragraph came together, I decided to ask for an appointment with the governor. He agreed to meet with me a week or so later, and I was given thirty minutes to discuss the ideas sketched out in my column.

I outlined the history of crafts as best I could. I talked about the absence of a marketplace for these creative riches and suggested that the governor petition his friends in the White House for money to fund a training program to allow a younger generation to learn the skills of their elders. Barron liked it.

"See Commerce Commissioner Smith, and let's get started," he said. "We can at least run it up the flagpole and see if it flies."

The winds were strong. The flag flew. Smith's first step was to inventory the scope of skills around the state. He then applied for federal training funds to develop an apprenticeship program for young people. He and his staff managed to locate a surprising number of West Virginia craftspeople with the ability and willingness to teach their particular proficiencies to others. The training program was set in motion.

Passing on these skills to a new generation and marketing the crafts produced were the impetus for the first Mountain State Art and Craft Fair held at Cedar Lakes near Ripley in the summer of 1963 as part of the state's centennial celebration. Smith invited Billy Edd Wheeler, Nashville recording artist and a native of Whitesville, West Virginia, to the opening luncheon as the featured entertainer. Wheeler delighted the entire crowd of VIPs with the debut of his now-famous song, "The Little Brown Shack Out Back." The musician warned the audience that it was still a work in progress, claiming to have jotted down most of the lyrics on the back of a paper bag on his way to Ripley. As I recall, that original version was longer and less "G-rated" than the version he later recorded, and I have rarely been privileged to see so many of the state's movers and shakers nearly falling into their soup with laughter.

A ribbon-cutting ceremony followed the luncheon. Spotting my young daughter at my side, Commissioner Smith asked Margo if she would like the honor of cutting the ribbon to officially open the fair. She shyly accepted the large pair of scissors and carefully snipped the blue and gold ribbons. Years later she confided to me that the significance of the formal ribbon-cutting had completely escaped her at the time. She simply dismissed it as another incomprehensible but harmless adult ritual.

The first Art and Craft Fair was a resounding success. It has remained an annual event and sparked the development of many other fairs and festivals which are now held each year in West Virginia. A gift shop offering the best of the state's craft products was later opened at the Cultural Center in Charleston. Tamarack, a showcase for West Virginia arts and crafts, was built near the Beckley exit of the turnpike. The Augusta Heritage Arts Workshop at Davis and Elkins College, started in the late 1960s and developed along lines similar to the apprentice program begun at Cedar Lakes, has achieved national recognition and evolved into a year-round academic discipline.

WHEN THE TOP ECHELON of state government met at the original state capital of Wheeling for the opening of the summer-long centennial celebration, the public seemed ready for an event of special significance. It was a colorful forty-eight hours along Market Street, Wheeling's main downtown thoroughfare. The governor and his entourage were dressed in period attire from the 1860s, as were members of the legislature. The storefronts were decorated with flags and bunting. Automobile traffic had been banned for the day and the streets were squeaky clean. Wheeling's downtown was fluffed and buffed and polished except for one aging eyesore, the former U.S. Customs House where the actual meetings and conventions that led to the separation of the western counties from Virginia had been held in the 1860s. The once fine building, which also served as West Virginia's first Capitol, had been allowed to deteriorate and was now occupied by commercial outlets selling beer, pizza, cigarettes, and who knows what else. It was a sad commentary on our stewardship of the state's historic buildings, standing in silent accusation on this centennial day.

Again in need of a subject for my column, I went back to my room at the McLure House and put together a piece in which I quoted Governor Barron as advocating the restoration of the Wheeling Customs House with state and local funds. That afternoon, just before the big event of the weekend at Wheeling's Capitol Theater where the governor was to reaffirm West Virginia's proclamation to remain in the Union, I asked him to read what I had written.

Standing backstage at the theater Barron scanned it, thought a moment, grinned, and said, "Sounds pretty good. Let's run it up the flagpole and see if it flies."

Finding the money through the years to finance the project was a continuous struggle, but today the state has a monument it can be proud of, West Virginia Independence Hall, now restored to its 1860 appearance. I confess to having a personal as well as civic interest in seeing the building restored, since it was there where my great-great uncle, Harmon Sinsel, fought to retain this state's symbolic kinship with the Old Dominion.

"I was born and raised in Virginia," Uncle Harmon told his fellow delegates to the Constitutional Convention, "and I have been ever proud of the name. I admit that Virginians have done wrong, that many of them in this rebellion have disgraced themselves, but that does not wean me from the name."

And it was in that same building where a wartime governor of a separated Virginia loyal to the Union, Francis H. Pierpont of Fairmont, laid out the continuing purpose of the western counties which were soon to adopt statehood.

"We have been driven into the position we occupy today by the usurpers of the South," Pierpont said. "We, representing the loyal citizens of Virginia, have been bound to assume the position we have assumed today, for the protection of ourselves, our wives, our children and our property. We, I repeat, have been driven to assume this position; and now we are but recurring to the great fundamental principles of our fathers, that to the loyal people of the state belongs the lawmaking power of that state."

BUT PUBLIC CEREMONY, roadside cleanup, and the governor's fondness for preaching patriotism were not enough. Barron was actually booed while delivering patriotic speeches at WVU football and basketball games. This rudeness was in part a testament to his slumping popularity. Thanks to the tape incident with Skeen, he had entered the governor's office under a cloud. Not long after he took office, rumors of indiscretion and illegality in his administration began to make the rounds. Matters worsened as two Charleston newspapers stepped up their writing about state government's illegal purchase of cars and office furniture, about favoritism in the purchasing of pharmaceuticals for state institutions, and about questionable practices in the acquisition and distribution of surplus government property.

It became evident that there was some substance to these recurring rumors after Truman Gore, Barron's appointee as finance and administration commissioner, eased his Purchasing Division chief, Boyd E. Hornor, out of office. In an interview soon after taking over the position, Hornor had told me that he planned to adhere strictly to purchasing regulations.

Since the purchasing of supplies and services is one of the most alluring and seductive areas for those with graft in their souls, I had sought out the new Purchasing Division chief to ask about his views on West Virginia procurement laws. The Department of Finance and Administration had been in existence for only three years, and I was curious to learn how Hornor intended to run his operation. The relatively new agency was an amalgamation of budget making, central accounting, and purchasing, and Hornor was determined to manage it in a businesslike manner.

Hornor was forthright in his statements about procedures he planned to introduce. Drawing on his rich background in purchasing and cost accounting, he said the state could realize vast savings by using methodology authorized by the 1957 law that created the department. He was so detail-oriented in his comments, even to a review of past questionable practices, that I called the *Gazette*'s attorney, Charles Peters Jr., to ask him to read the article I had written for evidence of libel. Peters, who later left Charleston to found the *Washington Monthly*, agonized over the piece before he finally said, "Let it go."

Hornor didn't last long after the story appeared. He was replaced by Curtis S. Wilson, who had been assistant commissioner of public institutions, and who remained as chief purchaser well into the next administration.

ALLEGATIONS OF FREEWHEELING PURCHASING and procurement practices were not the only cause of Barron's diminishing popularity. As a candidate, he had accepted financial support from various individuals of questionable reputation, one of whom he later discussed with me. This individual, whom I had known for many years, had contributed a substantial sum of money to the Barron campaign. After the election, this supporter wanted an appointment to a sensitive state post and personally requested it from the governor rather than asking someone to intercede for him. Barron told me he simply could not appoint the man to the desired office and wondered if I had any suggestions for an alternative.

"Have him down to the Mansion for lunch or dinner once in a while," I replied. "Leave him with the impression that you want his advice. Then later you might appoint him to one of the advisory boards or commissions where he'll be only one of several setting departmental policy."

The Alex Dandy problem was not quite as simple. Dandy was a fringe player and campaign contributor who became a persistent annoyance to the Barron administration. A self-described business consultant, Dandy had begun frequenting the halls of the Statehouse during the previous administration, when Barron was serving as attorney general. As the first of what he apparently expected to be a series of perks after Barron became governor, Dandy would dress in the manner his name implied and strut around the governor's reception room, greeting people as if he were an official goodwill ambassador for the administration. He often used the telephone in the reception room, calling people and leaving them with the impression that he had only a moment to talk before a scheduled meeting with the governor.

As far as I could determine, Dandy was never a member of Barron's inner circle. In fact, he became such an embarrassment that to even mention his name in Opal Barron's presence would make her livid. I was finally forced to interview him at editor Hoffmann's insistence and found him to be precisely as depicted by the rumor mill. He wouldn't give a straight answer to anything. "I love that guy," he kept repeating throughout the interview, referring to the governor.

Barron finally had to respond publicly to the Dandy situation. The final straw came when the governor went to Europe on a goodwill junket with Adjutant General Gene Hal Williams, a trip he had invited me on to provide press coverage. He had certainly not invited Dandy. But Dandy showed up in the Paris hotel where the governor was staying, and a story was leaked to the news services reporting that Dandy was a member of the governor's trade mission.

When questioned about it upon his return to Charleston, Barron growled, "Dandy has no more power in my administration than my dog Bozo."

At some point, Dandy had become an officer of Pioneer Construction Company, which was awarded government contracts for cleanup and repair work following the 1963 floods in Charleston and other areas of the state. Dandy, along with several other people in the company, one of them an employee of the Commerce Department, was indicted by a Kanawha County grand jury for falsifying state records relating to the flood cleanup. The case spilled over into the lap of Commerce Commissioner Smith late in his campaign for governor when he was criticized by the grand jury for sloppy handling of federal flood-relief funds.

Dandy was convicted of fraud for alleged influence peddling in the Pioneer Construction case but the conviction was eventually overturned by the

State Supreme Court. The next time his name appeared prominently in the press was in the late 1970s when he was charged with twelve felonies following the collapse of a bank in Cleveland, Ohio. According to federal agents, nearly $10 million in unaccounted-for deposits had been made to banks in West Virginia and other states. Agents in that case also linked Dandy to organized-crime figures. He pleaded guilty to two of the federal fraud counts and was fined twenty thousand dollars and placed on probation.

Finally, in 1991, after becoming involved in the top management of two grocery chains in Michigan, Dandy was accused of siphoning $10 million from the companies, demanding kickbacks from suppliers, and diverting $7 million from one of the supermarket chains shortly before its bankruptcy. He was convicted of tax evasion, obstruction of justice, mail fraud, and bankruptcy fraud; sentenced to twenty-three years in prison; and fined $2 million.

ANOTHER EMBARRASSMENT to the administration grew out of Barron's longtime friendship with Elkins attorney Bonn Brown, his former law partner and a frequent visitor to the Statehouse. Apparently resentful of the fact that Curtis Trent occupied an office next to the governor's, begrudging Trent the prestige, prerogatives, and access that were part and parcel of his position, Brown arranged through a friend, Finance Commissioner Truman Gore, to have an office and secretary assigned to him on the floor just below the governor's suite. This arrangement lasted less than a day. Learning about it within an hour after the office was opened, I walked in and asked the secretary if it was Brown's office. It was closed without explanation, and Brown went back to being a private attorney with the same easy access to the governor that he had had before.

YET ANOTHER SCANDAL, with links to Washington powerbrokers, erupted during Barron's last year in office. This controversy revolved around the quiet execution of a contract by Natural Resources Commissioner Warden Lane for the sale of three million board feet of high grade timber in Randolph County's Kumbrabow State Forest. The contract was with a Washington firm, Hardwood Company of America, which had neither an office nor a telephone. My own internal alarms first went off when I went to talk to Lane about the sale and was greeted not only by the commissioner but by the ubiquitous Brown.

In the succeeding months, the story snowballed, becoming headline news in Washington when Bobby Baker, President Johnson's former Senate aide, was linked to it. The whole affair blew up in Barron's face when timber operators in his hometown of Elkins learned of it. To them the deal was a shameless raid on public lands. The contract was so open-ended with renewal clauses that many millions of board feet could be ripped out of the forest at ridiculously low prices for the next three decades by a faceless Washington corporation with ties to big oil money in Texas.

In West Virginia, the revelations sparked a special legislative investigation which, like the Invest Right investigation and so many others, produced some juicy headlines but somehow never managed to bring out the names of the West Virginians who stood to profit from the deal. The story continued to drag through the press and eventually into the courts before the contract was finally voided by Kanawha Circuit Court Judge Frank L. Taylor.

RECURRING DISCLOSURES OF IMPROPRIETIES—and rumors of others, real or imagined—led to condemnatory resolutions in 1963 from the Charleston and Huntington chambers of commerce. The governor had reached the nadir of his popularity. When business organizations, many of whose members thrive on backroom deal-making, were openly critical and censorious, it became obvious that public scorn toward the administration was widespread.

The legislature reacted to citizen opinion by refusing to pass legislation that would have authorized a referendum on gubernatorial succession. The possibility that Barron could run for a successive term would never even make it to the ballot as an amendment for voters to consider. Barron had run his course. He was at the end of the political trail.

But why had it taken so long? Invest Right had been a covert presence in the Barron administration almost since his inauguration.

Chapter 10

The Ripple Effect

WHEN I BEGAN TO EXPAND my search for Invest Right, I turned to a technique used by Secretary of State Joe F. Burdette in his political campaigns. Burdette, a brash, self-assured career public servant, often talked about how he beat his opposition in his run for statewide office from his home base in one of West Virginia's smallest and least populous counties. Burdette's strategy was brilliant in its simplicity.

"Leaving Mason County," he would say, "I campaigned first in the neighboring counties and then moved out slowly from those areas where I was best known into those where I wasn't. In this way I used the ripple effect to build support, and by the time the campaign was over the whole state knew Joe Burdette and what he stood for."

The state had known Joe Burdette for a long time, as president of the State Board of Control, as assistant treasurer, as secretary of state, and as a savvy Democratic Party loyalist who knew where all the skeletons were and when they should be rattled or left alone. The only loss in his otherwise perfect record was his bid for governor in 1956.

I decided to make use of Burdette's methodology in my effort to locate Invest Right, hoping to save time. It made sense to start my search in the surrounding states. If I couldn't find Invest Right nearby, then I would spread out in a circular fashion until I had checked as far away as Alaska or Hawaii, if need be. Somewhere I would be bound to hit pay dirt.

Fortunately for the *Gazette*'s travel budget, I was saved a trip to Juneau. Turning first to Virginia for no other reason than the fact that West Virginia had once been part of the Old Dominion, I found nothing in Richmond. I turned next to Ohio because I had often traveled there. In the Capitol at Columbus I located my quarry.

Records in the Ohio secretary of state's office provided tantalizing clues. Invest Right had been founded March 8, 1961, less than two months after Barron's inauguration, with a capitalization of one thousand dollars. The agent of record was A. W. Schroath, and his firm's corporate headquarters were listed as Tuppers Plains in southeastern Ohio, where Schroath had a farm he had named Hickory Hill.

The very mention of Schroath's name—my first valid clue to a West Virginia connection—was a tip-off. Since the administration of Governor Meadows, Schroath had appeared occasionally in the news. In more recent years the Clarksburg businessman had gained prominence through his association with Finance Commissioner Truman Gore, also from Clarksburg, who was a close friend of Bonn Brown of Elkins, Governor Barron's former law partner. A few weeks after Barron's inauguration in January 1961, Schroath's automobile agency in Clarksburg had crept into print as the supplier of Oldsmobiles to four state officials, among them Gore and Road Commissioner Sawyers. Purchasing records disclosed no evidence that the cars had been purchased through the normal competitive bidding procedures.

The relationship between Schroath, Gore, and Brown was close. Schroath was president and Gore a director of Fleet Rental Leasing Corporation of Clarksburg; together with Brown they had other business interests. Whenever Brown went to Charleston, he shared Gore's apartment near the Capitol.

While the secretary of state's office in Columbus provided only the bare essentials about Invest Right, records in the Franchise Tax Department were more helpful. In that office I found additional documentation listing Brown as the corporation's president, Schroath as secretary, and an Eve Miller of 110 E. Palmetto Park Road, Boca Raton, Florida, as assistant secretary.

I might have been stopped dead in my tracks right there in the Tax Department if I hadn't wandered into the office during lunch hour. A nice young lady handed me the Invest Right file card, neither of us aware that it was not open for public inspection. Discovering this fact in another office, I offered up a quick prayer of thanks and caught the next plane home.

Who on earth was Eve Miller of Boca Raton? I kept asking myself that question as I scanned my notes during the plane ride home. The trail had begun to widen. The story was getting more interesting.

BACK IN CHARLESTON I ran into a problem of another sort. Both Chilton and Hoffmann were interested in what I had learned and, as a publisher who always wanted to be first into print with big stories, Chilton urged me to sit right down at my typewriter and tell all.

The problem was I had little to tell.

"I don't have anything yet but the name of the company, its officers, and a ton of suspicion," I argued.

"Christ, Tommy," he said in characteristic Chilton fashion, annoyed that I didn't want to rush headlong into print. "A corporation by the name of Invest Right with its headquarters in Tuppers Plains, Ohio, with direct links to the Capitol here in Charleston? The whole thing smells."

He was right, but I stood my ground. It smelled, but not enough. My reasons for delaying publication were complex, but chief among them was the gut feeling that if I waited and dug deeper I would find something vast, ugly, and corrupt. If, on the other hand, we went to print with what little we had, I foresaw a one-day headline and a "red alert" to Brown, Schroath, and their associates to cover their tracks more carefully.

I was to pay a price for not going along with Chilton. As the weeks wore on and I kept running down blind alleys in my search for information to support my suspicions, I decided in a fit of desperation to write a letter to a select list of state suppliers of goods and services asking them what they might know about Invest Right.

For several days I had sorted through the thousands of files at the Statehouse on qualified vendors, assembling a kind of *Burke's Peerage* of the most influential state suppliers. Unfortunately, this created a stir, and I had to fend off a lot of questions about what I was doing.

I took my list of state suppliers back to the office and had Anne Howard, the secretary I shared with Harry Hoffmann, type fifty original letters to each of the company presidents. Poor Anne. The result of all our efforts was a single response which told me absolutely nothing. But somehow my letter managed to find its way to interested parties at the Statehouse and its contents to the opposition press.

One of the least informative examples of investigative writing I ever read in my life appeared soon afterward in the *Daily Mail*. With facts laid out as they had been in my letter, plus the innuendo and limited data which had already appeared in the legislative report on alleged improprieties in purchasing, the *Mail* published a several-part series. Like the original legislative report, it was short on names and lacked detail and depth, but in scatter-shot style alluded to all sorts of wrongdoing. I was embarrassed and troubled. Chilton had seen the leading edge of a good story slip away to our toughest competitor, and he let me know that he didn't like it.

I had been sandbagged on two other occasions when trying to gather all the facts before writing sensitive articles. Several years earlier I had driven two hundred miles in an effort to interview Dr. Richard Lilly, who was being considered for the directorship of the Mental Health Department. I regarded a face-to-face interview with him as essential since the state was then thinking of shifting away from institutional care of the mentally ill to a more compassionate outpatient care system, but Lilly wanted to cling to the past. To me, any alternative seemed better than the "snake pit" style of care long practiced in traditional insane asylums, and I wanted to explore Lilly's reasoning in some depth. The opposition chose a different course, the telephone, and was in print with the Lilly story a publishing cycle ahead of me.

Sometime before this, less than a year after my arrival in Charleston, I had gotten wind of the messy way in which the state was doling out its insurance business to favored political figures, and I went to the Purchasing Department's files to try to prove or disprove the rumor with facts. I made the mistake of telling a young employee what I was doing during the five days I spent examining records and she leaked it to the *Mail* on my last day there. I lost the "beat."

I learned a lesson on that occasion. Never tell anybody anything when you launch a prolonged search of public records.

Chilton chose to remind me of these humbling experiences as the latest purchasing scandal was sketched out by the Mail. It made no difference to him that I was intent on telling the full story. Chilton wanted his reporters to be first on the street with enterprising stories and was sometimes willing to sacrifice content or substantive depth to meet a deadline.

I liked making the big score, scooping the opposition, as much as anyone. You learn to love the adrenaline surge, which can be as addictive as any drug. But after a quarter century in journalism I had become less interested in rushing into print than in writing a balanced and documented account. I was a devotee of the news-gathering philosophy of James "Scotty" Reston, former editor of *The New York Times* and a journalist who stands as one of the finest and most influential of the latter half of the twentieth century. He had a policy which became known as Reston's Rule to Reporters. Beware, he warned, of making the deadline but missing the point.

There was a time in my youth, before radio and television newscasts became the norm, when a newspaper's only competition came from the other newspaper in town. Reporters dashed around scheming and conniving to be first into print with their "scoops." Reputations were made on the "beats" a reporter had in his possession.

Much of this glamour had already faded by the time Chilton became publisher, but the excitement and thrill of getting the big story still floated around the newsroom, the ghost of another age. Radio and television, with their several-times-a-day newscasts, turned the newspaper into a chronicler of the day's intelligence, the recorder of history at the moment before it becomes history. Radio and TV largely offer a digest of the news; newspapers provide a broader report. Together they make the American citizen the best-informed person in all creation.

Nothing made me more aware of this condition than a rule we had at the *Gazette* about delivering copies of every story we wrote to the Associated Press. Regardless of how little or big the story was, everything was made immediately available to the AP. As a result, we seldom reached our readers first with our own stories. This rule, which grew out of our contractual agreement with the world's largest news service, permitted the opposition radio and TV stations, which also were AP affiliates, to go on the air with our enterprise reporting before the *Gazette* even rolled off the press. The idea that with diligence and hard work we could be there "firstest with the mostest" was dead, a relic of the days of Joseph Pulitzer, William Randolph Hearst, and the 1928 Broadway play *The Front Page*.

So, although the opposition had gone to the streets with a hint that corrupt practices might be at work in the Statehouse, as I had already suggested in my "Affairs of State" column when the legislative committee first released its report, many more months would pass before this suspected rip-off was proven and years before high state officials would go to prison.

ONE OF THE MORE INTERESTING ASPECTS of my investigation was the fact that no one seemed to care that their elected officials appeared to be playing fast and loose with public funds, and that it was costing the taxpayers money. No one, that is, except the Charleston and Huntington chambers of commerce, who passed resolutions, with a great display of self-righteousness, condemning the Barron administration of abuse of its public trust.

This was the irony of ironies. On my select list of successful state bidders were members of both chambers of commerce, none of whom had bothered to respond to my letter requesting information about impropriety, wrongdoing, or outright theft in the administration. That wasn't the way the game was played. You quietly used your political leverage, twisted arms, skirted laws and regulations to gain a competitive edge over other bidders, but never—except among the safety of your fellow aggrieved peers—did you publicly protest.

This kind of hypocrisy had predominated in West Virginia's halls of government for a long time. No public official becomes corrupt in a vacuum, and the chain of subordination begins with the man with the money: the businessman, banker, industrialist. It takes two to tango, and behind every unscrupulous politician is the man with the deep pockets.

The use of money to gain favors was rife throughout government, and the practice frustrated even some politicians. During a conference of state officials at The Greenbrier, which I was covering, I had lunch with an old friend from my college years, Senate President Ralph J. Bean of Moorefield. I cannot recall what precipitated the dialogue, but Bean just opened up and, in anger and frustration, poured out his political soul. Bean had been in the Senate for sixteen years, seven of them as president, and had seen a lot during that time.

He talked at length about the influence of business and industry on policy-making, particularly in the branch he knew best, the legislature. Some members were owned body and soul by the business community, were merely puppets who danced for whoever pulled their strings. Others were given the lobbying soft touch, with invitations to parties and dinners and other social events. "It's a serious problem," Bean said. "I'm not sure what the future holds, but West Virginia is in trouble."

He went on to talk about some members who refused to make a move without consulting their friendly lobbyist. He spoke about the difficulties involved in balancing the legislative process so that the public good as well as special interests would be served. "It's a constant battle," he complained bitterly.

A few months later I walked into his office shortly before the session began to find him red-faced and clearly upset. I chose not to ask about what had happened between him and one of the business-oriented senators who had just walked out the front door. I asked instead about a particular piece of legislation that was on the calendar that day.

"Don't ask me," Bean replied sharply. "I'm not in charge anymore. He and his buddies run the Senate." That fall Bean chose not to seek reelection.

ONE OF THE MOST EGREGIOUS EXAMPLES of out-of-control lobbying involved the effort during Barron's administration to pass legislation authorizing construction of a coal slurry pipeline. This would have allowed coal to be pulverized and moved as a liquid through the pipeline. Consolidated Coal Company, the state's biggest producer, already had such a line from its mines in southeastern Ohio to the Great Lakes. Along with other companies, Consolidated Coal wanted eminent domain rights eastward out of the biggest coal-producing state in America.

The coal industry was monolithically united in seeking passage of the measure. The railroads opposed it. The core of the disagreement was not so much the new method of moving coal to market as it was freight rates and the cost of moving the coal. As it had been trying to do for decades, the coal industry wanted to counterbalance the railroads' century-long control of costs beyond the point of production. Oil and gas had unseated coal as the country's preeminent energy source, and Old King Coal wanted to reclaim the throne.

One of the biggest battles of the decade broke out at the Capitol over the coal slurry pipeline issue. And in the legislative chambers, in hotel rooms downtown, in backstreet clubs and out-of-the-way brothels, money and favors flowed from the pockets of the warring industries into the pockets of the lawmakers.

During the Barron years criticism focused mainly on the governor's office, but the exercise of pocketbook power was not limited to the executive branch. It was everywhere. During the fight over the slurry bill, little thought was given to the small amount of coal that could actually be transported through the pipeline—or what effect the pipeline would have on another even more precious resource, water. Vast amounts of the water this state moved daily into other states would have been poured into the pipeline. Rather than arriving beyond the borders as a relatively clear liquid, it would have shown up at the eastern seaports as a gooey mess, the residue from an energy source of indeterminate quality.

The slurry bill passed both houses. It was signed into law by Barron. But despite the best efforts and enormous resources of the coal industry, the pipelines were never built. Other states through which the pipelines would have to pass refused to approve similar legislation. It still remains on West Virginia's statute books, a silent witness to the power of the almighty dollar in the state's legislative chambers.

Chapter 11

SINCE I SEEMED TO BE GETTING NOWHERE using standard reportorial techniques, I decided that the only way I might be able to pull together the Invest Right story was to work my way inside the defenses of those I was investigating. But this was like plunging into a deep forest where there were no roads or signposts.

I increased my attendance at seminars and conferences frequented by the members of the Barron inner circle. I socialized with them, commiserated with them, listened to their yarns, and spun a few of my own. Much of it was a waste of time, but I felt that I had to be on hand for the occasional slip of the tongue, or a disenchanted pol angry enough to vent his or her frustrations to me.

It was a difficult time for my family. I often arrived home after my daughter had gone to bed and was still asleep when she left for school in the morning. "Mommy," Margo asked one day at breakfast, "when are we going to see Daddy again?"

Was this procedural journalism? Hardly. For the investigative writer there are few recognized ground rules. The right to publish information carries with it the right to gather information. And when officials try to suppress that information, a reporter will have to employ creative methods to bring it to public view. As long as he keeps faith with his newspaper's stated policy and adheres to U.S. Supreme Court Justice Hugo Black's admonition to serve the governed, not the governors, the First Amendment privilege will not be dishonored.

My unconventional methods did not worry Harry Hoffmann, a self-described "dumb guy" who never attended college. Hoffmann had come up through the ranks, starting with the police beat in Wheeling where he covered, among other stories, the Big Bill Lias racketeering trial. He was well-acquainted with the seamier side of human nature, and he was as determined as I to break this particular story. But Chilton, a Yale graduate who moved directly into an executive position, was concerned. He was afraid that I might be compromised by my "insider" approach, and the newspaper as well as its reporter would be embarrassed if knowledge of it became public.

Chilton's concern was not without foundation. Reporters with the best of intentions have been occasionally drawn into the web of illegality through their own indiscretion, sacrificing not only their story but their professional reputation and entire career. There was also the problem of confidentiality of sources. I had first run up against the judicial system as a young reporter in Beckley when I refused to reveal the identity of a news source. On that occasion, I had been able to protect my source with the help of a gutsy editor and the implied power of the newspaper's opinion page. But by the time I began probing the Invest Right matter, the laws had become more definitive. The U.S. Court of Appeals for the Second Circuit (New York) had ruled in the case of *Judy Garland v. Marie Torre*, and Torre, a *Herald-Tribune* reporter, had been sentenced to jail for refusing to reveal her news source.

The unspoken but near-sacred pledge of the journalist to never reveal the identity of a source who wants to remain anonymous is the heart and soul of good journalism. Those willing to provide information are made aware of this fact whenever the reporter approaches them on sensitive matters. Indeed, the reporter is expected to choose imprisonment if necessary to protect this privilege. In journalism the reporter's right to preserve confidentiality of sources is as sacrosanct as that of the priest in the confessional.

Whenever such a right ceases to exist, the free flow of information begins to dry up, leaving the news media little more than an outlet for the dissemination of handouts and press releases. Without the ability to protect the news source, the reporter has an impossible task in trying to expose government corruption.

The precedent set by the *Garland v. Torre* decision served as a warning and a constraint during most of my years at the *Gazette*. Another case in 1972,

Bransburg v. Hayes, involving the Louisville *Courier-Journal,* went all the way to the U.S. Supreme Court, but the resulting decision only muddied the waters further. In a decision characterized as a 4½ to 4½ split, four justices swung in favor of the sanctity of confidentiality and four came down on the opposing side of the issue. It was left to Justice Louis Powell to state that competing interests should be evaluated on a case-by-case basis. In other words, confidentiality remained a legally imprecise and undefined principle for every reporter who thereafter set off in pursuit of a hot tip.

MY FIRST VENTURE INTO INVESTIGATIVE REPORTING took place while I was still a mere reporter with *The Raleigh Register* in Beckley. Reading in an overnight press report about a bill introduced in the legislature which would have expanded the jurisdiction of the criminal court in Raleigh County, I began to wonder about the merits of the legislation and the reasons behind its introduction. In those waning years of the 1930s, Raleigh County had both a circuit and a criminal court. The circuit court had jurisdiction, as did circuit courts everywhere in West Virginia, over matters of general concern, both civil and criminal. The criminal court was limited to criminal concerns. As a consequence, it was inferior in its jurisdiction, was less prestigious than the circuit court, and paid a lesser salary to the presiding judge.

At the time, Raleigh County had a hardworking prosecuting attorney in Warren Thornhill, who was responsible for a docket of cases unprecedented in the court's history. The criminal court judge was thus heavily burdened by his docket and had a backlog of untried cases reposing in the clerk's office files.

Why, I asked myself, would there be a move to increase the criminal court jurisdiction when it already was overburdened with work? I asked a few questions at the courthouse and learned that the criminal court judge favored the legislation and that the circuit judge did not. I then went to the records in the clerk's office, pulled together the information I would need to write a story about the backlog problem, and submitted it. The story was published the next day.

Tempers flared around the courthouse. The judge summoned me to his chambers and demanded to know who had assisted me in gathering my information. He threatened to send me to jail for contempt of court if I refused to reveal the source or sources of my information, and gave me three days to think about it.

I was the new kid on the block as a courthouse reporter, and, quite candidly, I was scared witless at the thought of going to jail and dishonoring my family name. But mindful of the journalistic principle that source protection in news gathering is sacrosanct, I resigned myself to my fate—and to having a rap sheet for the rest of my life.

When I told my editor about the judge's reaction to my story, Raiford Watkins exploded. "Nobody's going to intimidate my reporters when they tell the truth!" he bellowed.

He immediately telephoned the judge. To my relief, I didn't go to jail the following Monday morning. Rather, the judge apologized to me, and we both watched as his bill died in the legislature without ever reaching a vote in either house.

Who was this judge? Harley M. Kilgore, who would be chosen by Matthew M. Neely, then the kingpin of West Virginia politics, to run for the U.S. Senate. Kilgore went to Washington after winning an easy election, became an ally of President Harry Truman, and rose to the chairmanship of the powerful judiciary committee.

Our relationship healed after the courthouse imbroglio, and Kilgore's original charming manner resurfaced in his dealings with me. And in the early days of World War II, during my first tour of duty as an enlisted man at the Naval Operating Base in Norfolk, Virginia, he did me a great favor.

Parted from my bride of only a few months, unenthusiastic about the nightlife offered by wartime Norfolk, and unable to find any books of interest in the limited base library, I enrolled at the Norfolk branch of William and Mary College in a course listed as social psychiatry, which was the study of the effects of war on the children of Europe. I did so well with my grades that at the end of the term the professor wrote an unsolicited letter to my commanding officer.

This gentleman, Earl Gallimore, an Annapolis graduate who had been recalled to active duty from the operation of his newspaper in Florida, suggested that I apply for officer status. The war was only a few months old, and the Navy was in need of officers for the fleet of ships being built in shipyards across America.

If I was to be successful with my application, my CO advised, I would need some good references from back home. One of those who wrote letters on my behalf was Congressman Joe L. Smith; another was Senator Kilgore. My CO was impressed, and apparently so was the Navy personnel office in Washington. Nine months after I enlisted as yeoman, I was promoted to ensign and eventually to my own command, a rescue-and-salvage ship in the western Pacific.

That little episode in Kilgore's office had another residual effect. He had threatened me with jail shortly after the *Register* had reached the newsstands. It would be the following morning before I had the opportunity to talk with my editor about it. Needless to say, I spent the rest of that day alternating between anger and fear. Mostly I worried about where I would find a job in those Depression times—once I was freed from my incarceration for contempt of court. Before going to Beckley to work for the *Register*, the only job I had been able to find had been as a truck driver for a furniture store.

I was still in a state of emotional turmoil when I showed up that evening for my usual Friday night date with Margaret Bledsoe, the girl I would later marry. I told her everything that had happened, and although she was shocked, she was sympathetic to my plight. She had taken some journalism courses in college—one of her teachers had been an editor at *The Washington Star*—and she both understood and supported my refusal to disclose the name of my news source.

That was a benchmark evening in our relationship. It was a difficult night for us, perhaps the first time either of us had had to wrestle with the question of ethics versus personal welfare and the implied consequences, but out of it came a new closeness and a deeper understanding which propelled us into something far more substantive and durable.

THE YEARS FOLLOWING THAT NIGHT weren't always easy for my wife. I was the one who took unpopular editorial stands on various issues, but she was forced to endure the fallout from ill-humored resentment directed at me. There were occasions when she was treated rudely or shunned completely at social gatherings. Lifelong friends would cross the street to avoid speaking to her. We even dropped our membership in the country club her father and uncle had helped found. I was a pariah of sorts and my wife, who had been voted the most popular girl in her senior class in high school, was condemned by association.

Even our daughter, Margo, was not allowed to escape the acrimony sometimes generated by my editorial writing. Once when the president came to Charleston for a political rally, I was given special passes for my wife and daughter in the VIP section so they could have a good view while I covered the event. The social secretary from the Governor's Mansion was examining passes at the door. When my wife and daughter went through, she looked at my small daughter and said, "What a lovely young lady you are. But at the Mansion we don't like your father."

After we moved to Charleston, as a convenience when the two of them would drive back to Beckley for the weekend to visit my wife's family, we re-applied for membership at the country club so Margo would have swimming privileges with her cousins. We stated the reason on our application, but the application was turned down. We were blackballed and a little girl was disappointed because of the editorial position I had taken on illegal gambling years before my daughter was even born.

DURING MY YEARS AS A CARD-CARRYING JOURNALIST, I had been forced to develop my own personal reporting standards. I felt fortunate in having had Perley Isaac Reed as my professor at the WVU School of Journalism, one of the finest men I have ever known and a firm believer in ethics in newspapering. But there were no formal guidelines for reporters to follow throughout my years in the business, although a Code of Ethics was finally established in 1973.

One thing I always personally refused to do was tape telephone conversations. In a separate cabinet at the *Gazette*'s associate editor's desk was a non-beeping tape recorder that would have allowed me to tape any and all telephone conversations without the person on the other end being aware of it. But the contraption bothered me.

In those days before the passage of the Omnibus Crime Control Act of 1968, it was not illegal to tape phone calls without first informing the party that he or she was being taped. It would have made my work easier had I left the recorder intact, but one of my first actions after moving to Charleston was to rip out all the wiring. The cabinet sat there unused the rest of my time at the *Gazette*. I didn't want to be tempted by a convenient tool which would have made me no better than some of the people on the other end of the phone line.

I also refused to use pseudonyms or false identities in my telephone dealings with people. Nor would I identify myself improperly when interviewing a party face to face. On one occasion during a trip to Pittsburgh, working with a photographer borrowed from *The Pittsburgh Press*, I declined to go along with his suggestion that he shoot photos through a window at a Turtle Creek storefront office.

"We read the *Gazette*, and we like the way you go after the bastards," he said. "But the *Press* doesn't do much investigative reporting, so I really don't know how you want this handled."

I had him go inside the office with me where we identified ourselves, and he took his photos while I did my interview—an unpleasant one, I might add, since I was piecing together a story on the State Road Commission's illegal purchase of highway abrasives from this outfit.

I cannot pretend that I sat at the right hand of God during my years in newspapering. However, I had spent so much time in my earlier years having to justify my conventional practices that I had no desire to have to try to explain the use of unconventional reporting methods. Lawyers can make you look bad under the best of circumstances when you're on the witness stand during a libel suit.

WHILE I WAS FORCED TO DEVELOP my own investigative procedures during this phase of the Invest Right investigation, I first had to figure out just how certain officials were getting around or subverting standard practices. One of the steps I took in seeking answers was to solidify my relationship with the Purchasing Division and with other agencies that bought supplies and services in wholesale lots, particularly the Road Commission and Liquor Commission. This meant an increase in my visits to the offices of Finance Commissioner Gore, Road Commissioner Sawyers, and Liquor Commissioner Elmore. I also spent more time with members of their staffs than I had in the past and began developing friendships with suppliers of goods and services to these agencies.

The results proved interesting. All three of these officials appeared to be living better than their state salaries would allow. I could understand it in Gore's case, since he had come into government service more financially well-off than the others.

What seemed odd was that nearly every time I dropped by his office, Gore was either on the phone with his broker discussing investments or had investment data spread out on his desk, which he was checking against that day's stock-market report. He simply seemed to have access to an inordinate amount of money for personal investment purposes. Another state official I began paying more attention to around this time was Treasurer John Kelly, who also appeared to be living beyond his means, enjoying a lifestyle that included frequent trips to The Greenbrier and membership in the most exclusive of Charleston golfing clubs.

My conversations with these department heads went beyond pure reportorial business. I would take the time to chat about unrelated matters when inquiring into late-breaking political news or probing into the latest Statehouse gossip. Usually nothing of consequence came out of these conversations, but now and then a tidbit or two touching on the Invest Right matter would surface. This same technique, when used with staff people, proved even more productive. And then there were the vendors. They became a veritable treasure trove of information, especially those who were not getting as much state business as they felt they deserved. The rumors, innuendoes, and unrelated bits of information began to gel into something concrete. Concrete and ugly.

I HAD EXPECTED A COOLING of the renowned Barron cordiality as I dug deeper into the Invest Right story. While my efforts weren't general knowledge in Charleston, Governor and Mrs. Barron surely were aware of my more than casual interest in the seemingly unorthodox practices in the Division of Purchases. But their attitude never changed. Rather, both Opal and Wally became friendlier as the months wore on.

If the governor or first lady learned that I was somewhere around the Capitol, one or the other would often send word that I was welcome to stop by for coffee or a soft drink before going back to the office. The latchstring also was out for my wife and me at the governor's social functions. And if a special luncheon was arranged at the Mansion for such dignitaries as Franklin D. Roosevelt Jr., we received an invitation.

I went through a long period of self-loathing during the Invest Right investigation. I was well aware of the dilemma faced by the reporter who enters that narrow field known as muckraking or investigative writing. He has to keep reminding himself that he can never hope to be loved; he can only hope to be professionally respected.

I liked many of the people in what came to be known as the Barron crowd, especially the Barrons themselves. Using friendship as a pretext to listen and observe left me almost constantly angry with myself. Yet regardless of my own emotional turmoil, I kept at it for reasons I will never fully understand. I certainly felt no sense of accomplishment in the actual process of trying to put the story together and experienced little satisfaction each time I discovered another piece of information which brought me closer to the solution to the puzzle.

On one occasion during that period, I flew with Barron to Altoona where he was appearing in a parade with Pennsylvania's governor, David Lawrence, who had visited West Virginia several months earlier. Although I was there in a professional capacity to cover the governor's appearance, Barron insisted that I join him and Lawrence in the parade. We chuckled about it later, my riding along in the same convertible with the chief executives of two states, waving to the people lining the parade route as if I had the same VIP credentials. Riding past the crowd lining Altoona's streets, I wondered if some of them thought I was another Tom Stafford, astronaut and authentic VIP, whose name in those years appeared often in the national press. There was a quip then making the rounds of the West Virginia Statehouse: "Why don't they shoot our Tom Stafford into space and lose him?"

I traveled with the governor on another more somber occasion during those terrible, sad days following the assassination of President Kennedy in Dallas. The day after the president was shot, Barron flew to Washington to pay his official respects. As we were leaving the White House, we ran into a visibly grieving attorney general in the hallway. Both of us had known Robert Kennedy on the campaign trail three years before, and it was a difficult moment. No words seemed adequate to offer the brother of the slain president.

Barron was not the sort of politician who thrived on the usual arch banter and affected urbanity that went on late into the evening following events where he had been the honored guest. He would be pleasant, as all good politicians are in public, but he would bow out as quickly as possible. Opal was different. She loved the camaraderie, the give-and-take of conversation. A naturally warm and gregarious person, she genuinely enjoyed the company of other people, and no West Virginia first lady of my acquaintance was more outgoing and sociable than she.

There was a reason for the governor's after-hours monasticism. Early in his career he had developed a problem with alcohol, and he found it easier to simply avoid temptation. He would joke about it at social gatherings. As he stood drinking his nonalcoholic wine, he would sometimes smile and say, "You may be having a great time tonight, but I'll feel better tomorrow morning."

Only once during his four years in office did I see Barron fall from abstemious grace. It happened during a National Governors' Conference in Hershey, Pennsylvania. When I called Charleston to ask how I should handle the matter, Hoffmann replied, "Ignore it, unless he falls over in his soup at the state dinner."

After appearing publicly at a reception the first evening and at breakfast the next morning, the governor never left his suite. He remained there playing cards with friends until the conference ended four days later. Opal and Press Secretary Con Hardman served as his stand-ins, keeping in touch with official events throughout the conference and relaying important developments to the governor.

The outgoing and cordial Opal Barron acted as her husband's stand-in on more than one occasion, and sometimes had to deal with the standard annoyances that go hand-in-hand with political position and prestige. People from inside and outside the administration who wanted favors from the governor often regarded social events as an opportunity to approach Opal to ask her to intercede for them with her husband. One way she handled the problem was to draft me as her escort. The very presence of a newsman at her side turned away most favor-seekers. It was all by design, and on the few occasions when someone became verbally pushy, I was more than capable of pushing back.

Never in all the years while she was in Charleston did I attempt to pry secrets out of Mrs. Barron. Spouses as news sources, in my opinion, are strictly off-limits to reporters. They have the thankless task of trying to preserve family life and sanity in an incredibly stressful environment, and they deserve to maintain whatever privacy they can.

In the past the general rule was that an official's private life remained locked away from public view unless he brought it to the public's attention himself with a DUI violation or a frolicking romp with his paramour in the fountain in the public square. Until his alcoholism, sex life, or other indiscretions affected his ability to serve, the subject remained personal and private, a matter for the politician and his conscience. And his wife was untouchable.

This is why many journalists developed a disgust for the tactics used by Bob Woodward and Carl Bernstein after they so brilliantly unraveled the Watergate scandal. The feeling was that they tarnished their earlier achievements and destroyed a measure of their professionalism by writing a glitzy, gossipy, tawdry sequel about the backstairs goings-on in the Nixon administration. I could write my own paperback thriller, as could any number of Capitol reporters, about the peccadilloes of our state officials, but as long as what occurs offstage does not affect the governing process, it should be left alone. We all have skeletons in our closets; some people's are simply more embarrassing than others'.

THE INVEST RIGHT STORY started coming together after I developed my new method of investigation. I began picking up the names of corporations, or the names of individuals linked to these corporations. They trickled in slowly from a number of different sources, but trickle in they did. Rather than take the long route of trying to trace them through the secretary of state's office in half a dozen states, I acted on a hunch and turned first to Florida, the state of residence listed for the woman whose name appeared in the records of incorporation for Invest Right in Ohio. No quick trips to the state Capitol in Tallahassee were necessary. I had my own private news research center in Florida in the person of my brother Charley, who was then the bureau head of the Associated Press office in Tampa.

I also had another contact in Florida as well, an old acquaintance who was then editor of the *Miami Herald*. When I alerted him to my suspicions, I was interested to learn that he had an entire team of reporters whose mission was ferreting out governmental bribery and conspiracy.

Charley turned out to be a bigger help, however, than the *Herald's* entire team. In my brother I had a seasoned and trusted ally. Following his graduation from the WVU School of Journalism, Charley came to work for me in Beckley but left after two years for the Huntington AP bureau. A couple of years later he was transferred to the Baltimore bureau, and went from there to one of the prize assignments in all of the Associated Press, News Features in New York.

Charley was doing a superb job in New York, as General Manager Wes Gallagher told me later. "I had great plans for that brother of yours," Gallagher said. But Charley wasn't happy in New York, and when his young son had a run-in with a group of neighborhood punks, Charley decided that a change was in order. The following morning he asked Gallagher for a transfer south at the earliest opportunity.

Tampa was his next assignment, and he was ideally placed to help me in drawing the noose around Barron's top aides and friends. As soon as I heard about another corporate spin-off from Invest Right, I would call my brother. He would call Tallahassee, and one of the reporters in the bureau there would pull the facts together at the Capitol and message them back to Charley, who would relay them to me by phone.

These calls were always made from my home phone, and Charley would respond in kind. Secrecy had become a major consideration by this point in the investigation. Newspaper offices leak like sieves, and by then my worst problem was Chilton.

NED CHILTON WAS YOUNG, brash, and still relatively new to his publishing responsibilities. Circumspection was not part of his nature, and he loved talking about the bigger stories being developed by his newspaper. At the time of my Invest Right investigation, I was also working on a story that dealt with bond financing of National Guard armories then in the planning stage. From sources within the bond market, I had learned that some possibly illegal pricing policies had been adopted by state officials.

My research took me from downtown Charleston to Virginia and from there to New York City. An appointment with a top official in one of the biggest bond houses on Wall Street was arranged for me by my Virginia source, and I later phoned the official myself to confirm the meeting. When I arrived in New York on a Monday afternoon, I called his office again to reconfirm the appointment time for the next day.

"I'm sorry," his secretary said. "He had to leave town. He won't be back for two weeks."

With that I repacked my bag and headed home where I hoped to be able to retrace my steps and start over. But my efforts were futile. Through several phone calls to various sources, I discovered that the weekend before I left for New York, Chilton had upbraided one of the supposed principals in the affair at a cocktail party. The story was dead.

I tried to revive it as best I could, but after the reconstructed version appeared in print, one of the insider secretaries at the Statehouse laughed and said, "You didn't get us, did you?"

In a situation like this, a writer doesn't raise hell with his boss. He rants and raves in the privacy of his own home and vows to keep his mouth shut when working on important stories in the future. From then on, until I finally finished my Invest Right investigation, I seldom gave Chilton a progress report, preferring to keep only Hoffmann apprised of what I was doing and where I was going.

UNDER CONDITIONS LAID DOWN by Chilton when he organized the editorial board at the *Gazette*, I had broad latitude in the way I worked. I could choose either to report to him or to Hoffmann.

Shortly after taking over management of the paper, Chilton scrapped the outside board Frank Knight had named and appointed a new one composed of editor Hoffmann, vice president Bob Smith, executive editor Dallas Higbee, city editor L. T. Anderson, and me. Chilton served as chairman. To inform us about the changes, he took each new board member to dinner separately at Berry Hills Country Club.

Chilton was very positive in stating that as board members he wanted us to exercise independence of thought on policy matters. "If you're going to say what you think I want you to say, I don't want you on the board," he told us. "I want you to be honest and forthright."

He warned each of us that he might on occasion override us on particular issues, but by and large majority rule would be exercised. I can remember only one time when he chose to make a decision independently of the board. This was on the question then before the legislature of changing the status of Marshall College to that of a university. Chilton maintained that the rest of us were so locked into fixed attitudes about Marshall that he, a Yale graduate, was the only one who could be truly objective. When he finally decided to oppose university status for Marshall, he had our resident scholar, Harry Ernst—later a journalism professor at WVU—write the editorial.

During that interesting dinner at Berry Hills, Chilton told me that I could make my own assignments and choose where I needed to travel in doing them. "Just report to Harry or me once in a while about what you're doing." Also, he said he wanted me to begin writing a column entitled "Affairs of State." In this column, he added, I would have the right to express my own opinion; in writing editorials, however, I would adhere to board policy.

I learned to my delight what he meant by this independence a year or so later when he came to my desk with an editorial he had written. "Read this, Tommy, and let me know what you think about it." I told him afterward that I didn't agree with his position.

"All right," he commented, "but I'm going to use it anyway."

About an hour later I went back into his office and said, "Ned, I think you're on the wrong track," and set forth my own ideas on the issue at hand.

He listened politely for a few minutes. "You have a column running tomorrow," he countered. "Say whatever you want, but I'm using this editorial." The next morning, the *Gazette* hit the streets with Chilton's opinion on a local political issue on one side of the op-ed page and my differing viewpoint on the opposite side.

We were often criticized for what was perceived as our shifting editorial policy. My flippant response to such criticism was usually, "If you don't like *Gazette* policy today, wait a day."

Chilton could be mercurial in his moods and sometimes irritating. I usually found him willing to be objective. He also had a brilliant mind, could be in turn charming and abrasive, and was eminently professional in his work. And during our dinner at Berry Hills he advised, "If you disagree with me, you'd better be sure of your facts. I took a course in argumentation from Bill Buckley at Yale, and I'm tough in verbal combat."

He was that in spades. Hoffmann often said to me before editorial board meetings, "I just don't know how to deal with Chilton." On one occasion Ned waltzed me down the polemical garden path until I suddenly realized how he had boxed me in. He just sat back in his chair and grinned. Ned Chilton was a born scrapper who loved nothing better than challenging sophistry in others.

Although often frustrating, he was a joy to know in those years of his management at the *Gazette*—even when he came charging out of his office shouting out my middle name ("Freeborn!") in excitement, anger, or indignation. After I left the paper, we kept our friendship going through correspondence and telephone conversations. Now and then I would drop by to see him when I was in Charleston.

He had a special kind of appreciation for staff performance. Though more critical than many publishers, he was generous with perks. Bonuses to the staff came every Christmas, as did gift certificates and West Virginia hams. At one point, the Newspaper Guild targeted the *Gazette* for unionization, but after its organizers got a look at the salary scale and benefits, they changed their minds.

"We have nothing better to offer," they remarked.

Chilton's attitude toward his employees can be illustrated by what happened one Christmas Eve after he had attended a *Daily Mail* staff party.

"Do you know what they were serving?" he asked Higbee. "Punch and cookies!" He thought a moment, then decided, "On New Year's Eve I want a real party for my people. Have the Press Club cater it, and I want the best!"

On New Year's Eve one of the finest buffets money could buy was laid out in the center of the newsroom, with vintage wines and fine liquors on a nearby table. This affair became an annual event, with the paper put to bed early so everybody could relax and enjoy themselves.

Chilton was also committed to the idea of using the newspaper to better his community. One day he told me, "Tommy, we have a meeting with Bob Spilman." We met Spilman, a prominent Charleston attorney, for lunch at the Ruffner Hotel. Chilton was captivated by what he had to say. Spilman was proposing that the *Gazette* promote the formation of a community foundation for Charleston patterned after those in Cleveland, New York, and Pittsburgh. Such foundations encouraged people of means to bequeath or donate a portion of their inherited or acquired wealth to the foundation for investment; the income from the pooled investments would be allocated to charitable pursuits. "The people who participate create a living memorial to themselves in perpetuity," Spilman added, "and help the community at the same time."

Chilton was sold. "Let's get started on this," he said, turning to me. Out of that luncheon grew the Greater Kanawha Valley Foundation, which today administers millions of dollars in assets and income going to support education, health care, recreation, and other public purposes.

It was Chilton's dream that the community foundation idea would spread into other parts of West Virginia. Beckley and Parkersburg joined in the movement. The Clay family, which owned the *Daily Mail* for many years, created a $25 million foundation in the late 1980s. And the Shott family—owners of radio, television, and newspaper properties in Bluefield—developed an $18 million foundation.

I was told by other editorial board members that Ned changed over the years after I left Charleston. Hoffmann groused on one occasion, "He gets more like his father every day." Anderson also joined in the criticism, as did newer board members. True, Chilton could be unthinkingly rude and authoritarian. This lost him some good reporters over the years. In the case of such quality writers as Anderson and John Morgan, they retired as quickly as their benefits would permit. Hoffmann, too, headed into retirement, although he continued to write his "Politics" column until his death.

Despite his intellectual arrogance and abrasiveness with staff, and his fireball editorial writing, Chilton built the *Gazette* into a newspaper respected nationally for its honesty, integrity, and liberal views. The paper had a long way to go when he took over management on Frank Knight's death. Chilton's father, with an uncommon capacity for liquor, had permitted the paper to drift while he was in charge. It was on the verge of bankruptcy when the Chilton family hired Robert L. Smith as general manager in the early 1930s. Smith gave the paper financial stability, and later Chilton gave it that distinction so aptly described by another man of eminence in publishing, Jenkin Lloyd Jones: "Let there be a fresh breeze of new honesty, new idealism, new integrity. And there, gentlemen, is where you come in. You have typewriters, presses and a huge audience. How about raising some hell?" Chilton was one of the best of the hell-raisers.

MISCELLANY ⁕ A MOST EMBARRASSING MOMENT

Near the end of my years in newspapering, I was among the members of the Capitol press who gathered at the Daniel Boone Hotel to interview former President Harry Truman.

I had attended a Truman press conference in Chicago several years before. There I spent most of my time listening, leaving it to the Washington crowd to ask the tough questions. I found Truman to be adept at his craft. He fielded the questions with ease, never faltering or stumbling over his responses.

The next time I had a chance to interview him was at the Hotel Morgan in Morgantown. This was a one-on-one Q&A session, and the former president was a pure delight. Truman and I talked about many things, most of it pretty homey stuff. On that occasion I was only interested in profiling the little guy from Middle America who had been carried to greatness on the tide of events.

The last time I interviewed him was at the Daniel Boone in Charleston. He had offered to brief the media before going to the Civic Center to address a Jefferson-Jackson Day crowd.

Prior to leaving the office for the interview I had been stopped by Chilton and handed a slip of paper. He wanted me to ask Truman a question about international relations. I looked at what Ned had written on the paper, thought a moment, and asked, "Do you really want me to ask this question?"

"Sure," he said, and walked away.

I was the lead reporter at the press conference, so I asked my publisher's question first.Truman looked at me, frowned, and said, "That's the stupidest question I've ever been asked. Next question."

His reply was embarrassing enough. But I still had to go back to the office and tell Chilton what Truman had said.

Chapter 12

A SENSE OF PASSION

DURING A RECESS of the Board of Public Works I was sitting in the hearing room talking to Dr. Mildred Bateman, commissioner of mental institutions and a recognized authority in the field of psychiatric medicine.

"Tom," she said in her quiet way, "you're a nice person to be around at times like this, but you turn into a real bastard when you sit down at a typewriter."

How right she was. As Irish poet Thomas Moore once put it, I was not simply one of the angels who write but one of the devils who print. As an investigative reporter, I worked at being pleasant, just as I worked at being probing when seeking reportable information. Accuracy is the goal of the responsible journalist. One's own personal likes and dislikes often have to be set aside when reporting the facts of a given situation. The journalist has a professional obligation to maintain his objectivity. If that objectivity is compromised, he loses his journalistic credibility.

The task is more difficult for the investigative writer because the basic facts are harder to come by. He has few resources to work with when he sets out on an assignment. Unlike the courts and Congress, he has no subpoena powers. He often has no specialized investigative skills or investigators to assist him. He has only his personality and whatever interviewing techniques he may have developed. If on occasion he uses them with a toughness and assertiveness uncommon in other professions, he has no valid choice. The challenge of turning rumor and suspected wrongdoing into reportable fact is difficult under any set of circumstances, and in my time it was harder than it is today.

Now we have Freedom of Information laws to aid reportorial investigation, but those laws did not exist in the middle years of the twentieth century. All we had going for us was the First Amendment, which said Congress shall make no law abridging freedom of the press. A marvelous maxim this, until a reporter tried waving a copy of it in the face of a crafty public official. Typically, the official would lean back in his chair, smile and say, "Go to court if you don't like the way I run my office." He knew the score. Court battles cost money, and publishers showed no desire to rush to the courthouse every time a reporter ran into a roadblock on his beat.

There is another characteristic the investigative reporter needs if he expects to survive in his specialized field. Somewhere deep in his soul he needs a sense of passion and outrage that surfaces whenever he finds evidence of thievery and injustice. This is as essential as the ability to write a simple sentence.

Contrary to some pundits, I did not emerge from my mother's womb ranting and raving. She often said that I was the most placid of her six children. As a youngster I was never an alley brawler. I lacked the zest for football and other sports that my older brother, Jimmy, had. Only once in my early years did I take an unpopular stand. This was when I was a sophomore in high school and was serving as class president. Many of the students went out on strike to protest the firing of a popular football coach who had been winning games with ineligible players.

A meeting of the student council was called to decide whether the whole student body would join in the strike. The other three class presidents voted to walk out. I didn't. In a quick turnaround the other presidents changed their minds, and the threat of a student strike ended. But although my name was put in nomination during my junior and senior years, I never again was elected to the student council.

MY WHOLE PERSONALITY, my outlook on life, changed after I was transferred to a Navy ship in Delaware Bay early in World War II. We were assigned the task of forming convoys of merchant ships that would steam out into the Atlantic Ocean en route to New York City, New England, and Europe.

At the time, America was fighting a containment war in the Atlantic and Pacific, and we were suffering badly on both fronts. On the Murmansk run we were losing all too many ships to German submarine wolf packs. Added to those losses was the bloodbath in the Coral Sea and the massive casualties off Guadalcanal.

There in the Delaware Bay, which during the previous century had been the summer playground of the rich and famous, a quiet war, little discussed in the nation's press, was being fought. The Northeast had to be supplied with food, manufacturing materials, and military goods, and much of it came northward through the Inland Waterway from Florida to the Chesapeake Bay. There it was reloaded and, together with cargo from port areas around Norfolk and Baltimore, moved through the Chesapeake-Delaware Canal, where it joined cargo from the Wilmington-Philadelphia area and moved in a ragtag assortment of ships to the assembly point in the lower bay for the final run to New York. This last stage was a killer. The German submarine commanders had studied the coastal charts and knew precisely where to assemble their subs to inflict the greatest possible damage on American shipping.

The defense line was woefully inadequate. The only ships the Navy had available to patrol the sector off Cape May and Rehoboth Beach were lightly armed former fishing boats and pleasure craft. In fact, the flagship of this mismatched fleet was a former DuPont family yacht.

I was one of the young officers who made up the convoys for their final frantic run to New York. Our orders were to assemble the ships in three columns, with those carrying the least vital cargoes in the outer row—the one most seaward—and to set the group speed at the rate of the slowest ship in the convoy.

No one liked any of this, least of all the men aboard the merchantmen. They were laying their lives on the line, even though they were technically civilians. On the station ship we tried to ignore the role we were playing as best we could. We talked of forthcoming trips ashore, or of the last time at home with our families. Every one of us hated our assignment, but we kept our feelings to ourselves until early in the morning when the convoys would set out to sea. As the ships rounded Cape May Point into the Atlantic, we could hear the muffled sounds of mines exploding or ships being torpedoed. It was pure slaughter. In the aftermath we would stand at the railing, two or three of us, looking outward at the next convoy then assembling and talking bitterly of the terrible waste we were helping to cause.

I WAS A LONG TIME CATCHING UP with the war after that assignment. It was followed by protracted tours of training in sub-chasing at Miami, firefighting at San Diego, and gunnery at La Jolla. I was finally assigned to a firefighting rescue-and-salvage ship still under construction in California which eventually made its long, slow voyage across the Pacific.

The U.S.S. Cable towed strings of barges from one port to another and cleaned up harbors where the war had been fought and then moved on, places with such unfamiliar names as Tarawa, Tulagi, Kwajalein, Mios Woendi, and Finchhafen. We refloated sunken vessels and recovered the bodies of crew; sent divers down in heavily shark-infested waters to repair damaged craft; boarded crippled ships in the middle of naval engagements to fight fires, rescue the injured, and secure tow lines. Near Lingayen, we even raised what was as far as I know the largest Japanese sub to be salvaged during the war.

Eventually we shipped out of New Guinea at the tail end of a large convoy on our way to the offensive that broke the back of Imperial Japan. We were always positioned in the rear of the pack in case a ship broke down and needed to be taken under tow. On this voyage a fleet tanker that had been towing a barge of highly flammable aviation fuel broke her towline. We were ordered to retrieve the barge, which slowed us down and left us lagging unprotected ten miles behind the rest of the convoy. We finally arrived in Leyte Gulf a week later just in time for the greatest sea battle in history.

Although our ship and the tow we had alongside were straddled by bombs, we were ordered to make an airfield operational, a field which had just been taken by U.S. forces the day before. We did it by pushing our tow up against the beach. We also took part in the long effort to throw back wave after wave of attacking Japanese planes. The war might have ended for me during Leyte, when I heard the crack of metal against metal and looked down to see that I had just missed being struck by a stray bullet from another American ship. On another occasion I was hit in the head by shrapnel kicked up by a 20mm shell carelessly fired by an American LCI at a Navy fighter plane.

Except for a short tour of duty in Australia and the last invasion of the war in Borneo, my time in the Pacific was spent among the thousands of islands making up the Philippine archipelago.

One experience there brought home the whole bitter reality of war for me as no other throughout my tour of duty. Our ship had been dispatched to Manila, the first U.S. Navy ship to return following General MacArthur's escape south three years before. Our orders were to begin clearing wrecked and sunken ships and other debris from the harbor in preparation for the invasion of Japan.

We steamed past Corregidor Island only hours after Army paratroopers had retaken it and made our way cautiously toward Manila, not knowing what surprises the Japanese might have left waiting for us. We reached the city intact, to encounter the worst devastation I have ever witnessed. Much of the city had been leveled and the huge harbor itself was a mess, littered by scores of sunken vessels, some of them blocking entry to the docks. Many of the derelicts had been booby-trapped by the departing Japanese, and others harbored snipers left behind to make our work as difficult as possible. We had been given two weeks to clear the channel.

It may seem laughable that my first directive from our captain, Hartwell Pond, was to go ashore and locate screen wire. Overnight our ship had been invaded by mosquitoes and flies by the thousands, and if we were to remain there, we had to secure our position against this pesky, disease-carrying horde.

Locating an item as unwarlike as screen wire in a bombed out city was no easy undertaking. Another officer and I made our way on foot through what was left of the former business district and financial center, much of it destroyed by bombing raids and fires, detoured into a university being used as a hospital, and eventually found a makeshift Army supply depot in the suburbs where we bargained away several cases of beer for two rolls of screen wire.

It was a good trade-off. The Navy always had beer in its holds, and the Army had many of the mundane items that made life at sea livable.

My day-long tour of ravaged Manila was a sobering experience. I hadn't been ashore ten minutes before a small boy tried to sell me his teenage sister's charms for a dollar. In the financial district I found paper money, the currency of the realm only a few days before, strewn ankle-deep in the streets. The people looked beaten and hungry, beggars were on every corner, commerce was at a standstill.

Then we encountered what for me would be one of the most remarkable and moving sights of my life. We were in the middle of the old walled city, the Intramuros. Everywhere around us lay a wasteland of smoking rubble. Yet there at the entrance to a wrecked church stood a statue of Christ on the cross, resolute and untouched, a survivor of the hate and savagery that had brutalized the once lovely Pearl of the Pacific.

As I stood there transfixed by the sight of the statue standing untouched in the midst of all the devastation and destruction, I had the remarkable feeling that if I had been closer, I would have seen tears in His eyes.

I WALKED INTO A MINEFIELD of another sort within months after returning home from the war. This was when, in my first serious effort to shape public opinion as an editor, I opposed payment of a bonus to the veterans of World War II. Most other editors in West Virginia were years older than I was, and most of them were not veterans. They apparently felt unqualified to voice an opinion on this bonus for the second legion of young men in a quarter century to commit themselves to the effort to "make the world safe for Democracy."

I knew in advance that I was taking an unpopular position. Where public money is concerned, the average citizen tends to resent being denied an opportunity to pocket what he imagines to be his share. In this instance, I was seen as breaking faith with my fellow veterans.

They rose up almost en masse. Letters to our "Readers' Forum" poured into the newspaper. Anonymous phone calls kept me busy at night. On the radio program "The Public Speaks," I was labeled a turncoat. There was absolutely no support for my position, except from one lone voice on the floor of the West Virginia legislature where the bonus bill was being debated. This voice belonged to William H. File Jr., a friend of mine from Beckley who had also commanded a ship in the western Pacific and who, as his record showed, had served his country with courage and dedication.

He and I lost that fight. I thought I had written reasonably and dispassionately on the subject, but I went down in flames. The bonus payments, if approved, were to cost the state approximately $120 million. I argued that this money could be put to better use by paving crumbling roads, strengthening education, and building libraries, benefiting the entire public—including veterans and their families—instead of being distributed piecemeal among thousands of citizens.

The veteran's lobby struck me the most telling blow at a meeting of the local American Legion. I had joined the Legion after my return home for no other reason than to help support veterans' causes. At this meeting a resolution was passed informing the legislature that the Beckley post was 100 percent behind the bonus.

Although I had not been present at the meeting to cast my vote, the next day my name appeared in the opposition newspaper and on radio as a supporter of the bonus, along with the names of the other Legionnaires. I was, in other words, publicly branded a hypocrite, a fraud, a phony.

The bonus? In the end, I took my four hundred dollars. I knew I would have to pay it back in taxes over the years while the bond issue that financed it was being repaid to lenders, whether or not I actually accepted the bonus.

WHAT I REGARDED AS THE SOCIAL CONTAGION of gambling became another passion of mine after the war. Repelled by this shadowy enterprise, I committed myself to trying to eliminate it. Again I walked into a minefield.

A community will tolerate an occasional raid on the back-street pool hall or the local "numbers game" operation. But there are certain people in every town across America who believe that they are entitled to special and untouchable privileges, including the right to gamble in their private watering holes, more commonly known as fraternal organizations and country clubs, even if the practice is against the law.

So when I wrote my first antigambling editorial I struck a nerve that ran through several layers of our socially stratified community. There were the rich and the not-so-rich, the "country-club set" and the Elks, the status seekers on their way up, the scions of Old Money trying to hold their own against the encroachments of the nouveau riche, and the impoverished masses with no place to go. "At the baths," says the Yiddish proverb, "all are equal," but it ends outside the bathhouse door.

During this crusade I asked the local ministers why they weren't speaking out against gambling from their pulpits. The Kefauver Crime Investigating Committee had documented evidence tracing gambling in private clubs to the Mafia. I had charted the same trail in our town. I was invited to speak at a ministerial association meeting, but the members were decidedly cool in their greetings.

In my speech, I mentioned the story of Christ scorning the moneychangers in the temple. I quoted Voltaire's observation that "the more ancient the abuse, the more sacred it is." The ministers remained silent. I should have remembered that they numbered among their congregants people of wealth and influence who contributed generously to their churches—and who also belonged to private clubs.

Never underestimate the capacity for outrage among certain members of the self-anointed privileged class when they believe their pleasures or income are threatened. Beckley's elite struck back at our newspapers by canceling advertising and printing contracts.

Our circulation continued to rise, but circulation is not the bottom line on a newspaper's balance sheet. The moneymaker is advertising. They struck back on a more personal level as well, one I was unprepared for. My wife, whose roots reached back to the town's founding family and whose only crime was her choice of husband, was deemed guilty by association. We became social outcasts together.

These efforts at retaliation, however, failed. My publisher, Charles Hodel, a frugal and principled man of Swiss ancestry, came to my office late one afternoon with a copy of the trade publication *Editor and Publisher* in his hand. "Read this, please," he said. I scanned the piece buried deep inside the magazine and saw that an editor in the Southwest had lost his job after mounting a campaign against gambling.

Hodel looked me straight in the eye, paused for effect, and said, "That will never happen here. I will close these newspapers and lock the doors before I'll put a stop to what you're doing."

This kind of support was extraordinary. This man, who had hobbled out of an Ohio orphanage on one leg and risen to a position of influence in his adopted state, had lost large amounts of money backing me but refused to budge one iota from the pledge he had made the day he promoted me to editor. He was a paragon among publishers, a man of uncommon integrity and goodwill.

Gambling in Beckley's private clubs continued, but in time the economic effects began to take their toll on Main Street, and the city council called for a crackdown. One of my merchant friends whispered to me about how costly wide-open gambling had become to the business community. All too many customers, he said, were failing to pay their bills. Something had to be done. Once Beckley businesses began to feel the effect, gambling ceased.

I left for Charleston three years later, but gambling would not return to Beckley for almost two decades. Once a community alters course, it takes a long time to change it again.

SALLIE JOHNSON, A FAMILY FRIEND, came to my wife one day and said, "Our church would like to have a picnic at Grandview State Park. Do you think Mr. Stafford could help us with the permit?"

This was in the summer of 1954, a short time after the U.S. Supreme Court had handed down its landmark decision in *Brown v. Board of Education*, a ruling which brought an end to the "separate but equal" policy in public-school administration and set in motion the civil rights movement. Mrs. Johnson and her fellow church members were black.

She knew my sentiments on the racial question. Governor Marland had just issued his historic order pledging West Virginia's compliance with the court's ruling, and I had written an editorial supporting both his action and the Supreme Court's decision. In Beckley, as southern in its sympathies as any city in West Virginia, my position wasn't particularly popular. Even a close relative asked, "Can't you just leave it alone? There are so many other things you can write about."

I wasted no time after Sallie's inquiry in calling an old friend at the Statehouse, Conservation Commissioner Carl Johnson (no relation to Sallie Johnson) and asking him to process the picnic permit her church was requesting.

"Oh, Tom, can't we just forget that you called?" he begged. "This is a very sensitive matter."

"Carl," I countered, as mild-mannered as he, "haven't I been your friend? Hasn't the *Register* been supportive of conservation and the work of your department?"

"Yes," he admitted.

"Well, Carl, I would like for the *Register* to continue to be your friend, and I would like for Grandview to be available for this church group next Sunday afternoon."

"You'll have it," he promised.

Ah. I'd finally learned how to twist arms with the best of them.

With her seemingly simple request, Sallie Johnson, a quiet, ordinary, extraordinary woman, did something special for both black and white West Virginians. Thanks to her, the racial barriers came down not only at Grandview but also in the state-park system all over West Virginia. Precedent had been set, but calmly and civilly, without the fanfare that often stirred up opposition in other states.

On the whole, the citizens of West Virginia responded fairly well to the challenge of civil rights and racial equality. West Virginia's efforts were certainly better than those of other southern and border states during the years when desegregation was being implemented. The attitude of the courts in this state also helped make the transition to integrated schools smoother than in places like Alabama and Arkansas. On one occasion in Marion County, a protest against desegregation had been organized at one of the schools near Fairmont but had barely gotten underway when Circuit Judge Harper Meredith warned that he would put the demonstrators in jail if they didn't cease their picketing. "I'll fill the jail until their feet hang out the windows if I need to," he said.

Some time later Federal Judge Ben Moore, at one of the last hearings ever held by his court in Lewisburg, listened patiently for two days to the NAACP and the Greenbrier County Board of Education as they argued the segregation issue. Then Moore drew up a compromise, later known as the Moore Memorandum, which effectively eliminated resistance to integration in several holdout southern counties and brought an end to the problem in all of West Virginia. In the sixteen other states affected by the Supreme Court's decision, it was a different story.

I was a member of a group established to follow this explosive and divisive issue. In order to ensure that the general public would be adequately informed about what was happening in the aftermath of *Brown v. Board of Education*, the Ford Foundation funded a program to track the progress of desegregation and tell the story factually, without prejudice. I inherited my role in it from Frank Knight on his death. Knight had been part of the original team of editors and editorial writers recruited from the major newspapers in the region, one from each state, and I was his successor. Our work was compiled and published periodically as *Southern School News*, released to libraries and the news media nationwide.

It was an unexciting assignment for a West Virginian. Judge Moore's memorandum had made school segregation largely a non-issue in this state. But at Central High School in Little Rock, Arkansas, the trouble was so serious that the National Guard and later the Army had to be called out. The Selma March and bus boycott in Montgomery, Alabama, were spin-offs of the same issue. These shocking events commanded the headlines for months, but they were only the tip of the proverbial iceberg.

Once or twice a year the Ford Foundation's group of journalists would gather for a conference in either Nashville or Atlanta. Reporters from *Newsweek*, *Time*, *The New York Times*, *The Washington Post*, and other national publications also came to our seminars since we provided a distillation of desegregation issues throughout the South and border states.

It was appalling, the hate and violence that were erupting all over the Deep South. Police, courts, and community leaders refused to involve themselves in efforts by others—those they referred to as "outsiders"—to stop the rape, torture, and murder of innocent blacks. Most chose to sit in sullen defiance or work in active opposition as federal authorities struggled to enforce the law. "Look north," their apologists said at our seminars. "We're no guiltier than the people on the other side of the Mason-Dixon line."

They were right, as we all had to admit in the 1960s after the violent upheaval in Detroit, Los Angeles, and Newark. But the deep-seated animosities and callousness of some of the southerners in the program, people responsible for molding public opinion, caused the bile to rise in many of us. They were interested only in preserving a historic attitude, not in joining the effort to correct three hundred years of prejudice, injustice, and bloodshed.

These attitudes reared their ugly heads at every level of society in the years following the Supreme Court's decision in *Brown v. Board of Education*, sometimes in surprising situations.

Our daughter, Margo, brought home a friend from her second-grade class, Carmen Fountaine, to join her in her after-school "tea party." Later Margo mentioned to her mother that she and Carmen were talking about joining a Girl Scout Brownie troop being formed in Kanawha City. Carmen, the only black child then attending Kanawha City Elementary School, was also the only black child to sign up to join the Brownie troop.

When Carmen wasn't invited to be part of any of the Scout carpools that were being formed to drive the girls to meetings, my wife volunteered to chauffeur Margo, Carmen, and several other children to and from the meetings. One busybody Scout leader suggested to Margaret that she need not worry about Carmen.

"She can arrange for her own transportation," the woman said, knowing perfectly well that the little girl had no other means of getting to meetings. My wife simply smiled and assured the Scout leader, "It's no trouble for me."

We weren't alone in our feelings about the racial bias which existed in so many mostly-white suburban communities in those days. Carmen had many friends among her classmates at both Kanawha City Elementary and Horace

Mann Junior High schools. In her last year in junior high she was overwhelmingly voted the most popular girl in her class. In her first year at Charleston
High, she was nominated to the homecoming queen's court.

Since the days of rising expectations after the Supreme Court handed
down its decision in *Brown v. Board of Education*, a start has been made
but, as in the case of the Native American, it is only a start. The statement
made by the National Advisory Commission on Civil Disorder in 1967 still
resonates today: "Our nation is moving toward two societies, one black, one
white—separate and unequal."

Prejudice is not a birth defect. It is handed down, whether intentionally
or unconsciously, by one generation to the next, and each of us has the choice
and the responsibility of bringing this awful legacy to an end.

ANOTHER ISSUE OF INFLAMMATORY PROPORTIONS in the 1950s and '60s was the
practice of medicine and its effects on the elderly.

Soon after I moved to the *Gazette*, Knight informed Hoffmann and me
that the three of us had a lunch meeting scheduled with several concerned
doctors and hospital administrators.

They had quite a story to tell us. Hospital costs were rising rapidly and
in three areas—pathology, radiology, and anesthesiology—they were rising
at an alarming rate. We were promised help in gathering facts from hospitals
all over town. Hoffmann and I were to share editorial comment, and I was to
write a series of articles on the problem.

As it turned out, what we had expected to be a five-part series grew into
more than ten. I went to Johns Hopkins in Baltimore, where the same issue
had been addressed by the local newspapers.

I contacted hospitals in other cities and interviewed the administrators of
every hospital in Charleston. I talked to my wife's brother-in-law, a hospital
administrator in Beckley, and to several other relatives and friends who were
physicians. The situation was indeed serious, and when the series began appearing in the *Gazette*, it carried the tagline "Don't Dare Get Sick."

It was understandable that some doctors would be angered as their particular discipline came under review. The number of letters we received for

publication in our "Readers' Forum" began to mount. One evening three doctors who were enjoying an evening of relaxation in the bar at the Press Club sent a message back to us by one of our deskmen.

"Tell Frank Knight and Tom Stafford, 'Don't dare get sick,'" they said.

As far as I could determine, nothing much came of the series except a few cheers from patients who believed their bills were too high and a surprising number of ill-humored comments from medical practitioners. We had rather sharply suggested, "physician, heal thyself," but while we had expected the resentment to come mostly from practitioners who were actually gouging the public, it covered the entire spectrum of the medical community.

The ill will in Charleston was so intense that for several years my family elected to return to Beckley for our medical care, where my wife's uncle practiced medicine and her brother-in-law's family owned a hospital. It turned out to have been unnecessary.

Two old friends, John and Henrietta Marquis, took over as our physicians with understanding and hearty professionalism. But in those early years we chose to take no chances with our dearest treasure, Margo, whose beginning in life had not been the easiest.

The medical profession in the early 1960s began a frenzied attack on the national government when President Kennedy mounted his campaign to make Medicare a part of the Social Security system. Family practitioners, specialists, and surgeons joined in a common cry of "socialized medicine" in an effort to defeat this legislation.

I had recently completed a series of articles on the problems of aging, which was subsequently requested for use as background data by members of Congress who were drafting the Medicare legislation. My writing was generally supportive of the bill being pushed through the Senate and House, but with the medical profession hammering out the same tune day after day about how America was about to be swallowed up by the monster of socialism, I couldn't resist aiming at what I termed its "Achilles' heal."

How, I asked, was Medicare any more a creature of socialism than were the construction programs that had grown out of the Hill-Burton Act, which the medical profession had pushed through Congress some years before?

Were not the doctors as guilty of siphoning off public monies for the hospitals they practiced in as were the elderly in wanting help in paying for the rising costs of medical care? And where, I asked, was West Virginia's finest monument to socialized medicine? At West Virginia University's medical school and hospital, which served the doctors as much as the patients.

The doctors lost that battle but ultimately won the war. Medicare was approved by Congress and became law. The medical profession discovered that it could live profitably with socialized medicine. In fact, health care providers became so adept at it that when State Welfare Commissioner W. Bernard Smith released to me the annual report on payments to physicians and hospitals statewide, the information turned into a bombshell as soon as it hit the paper.

The medical profession screamed bloody murder. The annual report was thereafter stamped "Unreleasable to the Press."

Chapter 13

AFTER ALMOST TWO YEARS of trying to decipher the puzzle of Invest Right, I began to realize that some as yet unidentifiable persons were becoming worried. Just how worried became apparent when I received, first, an offer of a money deal to try to persuade me to drop my investigation, followed by threats of possible injury or death.

I knew, of course, the people who approached me. I had known them a long time. But they were only the messengers. What I didn't know was the identity of the party or parties they were representing.

These overtures, if you can call them that, acted as a stimulant rather than a deterrent. What the opposition wasn't aware of was that I had been looking for facts with so little in the way of concrete results for so long that my interest was beginning to wane. I would go home in the evening and pull out a large chart I had roughed together that listed the names of the companies I had uncovered and their officers. I would study the various listings long into the night, double checking them against my notes and searching for any clue that might set me on the right trail.

Until the offers and threats were made, I didn't realize how important a story I was pursuing. Intuition told me I was onto something big, but so far it was more conjecture than anything solid, let alone reportable. Now I was becoming convinced that Invest Right and its series of spin-offs were all part of a giant scheme to fleece the government and make a small group of people wealthy at the expense of the taxpayers.

Throughout most of my years as a journalist my wife and I struggled to make ends meet. Like so many families we had a mortgage on our house, tried to set aside some funds for our daughter's education, banked a little each month for our retirement years, took less than exotic vacations, and tried to make each dollar stretch as far as possible. In other words, we were always a little bit broke. But I was no different from most other newspapermen. Even those of my colleagues who rose to positions of prominence and influence professionally seldom died rich. Journalists were like teachers and ministers. Service was their mission, as well as their reward.

I had received my first offer of a payoff a year or so after I became editor at Beckley. A big, burly black fellow came to the door of my office one day, stood there a moment, and said, "I've got a proposition for you."

"What's that?" I asked.

"We'll pay you eighty dollars a week if you'll give us the Clearing House number from your teletype machine each afternoon. You just call a certain phone number with this information, and you'll be paid in cash at the end of the week."

When he told me what he wanted, I knew right away that he was delivering a message from the people who ran the numbers racket in Beckley. I also knew that they didn't need me to supply the information. A phone call to Charleston, Pittsburgh, or New York would have been a whole lot cheaper. Clearly, although my antigambling campaign was running up against strong opposition, the gamblers were looking down the road and seeing trouble ahead. They wanted to shut me up, and they were willing to buy my silence. I was making seventy-five dollars a week at the time, so they figured I'd jump at the chance to more than double my income, tax free.

I didn't even pause to think about it. I told him, "Thanks, but no thanks." If I had taken that first eighty dollars I could never again have raised my voice against gambling in any form. I had no interest in signing my own gag order. Once you accept such "gifts," you lose your right to express you opinion, as well as your professional and personal freedom of choice.

Other offers came my way as the years wore on, but the more creative of them began to surface after I reached Charleston. In those years, the *Gazette* was often labeled the "fourth branch of government," and with good cause.

No other member of the news media in West Virginia had the power and in-fluence wielded by this single newspaper.

There was the time Chilton came to my desk and said, "Tommy, I want this bill passed." He pointed to a particular listing in the House of Delegates *Journal.* I smiled and said, "Oh, you want some dirty journalism."

"Don't say that," he replied, frowning. "Just get this bill passed."

A similar conversation took place a year or so later, also during a regu-lar legislative session, when Chilton wanted a particular bill killed. The one he had wanted passed authorized daylight savings time; the one he wanted defeated would, if passed, have set in motion a program to rid the Eastern Panhandle sheep-raising counties of the black bear population. Neither was an especially crucial piece of legislation. Not surprisingly, the first bill passed, and the other died. When the *Gazette* chose to unleash its power, the effect could be awesome. And it was unleashed in many different ways while I was there, on major as well as minor legislation, on vital community issues, and in political campaigns.

Attempts to curry favor or buy influence were seldom as crude as that first effort in Beckley. *Gazette* staffers were approached frequently by lobbyists, public relations representatives, and others wanting to shape their thinking. Invitations to lunch or dinner were common. For the price of a few bucks, these people sought to subtly shape news stories or editorials, which, if pub-lished to their satisfaction, were worth sizable returns in dollars or favors for their clients. The same approach was used on the golf course, at cocktail par-ties, at banquets, and at receptions. Offers included tickets to football games at WVU, all-expense-paid trips to the races at Charles Town, or weekends at The Greenbrier "for you and the little lady."

The practice of influence-peddling is not pretty, and it can snag even the wariest newsman, as it did one of our divisional editors who accepted a trip to Europe to view a new car and then came home and wrote about it. Enough is enough, Chilton groused, and promptly invoked a shrewd rule. He directed all members of the staff to report to him—in writing—every instance of favors he or she accepted. The very thought sent chills up our spines. In a short time the number of questionable instances plummeted to a manageable level.

To try to avoid the numerous pitfalls, early on I adopted Harry Truman's maxim, "Only what I can eat or drink in a day." But even that sometimes ended in a hangover. I came to believe that accepting anything, whether something as simple as dinner from a lobbyist or as lucrative as a wine account, is a questionable practice and involves a certain risk to the journalist's professional impartiality. Such practices differ only in degree. Those with the cash naturally want something in return for their payment, and whether they use simply a nice dinner or the stronger seduction of monetary payoffs as a means to their end, they are attempting to corrupt an honorable calling.

The money deal I was offered by a messenger from Invest Right was one of those state wine or liquor accounts. Hints had been dropped in the past that one might be available to me if I would moderate or soften some of my more critical political analysis, but this was a genuine, bona fide offer. It was worded to let me know that the account would pay me about twice my salary.

I turned down the offer without so much as a second thought. Liquor and wine accounts, which were controlled by the state liquor commission but paid by the companies that supplied beverages to state stores, had been accepted previously by a few editors around the state. While those editors certainly lived better as a result, their reputations as professionals were forever tainted, and they forfeited any semblance of respect from their associates on their own and other newspapers.

WHEN BRIBES FAILED TO WORK, they were sometimes followed by threats. The threats I received over the years ranged from the frightening to the comical. The one that came while I was pursuing the Invest Right investigation was upsetting and remained so for as long as I was working on that particular story.

One afternoon at the Statehouse, I ran into a public official in a back hallway. A friendly sort with an inherent interest in just about everything going on in government both above and below the radar, he said, "Let me give you a little advice."

He was aware that I was trying to put together a story on Invest Right, he knew the people who allegedly were a part of it, and his advice was to back off, quit, give up the chase, cease, and desist.

"This is a rough crowd," he warned. "They're playing for high stakes, and they don't want anybody getting in their way."

I thanked him noncommittally, and he, reading my mind, said more emphatically, "You're a fool if you continue with this investigation. You might not be around to finish it."

My past experience with threats of bodily harm had led me to the conclusion long before this encounter that those coming by telephone or messenger were rarely serious. Scare you, yes, that's what they wanted. But they weren't prepared to go as far as harming you themselves.

During my brief stint as a police reporter, a young tough had threatened to rough me up for reporting in the paper that he had been drunk and disorderly in a beer joint. He harassed me verbally several times on the streets after this incident, and finally did it once too often while I was standing with some friends in front of a local hangout indulging in a little girl-watching.

"Come over here, Doc," I said, walking to the curb. It was a ridiculous little act on my part. I assumed the stance of a young Jack Dempsey and growled, "Okay, I'm ready."

This lad looked at me startled, then turned and walked away. Afterward he was coolly cordial to me, and for this I was grateful. I had never boxed in my life.

My next experience was sharply at odds with that one. I had covered the trial in criminal court of a young, husky ex-football player who was charged with breaking and entering. After the trial he warned me that following his release from prison he would be looking for me. A year or so later I ran into him in the courthouse. He had just been released from the state penitentiary at Moundsville, and he said, "I made you a promise. I'm gonna get you, Stafford."

I was truly alarmed this time. He had a nasty reputation as a tavern brawler. But he never got back to me. That same night he was picked up on another robbery charge, and I never saw him again.

While I was carrying on my crusade against gambling, telephone threats became a common occurrence. Among those offering advice was Robert Byrd, then a member of the legislature.

"You'd better start carrying a gun," Byrd told me.

I even received a few phone threats during the brief period when I was opposing payment of the veterans' bonus. Yet the one that imprinted itself most indelibly on my mind was the threat that came from Harold "Punchy" Neely of Hinton, Republican nominee for governor in 1960.

With the help of his sponsor, outgoing Governor Underwood, Neely had no trouble winning the primary election, and his chances looked good in the general election, where his opponent was Attorney General Barron. Neely had developed the growing conviction during much of the year-long campaign that he would win.

This was largely because of stories about his opponent that muddied Barron's political image, including Orel Skeen's accusation that Barron had tried to buy him out of the primary race. These developments damaged Barron to some extent, but Neely was his own worst enemy, displaying little understanding of the overall workings of government during his campaign appearances. As Hoffmann remarked when the *Gazette* editorial board was discussing endorsements over a few drinks at Berry Hills Country Club, "If Wally Barron is elected and someday we drive up the Boulevard and see the Capitol gone, we'll know where to find it—in Elkins. But if Punch Neely is elected, and we drive up the Boulevard and find the Capitol gone, we won't know where to find it, and neither will Neely."

On the Sunday before the general election, a column of mine appeared in which I said that our choices for governor were poor. This infuriated Neely, and on election night, after it became obvious that Barron was winning, Neely called me.

It was one of the busiest nights of my life. I was responsible for the lead election story, and I was about halfway through ten editions of the paper, having to update the story every half hour with new facts and figures as they came in. Then I got a call from Neely, who was at the Governor's Mansion watching the returns with the Underwoods.

At the *Gazette*, we were more interested that night in the presidential race than in the governor's race. Jack Kennedy was in a dead heat with Richard Nixon, and we were all pulling for Kennedy. Neely, understandably, was concerned only with his own race.

"Stafford," he shouted through the phone line, "the next time you see me on the street, you cross over to the other side. It won't be good for you if you don't!"

As it turned out, the next time I saw Neely was in the dining room of the Press Club. He looked up from his table as I walked in, got up, and came across the room with a big smile on his face.

"Hi, Tom," he said, shaking my hand.

THE WARNING ABOUT THE INVEST RIGHT CROWD that was passed along to me in a back hall of the Statehouse was not one that I took lightly. It came from Deputy Attorney General Philip J. Graziani, a native of Elkins who had been a prominent figure in government from the time he first went to Charleston as a member of the House of Delegates in 1958. Graziani, working in concert with C. Donald Robertson, of Clarksburg, who had been elected to the House two years before, and James F. Haught, of Parkersburg, also elected in the 1958 freshman class, tried to dominate the legislative process from the moment of his arrival on the Capitol scene.

This trio of articulate young men chose to make a bid for immediate visibility through the use of debate and parliamentary procedure. Using the ruse of the pass-off, one of them would gain the floor then yield to another of the trio, who in turn would yield to the third one, thus enabling them to control debate on sometimes important, sometimes trivial issues. This practice became so common as the session wore on that one day, in an unprecedented action, the entire press corps walked out of the chamber in an effort to give them a message. They had so trivialized the legislative rules of order that both the press and many of the members had become fed up with their antics.

Graziani, Haught, and Robertson had been active as officers of the Young Democrats before their election to the House. They were smart, shrewd, and adept at their political craft. The legislature was only a stepping stone for them. Robertson succeeded Barron as attorney general in 1960 and would be reelected to that office in 1964. Graziani became Robertson's right arm as deputy attorney general. After Kennedy's election to the presidency, Haught became state director of the Federal Housing Authority, with the blessing of Democratic National Committeeman and former Kennedy campaign director Robert McDonough.

When Graziani stopped me in the hall and warned me about possible bodily harm from unspecified parties, I listened with appreciation and concern. By this time he was one of the best informed people in government and always knew what was going on behind the scenes. He was Robertson's ear at the rumor mill, one of the most gifted people of his time at separating fact from fiction in the gossip that circulated constantly through the halls of the Statehouse.

As I had for years, I wondered what my price would be for backing off a story. I knew it wasn't money. I had already turned down enough lucrative deals to know that money wasn't enough of an incentive. I had also lived so near the edge during my wartime years that I didn't place much value on the ninety-seven-cents-worth of bone and tissue which was me. Risk of harm to my wife or daughter, I had come to realize, would have been my only bargaining chip.

As fate would have it, the one who paid a price was Graziani. He was gunned down in front of his home shortly before he was scheduled to testify as a government witness in a federal housing case involving his former associates Robertson and Haught. Graziani had distanced himself from his old cronies at some point before the shooting took place, although at the time he was classified under the witness designation of "unidentified co-conspirator."

As he returned from a party late in the evening of April 10, 1972, Graziani was shot twice in the head. He was listed as critical for several days but survived. After his recovery, he moved with his family to Gary, Indiana.

In October 1972, Robertson pleaded guilty to two out of five federal charges involving bribes paid by a contractor bidding on public housing projects. He was sentenced to two concurrent five-year prison terms and fined five thousand dollars.

Graziani later retired and moved back to Elkins. During a conversation with him in 1988 I was shocked to learn who had been behind the attack on him. Patrick Casey, prosecuting attorney at the time of the shooting, was able to place this prominent Charlestonian near the scene of the crime on the night when it took place, but had insufficient evidence to present the case to a grand jury.

According to the *Gazette*, a suspect who was tried in 1973 for Graziani's shooting claimed that former State Attorney General C. Donald Robertson had ordered the hit on his former friend and associate.

Chapter 14

The Threat of Libel

During a recess of the Republican State Convention at Clarksburg in the summer of 1964, Mary Heineman, a delegate from Randolph County, came to me and quietly asked, "How are you doing with your investigation?"

By this time most of the insiders in both political parties knew what I was doing, so there was no need to act coy. "I've hit a snag," I replied.

I had my corporate chart all filled in. I knew that kickbacks for goods and services delivered to the state were being channeled into some of these corporations. What I lacked was an admission from even a single source that he or she was paying tribute. I seemed to have reached a dead end and was beginning to think that I might have to forget the whole thing. I explained my problem to the delegate and was told, "Maybe I can help you."

She gave me the name of Harry Cupp, an Elkins businessman and maverick political figure who had run for public office on both the Democratic and Republican tickets. I had been acquainted with Cupp for several years but didn't know how reliable he might be as a news source on so sensitive a matter.

After my return to Charleston, I called him and received a promise of help with facts and figures. It wasn't until I went to Elkins a couple of weeks later that I came to respect Cupp as a gutsy guy who kept his word.

The time had also come for me to pay a visit to Boca Raton, Florida, where some of the principal players in the operation had their homes and businesses. But first I wanted assurances from the *Gazette* editorial board that I had the members' full support for the story I was researching. My reason for asking for a special editorial board meeting—with our attorney, Paul Chambers, present—was my concern about a possible libel suit from one or more of those I might name as heavy players in this conspiracy. Barron had twice shown no reluctance in seeking a political advantage by filing lawsuits against his adversaries. I suspected that some of his associates might be equally aggressive if they found themselves trapped in a corner.

The threat of libel is often used to cool a newspaper's ardor for factual reporting. The economics of the newspaper business is loaded with traps. Most newspapers operate on narrow profit margins. With judicial action as expensive as it is, all too many papers are loath to go to court to defend their rights. Politicians and public figures are aware of this and more than a few of them take advantage of it.

I was threatened with a libel suit on more than one occasion during my career in newspapering. When I was editor of the *Register* in Beckley, one of my reporters, Audrey Wood, spent weeks pulling her facts together for a hard-hitting series of articles on inefficiencies in one particular branch of county government. The head of the department under scrutiny called our attorney, Herbert Stansbury, and warned him that if I didn't cancel the series, he would bring suit. Our information was sound, so I advised Stansbury to tell the official to "sue and be damned." The aggrieved county official left town until our series ran out of steam.

A three-hundred-thousand-dollar libel suit was actually filed against the *Register* after we criticized the favored treatment given a jailed gambler. The suit was quietly withdrawn after the party who filed the suit learned of tapes of conversations we had in our possession.

Another time in Charleston, a department head called me in a state of high dudgeon and threatened a libel suit if I didn't stop investigating an office rental deal he was negotiating.

"As a lawyer," I told him, equally angry by this time, "you know better than to threaten me with libel when all I've done is ask questions. Wait until I start writing before you think about a libel suit."

He never sued.

I was fortunate in both Beckley and Charleston to have publishers who respected the First Amendment as the cornerstone of their profession. It is primarily the larger and more successful newspapers that spend big sums of money in the courts defending their publishing rights. Few smaller newspapers can afford to hire the legal talent necessary to wage such battles. As a result, most public officials enjoy a free hand, with little fear of journalistic criticism.

I CERTAINLY DIDN'T WIN all my court fights. Not long after I moved to the *Gazette*, I assembled data indicating that preferential treatment was being given political figures in the awarding of state insurance business. After finishing the story, which named names and listed the premiums they received, I wrote an editorial critical of the condition and of those receiving the larger shares of the business. Knight and Hoffmann followed with another editorial saying the *Gazette* would not be intimidated after two of the five named in my story brought libel suits for a hundred thousand dollars each.

The truth of the news stories and editorials was not the issue in these lawsuits. We had the facts from state records, and both suits were filed by members of the legislature who were also in the insurance business. Our problem was that the libel suits were filed in Wyoming County where the plaintiffs lived rather than in Kanawha County where the *Gazette* was published.

Plaintiff Paul England hired R. D. Bailey, political boss and former candidate for governor, as his attorney. The other plaintiff, Paul Bower, hired Grove Mohler as his counsel. It was a shrewd move on England's part. Libel suits can be filed and heard wherever a newspaper circulates, and we knew we were in trouble. Bailey was such a powerful force in Wyoming County that he ran his private law practice from an office in the county courthouse.

When the suit was finally heard, Bailey's arrogance in the courtroom was unbelievable. His questioning of me was imperious and insolent, in part because I had chosen not to support him in his 1948 gubernatorial campaign while I was editor of the *Register*. The phrase "badgering the witness" acquired a whole new meaning for me during that trial. And during closing arguments, Bailey wandered so far from the evidence in his summation that our attorney, Charles Peters, of Charleston, objected.

"Objection overruled," attorney Bailey shouted and kept right on talking, without losing a beat or even glancing away from the jury. The judge, Robert

M. Worrell, who by the rules of civil procedure should have ruled on the objection, opened his mouth, turned red-faced and said nothing.

After the trial was over, one juror whispered to Knight that after two hours of deliberation, the jury favored the *Gazette* by a vote of 11 to 1. This was at adjournment time on Friday. By the time the jurors returned to their deliberations at the beginning of the following week, it was a different story. The jury met only briefly before returning a verdict against us and awarding England five thousand dollars.

By this time, we knew the score. When Bower's case went to trial, we realized that only a miracle could help us. One jury had spoken, and it was a foregone conclusion that in a rural county like Wyoming the second jury would almost certainly endorse the England verdict. There was no miracle. Bower was awarded eight thousand dollars. The *Gazette* appealed the verdict to the State Supreme Court but lost there as well. Bailey's power extended all the way to Charleston.

In the end we lost the battle but won the war. England surprised us all by cosponsoring a bill in the legislature that would create a nonpartisan insurance board with the responsibility of awarding the state's insurance business. His cosponsor was Senator Jack Nuckols, of Beckley, another legislator who had been named in the original *Gazette* stories on the issue.

Governor Marland, who signed the bill into law, was obviously a party to this move. He had appeared in court as a witness and testified to the accuracy of the *Gazette*'s allegations. England and Marland were both residents of Wyoming County, and Wyoming was in Nuckols's senatorial district. Nuckols later served as Marland's campaign manager during his Senate race. There were close ties between the three men. A pattern of complicity for reform existed, and in joining together they helped the *Gazette* wipe out a sleazy system of political favoritism that Marland had inherited upon his election to office.

We paid a heavy price for our victory. Although the jury awards were token findings, the *Gazette*'s court costs and attorney fees were expensive for those days, amounting to seventy thousand dollars. But it was not the worst loss we suffered during this period. Within days of the end of the last trial, Frank Knight died of a massive cerebral hemorrhage, ending a brilliant career in journalism.

I CAME TO BELIEVE that none of the three libel suits to which I was a party would have been filed if today's case law had been in existence while I was a practicing journalist. The libel suit known as *New York Times v. Sullivan* changed the ground rules.

In that case, the U.S. Supreme Court ruled that public officials must prove intentional malice on the part of the newspaper and its writers, must show that the alleged libelous material was published with the knowledge that it was false, or must prove that it was published in reckless disregard of the truth.

In a later case, *Curtis Publishing v. Butts*, the libel standard was extended to public figures who enjoy a certain degree of celebrity. In all three of the cases I was involved in, the adversaries were public officials and the information I used was true.

When I requested the meeting with my fellow editorial board members on the Invest Right story, we were working under the same legal constraints that existed when we tangled with Bailey and his associates in Wyoming County. Understandably, the members present were apprehensive as I laid my chart on the floor and began explaining how a federation of corporate entities was tied together in a massive scheme to skim off tax dollars for personal gain.

Attorney Chambers, as expected, cautioned me to go easy and be certain of my facts before I started writing.

Publisher Chilton said, "Let's get moving on this."

City editor L. T. Anderson said, "If Tom puts this together, he deserves a special bonus."

And Vice President Bob Smith, editor Hoffmann, and executive editor Dallas Higbee urged me to continue my investigation.

In other words, I had all the support I needed to keep going with my effort to expose a degree of corruption in government as unprincipled as anything I had seen in my lifetime.

My investigation moved quickly after that meeting in Chilton's office. I flew down to Tampa on a Saturday and spent the weekend going over my notes with my brother Charley to see if he could find any loose ends. On Monday morning I flew to West Palm Beach where I picked up a rental car for two days of interview work in Boca and West Palm. Following the interviews, I flew to Tallahassee, where I spent a day at the Capitol checking the records of various corporations that had been formed by the Invest Right crowd, and finally flew home.

Back in Charleston I filled Hoffmann in on the results of my Florida trip, then recruited reporter John Yago to accompany me to Elkins for my wrap-up interviews. I wanted to make this one last trip before finally sitting down at my typewriter. I had decided to take Yago to Elkins with me because I would be confronting one of the lead players in this story, lawyer and Barron-confidant Bonn Brown. I wanted a seasoned newsman as my witness.

IN THE PURSUIT OF THE INVEST RIGHT STORY, most of my activity had been in the netherworld of news gathering. I had used almost exclusively the journalistic devices of deep background, off-the-record interviews, and non-attributable inquiry—a dangerous area to work in if your sources choose later to deny what they told you.

Investigative writing was a form of journalism that first asserted itself loudly and raucously after the Civil War, when newspapers, lusting for readership, turned to sensationalism as a means of outselling their competition. Among those with a greater social conscience than most was *The New York Times*, which turned its crusading attention to "Boss" Tweed and Tammany Hall. In spite of his attempt to bribe the editor with a $5 million payoff, Tweed went to jail, and crusading took on new dimensions.

Most notable among this breed of newspaper was Joseph Pulitzer's St. Louis *Post-Dispatch* and later his New York *World*. By blending sensationalism with idealism, Pulitzer gave the *World* such vitality that even today it is recognized as one of the finest newspapers ever published.

During this era and on into the early years of the twentieth century, magazines honed their own investigative skills. *McClure's*, the most widely read of the genre, boasted contributors such as Lincoln Steffens, who authored "The Shame of the Cities," and Ida M. Tarbell, who exposed the Standard Oil Trust.

With the entry of William Randolph Hearst onto the New York scene with his *Journal*, investigative writing lost some of its appeal. Hearst's style of journalism, based on crime news, scandal, and gossip, to some degree chilled reader interest in quality muckraking. Some newspapers, however, continued to offer seriously investigated news, which managed to outlast the scandal-mongering variety of journalism that began declining in popularity in the Depression years of the 1930s.

Today, newspapers that take on the tedious and protracted task of exposing wrongdoing are still, by and large, those in the big cities. Even without the threat of libel suits, it is an expense most smaller papers are unwilling or unable to bear. While there are a few like the *Gazette*, such efforts are restricted primarily to newspapers like *The Washington Post*, whose investigation of the Watergate scandal ultimately brought down the Nixon administration.

When I was finally ready to drive to Elkins to interview Brown, I had all the facts I needed to write the story. There was only one more thing to do before I actually started typing. I wanted the parties I intended to write about to have an opportunity to comment. Fairness and accuracy are essential to credibility in news writing, and the subjects' right to speak on their own behalf had to be honored. While it is sometimes difficult to confront the persons you are accusing of possible indiscretions, there is absolutely no other recourse when the story begins to take on the dimensions of this one.

Brown had brushed me aside when I tried to talk to him two days earlier as he stepped off a plane in Charleston on his way home from a trip to Florida. But as it turned out, all of the Invest Right group, although not pleased with my questioning, were cordial except Schroath. His response when I contacted him was, "It won't make any difference what I say. You're going to write whatever you please."

Chapter 15

Striking Gold

Why, I would ask in a series of articles, would a company in Elkins with half the state's tire recapping business pay money through a Florida corporation to the West Virginia State Democratic Executive Committee?

Why would a corporation created by West Virginians in the state of Ohio provide business consulting services to suppliers of goods and services to the State of West Virginia?

And why would other Florida corporations, whose officers were West Virginia officials or friends of the governor, be used as conduits for monies flowing out of and back into West Virginia?

For reasons never explained, except in the vaguest of terms, by the legislative committee investigating state purchasing irregularities, pages 58 through 61 of the committee report—pages relating to Invest Right—were deleted from the published version and quietly filed in the legislative auditor's office. These pages had been mimeographed for inclusion but were pulled from the report, and the remaining pages were renumbered.

The reference to Invest Right in these censored pages was not in itself incriminating. But some months after the report was released, a committee member with more conscience than his peers admitted to me that there had been speculation within the committee that the corporation had been brought into existence, in part, to offer its services for a fee to "assist" firms doing business with the state.

By their failure to publish a complete record of their findings, let alone act on the results of their investigation, the members of the legislative committee helped give official sanction to bribery and kickbacks, and the resolute silence of officials in both the legislative and executive branches gave graft and corruption a license to operate freely in every area of state purchasing.

This was an unconscionable condition, which seemed to bother no one at the Statehouse. So I began an inquiry that took me from that first encounter at the Charleston Press Club through three state capitols, to Florida's richest beach resorts, to the offices of corporate attorneys in two states, into a vast array of file cabinets, and to interviews with some of the most unsavory characters I have ever encountered. It was a long, lonely, frustrating search, but it finally paid off.

THE DISTANCE FROM CHARLESTON, West Virginia, to Boca Raton, Florida, was a safe 975 miles. There were probably other reasons why Governor Barron and his jolly band of buccaneers chose Boca Raton as the headquarters for their organized looting of West Virginia.

But their very choice of location was a classic Freudian slip. Sun-kissed little Boca was as rich in history as it was in business potential when I arrived there in the early 1960s. Located on Florida's Gold Coast between West Palm Beach and Miami, it was one of the few communities in south Florida to retain its original Spanish name, which translates as "rat bay." It came into existence as the stronghold of pirates such as Blackbeard who needed a handy refuge after their attacks on Atlantic and Caribbean shipping. Pirates had founded the town; a new gang of twentieth-century pirates had chosen it as the staging area for their own illicit enterprises.

The link between the conscious and the subconscious mind is strong and these men, confident that no one would be able to untangle their web of corporations, left the proverbial trail of breadcrumbs that would lead to their ultimate exposure. "Invest Right," the mystery woman who lived in Boca, a former West Virginia auditor with a packet of inactive corporate papers in his files, a former Army officer and retired CIA agent, and Boca Raton's early history were all clues that even a mystery writer would have found intriguing.

Who, for instance, was Eve Miller? All I knew was that her name was listed as a corporate officer of Invest Right in the files of the Ohio Franchise Tax

Department. Was she a housewife or career woman? Was she a link between the West Virginia Statehouse and Florida's Gold Coast? Was she an integral part of an expanding corporate empire?

As I later learned in an interview with her, Miller was a competent, charming woman in her early fifties who divided her time and energies between home and children and a real estate agency in Boca Raton known as Gold Coast Homes. The office where she worked was also an interesting place behind its modern façade. It was the nerve center of a string of corporations in which West Virginians Bonn Brown, Al Schroath, and Truman Gore were associated. And the chief executive officer of most of those corporations was Edgar Lawson, an expatriate West Virginian.

The three West Virginia residents who formed the core of the Invest Right alliance were prominent members of their communities. Gore came from one of the oldest and best-known families in central West Virginia. As a graduate of the University of Pennsylvania and its Wharton business school, with additional academic work at Cornell University, he had prepared himself well for a career in business. He was involved in real estate development, oil and gas well drilling and securities investment before he became Governor Barron's commissioner of finance and administration. In this latter position he was also responsible for the purchasing of goods and services for state government.

Schroath, owner of one of the largest auto agencies in central West Virginia, was successful in other fields as well. Besides his car dealership, he and Gore were partners in Fleet Rental Leasing Corporation, and together with Brown had other business connections. Schroath had dealt with the state through several administrations in the sale of automobiles. Early in Barron's term his name had crept into print as the supplier of Oldsmobiles to four state officials, cars which had been acquired without benefit of competitive bidding procedures. Gore and Road Commissioner Sawyers were recipients of two of those cars.

Brown, another scion of an old West Virginia family, had a successful legal practice in Elkins. He was former state commander of the American Legion, former chairman of the state Democratic Party finance committee, and would make a respectable showing in his run for the governorship in the 1964 primary. The theme of his campaign would be centered on business creation for the state, and his slogan would be "Brown Means Business."

As a team, they were a power to be reckoned with. And with the addition of Lawson in Florida, they had the capability of setting their sights far beyond the West Virginia border.

Lawson was an interesting study. A former Elkins resident and Schroath's brother-in-law, he had been active in Republican politics and served as state auditor before the GOP was pushed out by the 1932 Democratic landslide. After being turned out of office, he was indicted on a charge of fraudulent sales of securities. The trial ended with a hung jury but also ended Lawson's political career. He later ran for governor, but he lost in the primary.

Leaving Charleston in 1958, he teamed up as chief executive officer with Miller and her husband John in real estate development in Boca Raton. Together they formed and operated Gold Coast Homes and Gold Coast Mortgages. In 1961 Gold Coast went interstate as Boca Raton Capital Corporation. Among the original stockholders of this new company were Brown, Schroath, and Gore, who just happened to come aboard eight months after Barron was inaugurated as governor.

WITH THE OLDEST LAW FIRM in West Palm Beach serving as counsel, this foursome was also busy setting up other corporations, all using the Gold Coast Homes address. This flurry of corporate creations was made easy, Lawson explained to me, by the fact that he happened to have on hand a batch of inactive corporate documents for use as he needed them.

They formed Georgetown Homes, Inc., to develop real estate; Atlantic Management Service, Inc., to provide business counseling services; and First Southeastern Capital Corporation, to engage in everything from manufacturing to the ownership and leasing of airplanes. Later, Brown, Schroath, and Gore formed another corporation known as Dixie Service Center to build and operate a service station in Boca, and bought a tract of beachfront property which they said they planned to develop sometime in the future.

Lawson was an easy person to interview when I visited his storefront office in midtown Boca Raton. He answered my questions without hesitation, and through conversations with other businesspeople in town, I found that he was a respected member of the community. Typical of what others had to say about Lawson were comments by Ed Melvin, manager of the chamber of commerce: "He's a credit to the community. What I know of him . . . I'd like to have a dozen of him."

Lawson was best known for his association with Boca Raton Capitol Corporation, of which he was executive vice president. Both banks in town and some of the more influential businessmen had stock in the company, said Melvin. "It's a clean operation," he volunteered.

Melvin further recalled that Lawson had arranged a "coffee" two years previously for leading businesspeople where he introduced a "former governor" among the "prominent" West Virginians present. The former governor turned out to be then-Governor Barron, and those with him were Brown, Schroath, and Gore. Melvin added, "We like having these wealthy West Virginians come down here with their money. It's good for our economy."

Lawson was a man of many corporate identities. Working with the law firm of Stewart, Call, and Van der Hulse in West Palm Beach, he had formed so many corporations, he said, that some weren't even active at that particular time. He also talked proudly about helping to organize City National Bank in Kanawha City before leaving Charleston, and about having been asked to organize the Chemical Bank and Trust Company in South Charleston, an offer he refused because of the press of other business.

IN THE SPRING OF 1964, Brown, Schroath, and Gore severed their connections with Capital Corporation; according to Lawson, their reason for doing so was a lack of return on invested capital. Kenneth I. Van der Hulse of West Palm, who served as counsel and secretary of the company, intimated the same when I contacted him at his office. Van der Hulse told me that he was secretary of some forty corporations; he then observed that, while Florida was a place of opportunity for resourceful businessmen, not all ventures were profitable.

When I first went to see Van der Hulse, he tried to cut the interview short by saying that he had already talked with federal investigators about the affairs of the West Virginia group.

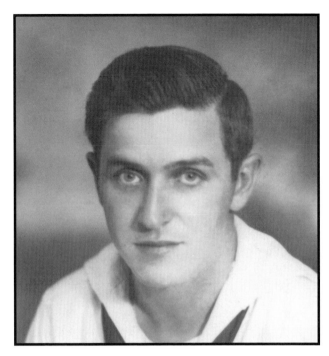

LEFT
Yeoman
Thomas Stafford,
1942.
Photographer unknown.

BELOW
Stafford and
crewmates on
the deck of the
U.S.S. Cable, 1945.
Stafford is in front
row at left end.
Photographer unknown.

Okey Leonidas Patteson. As governor one of Patteson's most controversial decisions was to locate the state School of Medicine, Dentistry, and Nursing in Morgantown.

Photo Courtesy of the West Virginia State Archives.

Matthew Neely. On January 12, 1941, Doddridge County native Neely resigned from the United States Senate to become governor of West Virginia.

Photo Courtesy of the West Virginia State Archives.

From left, Jennings Randolph, President Franklin D. Roosevelt, Gov. H. Guy Kump, Sen. Matthew M. Neely, Homer A. Holt during Roosevelt's visit to Thomas, W.Va., on Oct. 1, 1936. Photo courtesy of *The Charleston Gazette*.

Thomas F. Stafford, new editor of *The Raleigh Register*, Beckley, 1947.
Staff Photo, *The Raleigh Register*.

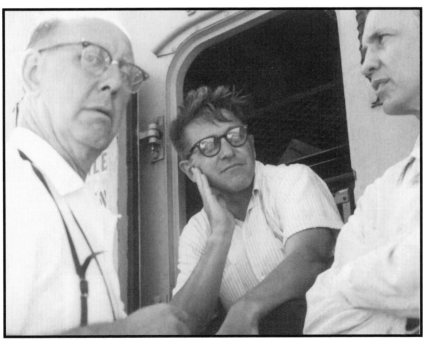

Stafford (center) aboard the Navy cruiser *U.S.S. Northampton* out of Norfolk, July 1959.
Photographer unknown.

In the Capitol
rotunda at the
inauguration of
Cecil Underwood,
January 1957.
Tom Stafford (left),
Judy Henderson
(center), and
Margaret
Stafford (right).
Photographer unknown.

Stafford with a group of West Virginia politicians and their wives at
The Greenbrier, early 1960s. Stafford is seated at center rear. Others
present include Barbara Boiarsky, wife of State Legislator Ivor Boiarsky
(at Stafford's right); State Commerce Commissioner and later governor
Hulett Smith (at Mrs. Boiarsky's right); Ivor Boiarsky (at Smith's right); and
Smith's wife Mary Alice (seated at Stafford's left). Photographer unknown.

Reception at the Governor's Mansion following inauguration of Cecil Underwood, January 1957. Right to left: Thomas F. Stafford; wife Margaret; his brother-in-law R. Virgil Rohrbough, the new State Superintendent of Schools; and Stafford's sister Mildred (Bee), Rohrbough's wife. Photographer unknown.

Thomas F. Stafford (foreground) seated at the press table during a session of the West Virginia Legislature in the late 1950s or early 1960s. Photographer unknown.

ABOVE
Stafford greeting Congressman John Slack at what is now Yeager Airport in Charleston, late 1950s or early '60s.
Photographer unknown.

RIGHT
President John F. Kennedy speaks at the state Capitol on West Virginia Day in 1961.
Photo courtesy of *The Charleston Gazette*.

A breakfast hosted by Governor Wally Barron in the early 1960s.
Left to right: former Governor Homer Holt, Governor Barron, former Governor Cecil
Underwood, former Governor Okey Patteson. Photo by Emil Varney; courtesy of WV State Archives.

Stafford and friend in entrance hallway at the Press Club in Charleston in the
mid-1960s. This is the hallway where Stafford was handed an annotated
report that started him on the Invest Right story. Photographer unknown.

Thomas F.
Stafford,
Elkins, 1979.
Photo by Eldora
Nuzum, editor, *The
Inter-Mountain*,
Elkins, West Virginia.

Arch Moore campaigns with Gerald Ford in September 1980.
Photo by Lawrence Pierce; courtesy of *The Charleston Gazette*.

"I've been told that by other people," I replied. "May I have a few minutes of your time to check out a few things?"

He agreed to talk briefly and confirmed some essential facts I had picked up elsewhere.

Brown, Schroath, and Gore may have been displeased with the return they received from their Capital Corporation investment, as Lawson said, yet when they disposed of their holdings, the gross worth of the company was $1 million. Apparently they were men with larger-than-life expectations, for the corporation's assets had more than tripled in value during the less than three years they had been stockholders.

In response to later questions about the Capital Corporation experience, Brown said he sold out because he was too far from Boca Raton to give it proper attention. Gore said much the same thing, explaining, "I couldn't be there to help in the management."

Both Gore and Brown complained that they lost money on the deal, money they hoped to recoup in other ways, one of which was the formation of yet another enterprise, First Southeastern Corporation, and the movement of a share of their invested Florida money to Hollywood, Florida, a play-spot farther down the coast.

First Southeastern was a corporate entity Lawson established in August 1961, seven months after Barron took office. Schroath, Lawson said, came to him and asked if he had any charters lying around. It just so happened that First Southeastern was available, and he sold it to Schroath for eighty dollars.

First Southeastern was a catchall operation that could engage in almost any type of business activity. Brown, Schroath, and Gore transferred the assets of several of their companies to it, Lawson told me. Brown and Schroath both confirmed that it was used to liquidate other companies, among them the daddy of them all, Invest Right.

Atlantic Management Service was also among the dissolved corporations, but before it disappeared, it left a trail that led me all the way to Brown's law office. It seemingly came into being only briefly, a faceless enterprise whose very records traveled the short distance between Boca Raton and Hollywood, via Elkins.

Under its charter, Atlantic Management had the authority to engage in every aspect of acquiring, holding, and managing property. "It had broad powers," Lawson explained, "including advice and counseling services." Miller's comment was that it was a consulting service "similar to Invest Right." But Atlantic Management and Invest Right had both been sent to the corporate graveyard by the time I arrived in Boca Raton.

In speaking of Invest Right, Miller said, "I don't know much about it. I just sign papers when they're put in front of me." Schroath said he didn't know who his fellow officers were in Invest Right. And Brown said he was not an organizer, officer, or stockholder. When apprised of the fact that his name was carried in records at the Ohio State Capitol as president, he brushed it off by saying, "Someone else must have put it there."

The responses regarding Atlantic Management were much the same. Brown said he had no connection with it although its books were sent to him by Van der Hulse, then forwarded by Brown to an attorney in Hollywood, Florida.

I also talked to one Joseph R. Evans of Boca Raton. Described as a former Army officer and retired CIA agent, as well as assistant treasurer of Atlantic Management, Evans also played the innocent game. "I didn't know I was an officer," he said and suggested to me that I "see the boys up in West Virginia."

"WEST VIRGINIA" MEANT A TRIP TO ELKINS and a conference with Brown who, from all indications, was the lead player in this corporate odyssey. I was looking forward to it. Although my intention was to get Brown to admit that he had engaged in questionable practices, I was not the least bit bothered by my role. After two years of pursuing the Invest Right investigation, I was seething with anger and disgust.

Unemployment was rampant in the coalfields and factory towns of West Virginia. The only meal many children got each day was their subsidized hot lunch at school. Our teachers and college professors were among the lowest paid in the country. Roads were in a bad state of repair. West Virginia and its people had a long shopping list of needs, but at the head of it, unknown to the electorate, sat a priority item—the further enrichment of a handful of the wealthy and powerful.

Also waiting for me in Elkins was Harry Cupp with evidence that Brown and company had been paid kickbacks on state business. Atlantic Management, Cupp had said in an earlier letter, "operates on verbal and written contract with various tire distributors and garages in West Virginia." Cupp didn't go into detail. It wasn't until I arrived in Elkins that he handed me copies of two cancelled checks written by Sayre's Tire Service in Elkins to Atlantic Management.

One check was for three thousand dollars and was made payable to "Atlantic Mgm. Ser. for use of Bonn Brown." The other was for $630 and was made payable to "Atlantic Management Service, Inc." Cupp said more checks of a similar nature were available.

State records indicated that Sayre's Tire Service held the state recapping contract for Northern West Virginia during 1962 and collected thousands of dollars for services rendered. The owner, Raymond Sayre, had died, but his widow said the company received large sums of money from the state and that certain checks were written to Atlantic Management.

While I was talking to Mrs. Sayre at her home in Elkins, she received a long distance telephone call. Interestingly, it was, according to Mrs. Sayre, from someone in the State Purchasing Division promising her additional tire business.

A short time later, when I questioned Brown at his office, he acknowledged receiving the three-thousand-dollar check but said it was for the "Democratic campaign fund." When I asked why a contribution to the party would be made through a company in Florida, he offered no explanation. He also said he had no recollection of the $630 check.

Lawson, when queried by telephone in Boca Raton, drew the noose a little tighter. "I wouldn't know why a check came through Atlantic Management for the use of Bonn Brown." He explained that Brown "represented a great many companies that paid money to Atlantic Management."

WHEN I RETURNED TO CHARLESTON, I related my findings to Hoffmann, and he decided that it was time for me to close down the investigation and start writing. I had the framework of the overall operation, he reasoned, and anything more would be a compounding of wrongs already committed. Besides, he added, the general election was only days away, and thereafter Brown, Barron, and their friends would fade into history.

His observation carried overtones neither he nor I could possibly imagine at the time.

MISCELLANY ⚬ DRIVING CAREFULLY

EVEN THOSE WHO PROFESS before God and country to be law-abiding citizens sometimes fall from grace.

Upon my arrival at the airport in West Palm Beach to look into Invest Right's Florida connection, I went to the car rental desk to arrange for transportation. I routinely handed my driver's license to the young woman behind the counter so she could process the papers.

"Is this the only license you have?" she asked.

"Yes," I replied. "Why?"

"It's two years out of date, Mr. Stafford."

I turned on all the charm I could muster under the circumstances, explaining weakly that my state's Motor Vehicles Department did not send out reminders when licenses were about to expire.

A few minutes later, I was on my way to Boca Raton.

"Drive carefully," she had advised with a great Florida smile.

So for two days, while I was trying to assemble information on what I believed was illegal activity on the part of certain West Virginians, I too was in violation of the law.

It goes without saying that I was probably more observant of traffic regulations during that trip than at any other time in my life.

Chapter 16

Going to Press

I HAD BARELY FINISHED the first of a four-part series on the Invest Right story when I learned that efforts were being made to stop publication before it even reached the *Gazette* copy desk. Hoffmann called and said, "They're trying to kill it."

I hadn't told anybody that I had actually begun writing, and I was doing the writing at home. Hoffmann hadn't breathed it to anyone either, other than possibly his wife, Veronica. It was clear to me, as well as to my editor, that word had leaked back from Florida and Elkins that I had been asking some hard questions, and the assumption in the political community was that the story was about to hit the streets.

With the information I had in hand, the Invest Right story didn't appear to be anything earthshaking. After two years of investigation I still didn't believe that I had found my "smoking gun," the analogy that would later be used in the Watergate mess. And I hadn't quite tied Governor Barron into the kickback scheme.

But nobody on the outside knew this. They only knew that an important election was days away, and the Democratic candidate, Hulett Smith, was ahead in the polls by a slim margin. But Smith had stumbled badly during a question-and-answer session on statewide television with his Republican opponent, former Governor Cecil Underwood. His backers were fearful that my Invest Right series might tip the scales against the Democrats on election day.

Apparently it wasn't enough for Democratic Party officials that I had already exposed the state's loss of millions of dollars in highway funding during the Underwood administration. Penalties of almost $9 million had been assessed on road construction projects receiving federal matching funds. Among the projects racking up penalties was a section of I-64, which was routed around the Guyan Country Club in Huntington where Underwood was a member. It cost the state almost a million dollars to divert the road around club property for the purpose of saving two greens, two tees, and a fairway. I had pursued this story for months but wasn't able to pull all the facts together until I had the opportunity to sit down with Road Commissioner Burl Sawyers and U.S. Senator Jennings Randolph, chairman of the Senate subcommittee on roads.

The overall impact of the penalties was even greater, according to Sawyers and Randolph. By having to absorb this added expense into an already tight Highways Department budget, West Virginia would lose the ability to match as much as $80 million in additional federal money.

Smith and his organization wanted a clear path to the finish line on election day. They were tickled pink when stories appeared that were critical of Underwood and the Republicans, but they wanted nothing said that might implicate their Democratic friends in the Barron administration. It was "politics as usual," but it disturbed me.

I remembered the night some seven years before when I sat down in a secluded section of the Charleston Press Club with Smith; his wife, Mary Alice; UPI writer Bill Barrett and his wife, Melba, who also happened to be Hulett's secretary; and Jim Harris, who later became administrative assistant to Senator Randolph. That evening Smith told us, "I'm going to run for governor in the next election, and I'm asking you to help me."

Hulett had risen from political obscurity to statewide prominence in 1956 as campaign manager for Congressman Robert Mollohan during his bid for the governorship. Mollohan wasn't destined to realize his dream. The deal Mollohan made to allow strip-mining on state property at Pruntytown while he was serving as superintendent of the Boys' Industrial School was more than the voters would accept. Smith had not been seriously damaged by this disclosure, although the Democratic Party lost control of the Statehouse for the first time in twenty-four years. Despite a move by some Democrats to oust him from the state party chairmanship, a perk awarded Smith after Mollohan won the primary, Smith managed to hang on. He was instrumental in helping the party regain a measure of its old vitality in the off-year elections two years later, and by 1960 he was a factor to be reckoned with when he announced his run for the governorship.

The help Smith was asking me for was to develop his image and steer him around political traps in his next campaign. Creating and marketing an image for Hulett was no problem. This was the era of the Kennedys, the Rockefellers, and others from wealthy backgrounds who were seeking an outlet for their energies in public service. Smith was a Mountain State version—rich, friendly, good-looking, squeaky clean in reputation and demeanor, with a wife as wealthy and charming as he. Despite growing up during the Depression, coming of age during a world war, and launching a career during the state's postwar slump, Smith's life had been one of privilege. He had the finest of homes in the Beckley suburbs, an attractive young family, a strong commitment to his church, and a degree in economics from the University of Pennsylvania's prestigious Wharton School of Finance and Administration.

Hulett's father, Joe L. Smith, had been elected to Congress two years before FDR arrived in Washington with his New Deal. The elder Smith, a bank president and businessman, understood the wrenching consequences of bank failures, the impotence of the national leadership following the stock market crash, and the effects in the coalfields of so much overproduction that coal operators were pleading for the socialization of their industry. Hulett followed in his father's footsteps, first into the family businesses and then into the political arena.

Advising him on ways to avoid the political pitfalls that had caused problems for others was more difficult than honing his image. We had our differences on issues such as taxation and campaign methodology, but Hulett managed to make it into the winner's circle on his second attempt at the governor's office with the two of us still on speaking terms.

I WAS PERHAPS JEOPARDIZING my professional credibility as a political writer by accepting this assignment from Smith. There are those who would say it was not good journalism. But at the *Gazette* such activity had been standard operating procedure since our publisher's grandfather had been elected to the U.S. Senate in the early twentieth century. In fact, my first sideline task after moving to the *Gazette* had been to help in the ill-fated effort to elect Senate Clerk Howard Myers as governor. Myers, the hand-picked candidate of the business community, had editor Frank Knight's blessing, and I was expected to help in writing press releases. It was a hopeless cause. Myers, an unexciting campaigner, was soundly beaten.

The *Gazette*, as the Myers candidacy illustrates, had a passion for involving itself in politics. In 1960, however, when Barron, Skeen, and Smith were the contenders, the paper's policy-makers had no real interest in any of them. The *Gazette*'s enthusiasm that year was national, when the country's attention focused, if only briefly, on West Virginia and the voters' decision on the issue of whether a Catholic could be elected president. Kennedy was the man of the hour in the country and in our newsroom, and remained so throughout his short tenure in office.

It wasn't until the 1964 election that our editorial board again found supportable choices for governor. Going into the primary, Hulett Smith, House Speaker Julius Singleton, and Elkins lawyer Bonn Brown were the most viable candidates. Although Chilton and Hoffmann thought Brown showed promise, they swung behind Singleton while I chose Smith.

Although I thought highly of Singleton, I had several reasons for backing Smith. Hulett's brother Joe and I had known each other at WVU; when I arrived in Beckley as a struggling reporter, he introduced me around town. He remained a true friend, and even gave me the opportunity of meeting my future wife at a party at his parents' home. Hulett's father, too, had been good to me. I felt I owed the family my support.

In addition, my wife had grown up in Beckley, had been a schoolmate of Hulett's, and had attended Arlington Hall with Mary Alice. Margaret's father had joined with Smith's father in founding Beckley's largest bank. Her sister, Phoebe, was married to Mary Alice's brother, Albert Tieche.

Also in Hulett's favor were the recommendations of my statewide network of political sources, an informal polling group who had never given me an inaccurate reading in the past. When I canvassed these sources before the primary election, I found that Singleton, despite his reputation as a knowledgeable and respected public official, had absolutely no chance. And with what I had in my files, I wasn't interested in lifting a finger to help Brown.

The results of my telephone poll regarding the relative strengths of the three Democratic candidates had been solid enough to convince me that I was right in supporting Smith. When I began traveling the state, taking street-corner and courthouse soundings in a wide range of counties, I found opinion leaning heavily in Smith's favor. His efforts as commerce commissioner in the Barron administration may also have helped his cause by giving him statewide exposure during the previous four years, an advantage his opponents lacked. Hoffmann, who favored Singleton, disliked hearing my reports about the lack of support for his candidate and became so angry at the situation that he almost called me back into the office. But when the returns rolled in on election night, Smith won all but Brown's and Singleton's home counties. The primary was a landslide.

Two days later, while recuperating from the rigors of campaigning at The Greenbrier, Smith told me, "This isn't the end. There are other races to be run . . . and won." He didn't elaborate, but I assumed from this conversation that his aspirations equaled or exceeded those of his congressman father. As it turned out, however, after winning the governorship Smith never again sought public office.

Smith's general election campaign was not as easy as the primary had been. His opponent, Underwood, was a seasoned campaigner, an experienced speaker, and one who showed himself to be a shrewd politician when he was on the ropes. It was a fight right down to the wire, and only an overwhelmingly Democratic registration would put Smith in the governor's office.

Perhaps Smith also made an impression on the voters when he expounded on his campaign theme of an "Administration of Excellence." This was his promise if elected governor. "A new look for West Virginia" was his pledge.

Then Clarence Elmore—state liquor commissioner under Barron, and Smith's chief campaign strategist—showed up at Hoffmann's door and asked that the story I was writing about the Invest Right group's exploits be killed.

Excellence in government. Maybe it took a holiday that morning.

Chapter 17

A Promise Curtailed

"I have pledged that I would give this state an 'Administration of Excellence'—an administration which will demand the highest standards of ethics, integrity, and honesty from dedicated and qualified public servants, and never tolerate incompetence or mediocrity."

This pledge by Governor Hulett C. Smith in his inaugural address on cold, blustery January 18, 1965, had been the source of a disagreement in the governor's office only two days before. The office was warm. The atmosphere was chilly.

Barron had vacated the office and Governor-elect Smith had just moved in. During this short transitional period, Smith asked me to perform one last task before he took office, another of those efforts to help prevent future embarrassment to his administration. "Read this inaugural message," he asked, "and let me know what you think of it."

I took the copy of the speech home that evening and was concerned when I found how far out on a limb he had gone with his promises. An "Administration of Excellence"? Too much had already happened for the governor-elect to be able to make good on that particular promise.

Two weeks earlier I had invited him to join me for lunch at Clement's restaurant, upriver from the Capitol. Our conversation covered a broad range of topics, but chiefly I wanted to talk to him about some of his planned appointments to major positions.

Already I knew that the liquor commissioner, politically controversial Elmore, was slated to remain as a holdover from the Barron administration. Smith also planned to keep Barron's commissioner of finance and administration, Truman Gore, whom I had just exposed as a member of the Invest Right group. But I knew that offering cautionary advice about these officeholders would be an exercise in futility. So I concentrated instead on one person, trying to warn Smith about potential problems down the road.

"Hulett," I said, "Curtis Trent has to go. He may be as good in his job as Governor Barron says he is, but Trent has been the central figure in so much controversy that you can't keep him if you want to maintain your image."

Smith's reaction was not favorable. A newspaperman was trying to advise the new governor on his plans to shape his administration. I got the distinct impression that my old friend felt I had gone too far, that I had invaded territory reserved for a privileged few, advisors like State Democratic Chairman James M. Sprouse, Democratic National Committeeman Robert P. McDonough, Robert D. Bailey of Pineville (later to be named secretary of state), former Tax Commissioner Milton J. Ferguson, and Liquor Commissioner Elmore, who had served as Smith's chief advisor during the recent campaign.

So I tried another tack. "I'm not here to deliver a message from the *Gazette* editorial board," I said. "This is personal, between old friends. I'm simply trying to make you aware of a fact of life in this town. The *Gazette*, as you well know, is a very powerful newspaper, and I certainly wouldn't want to be in your shoes six months from now if you keep Trent in your administration."

I concurred with the new governor's opinion that Trent had done some good work for Smith during his gubernatorial campaign. He had been a good soldier in the trenches. "But with Trent anywhere around you," I told him, "your administration will be off to a bad start the day you take office."

A few mornings later, Hulett called me at home with what he believed was a solution to the problem. "What do you think of this?" he asked. "I'll take care of Curt by hiding him, sort of, in the administration."

"You can't hide a person with the kind of profile Trent has," I replied. "You have no choice. He has to go."

Next came Smith's request that I review his inaugural speech, and when I returned it to his office with the strong suggestion that he start over again on a new speech, he asked, somewhat piqued in tone, "What's wrong with it?"

"Try as you will, Hulett," I told him, "you can't have an administration of excellence. With all the problems you have facing you as our next governor, you can't perform excellently. If you want the idea of excellence, say, 'I will strive for,' or 'I will endeavor to,' or 'I will try to give you an administration of excellence.'"

I lost that round, but in the end so did Smith. The word *excellence* became a millstone around the neck of his administration throughout his term. But I won a round, too. Within an hour after his inauguration, Smith announced that Curtis Trent had resigned as administrative assistant.

As I HAD DISCOVERED during his election campaign, Smith really didn't want advice. He only wanted support for his own ideas. Disagreement was not welcome. Never was this attitude made clearer to me than on the night before the inauguration when my wife and I were the only ones among family and friends not invited to a reception and dinner for the Smiths at Berry Hills Country Club. Once again I had become a pariah, and Margaret was condemned by association.

In my situation it was par for the course, part of the package deal when I signed on for a career in investigative journalism—although it was somewhat surprising in this instance, since my advice and assistance had been specifically requested. But for Smith to hurt and embarrass a longtime friend like Margaret was petty and childish. I had expected better of him.

His ill humor disappeared soon after he took office. A few days after the inauguration, he said he would like for me to become one of his closest advisors. I was pleased by the invitation until I began to consider the ramifications. For a journalist assigned to write about state politics, it would be a conflict of interest. The ethics of my calling placed me in a potentially adversarial position, and in order to retain any objectivity I had no choice but to decline the offer.

Chilton helped me in this regard. Smith hadn't been in office long when Chilton said, "Tommy, you've got to give up covering the governor's office." He expected me to object, since the governor's office was, and is today, the focal point of state politics, but I knew he had a point. "Your family relationship makes it difficult for you to be objective," he explained. "I've been getting feedback from people around town, and this is the way they feel."

As far as actual family relationship was concerned, I tried to explain, our only real link was through my wife's sister, who was married to the first lady's brother. "You may not call it a relationship in Beckley," Chilton responded, "but here in Charleston we think it's pretty close."

John Morgan was Chilton's selection as my replacement, and there could have been no better, more capable choice. Morgan was throughout his career an accomplished newspaperman who commanded the respect of both his associates and news sources. And his book, *West Virginia Governors*, is a classic of political reference works.

THIS CHANGE IN ASSIGNMENT was not about to put a crimp in my investigative writing, as I soon realized when an employee of the Department of Motor Vehicles called and asked for a meeting away from the office. She wanted to talk about the strange and, in some respects, inexplicable activities of her boss, Jack Nuckols.

Our meeting took place over coffee in a downtown restaurant. With her was another female employee from Motor Vehicles. We talked at length about conditions in their respective offices, but when I asked them to go public with the information, they declined, saying they feared reprisals from Nuckols. Others also would be willing to talk, they added, but would not allow their names to be used.

The information I gleaned from them, if true, meant that Nuckols had to be fired, but without something more concrete or someone willing to speak on record I was powerless to act. I said I would be back in touch with them, and after spending a couple of days thinking about how to proceed, I decided to bring Smith into my confidence. I called him at the Governor's Mansion and outlined what I had learned. My suggestion was that, while I couldn't touch the story because of a possible libel suit, I could get these employees to talk in confidence to a State Police investigator if one could be made available.

Smith promptly made the arrangements at his end, and I got back in touch with the two women. Within days I began receiving phone calls at home from various employees of Motor Vehicles. When I promised them that their identities would be kept secret, they gave me their names and phone numbers. I passed this data along to the designated investigator, and an explosive dossier was assembled on Nuckols.

About this time I had to go into the hospital for the first of what was to prove an almost endless series of such trips over the next twenty years. I had developed a stomach ulcer, which had hemorrhaged. While I was still recuperating at home one Sunday, Governor and Mrs. Smith came by the house to see me, and the first thing he said was, "What are we going to do about Jack Nuckols?" I smiled and replied, "It's not what we're going to do. It's what you're going to do."

The second of Nuckols's two terms as Motor Vehicles commissioner was coming to an end. When the day for review action arrived, Smith dismissed Nuckols and named James Kay Thomas—a longtime power in Kanawha County politics who had served as Speaker of the House of Delegates and attorney general—as the new commissioner. On November 12, just ten months after Smith had taken office, Nuckols was indicted by a Kanawha County grand jury on charges of falsifying state records to "defraud the State of West Virginia and to assist Jack Nuckols and other persons to obtain money to which they were not entitled." Indicted with him was Fred Vines, of Flat Top, caretaker at Flat Top Lake resort, where Nuckols had a summer home.

Nuckols was accused of padding the state payroll with Vines and four others, and of various other acts of personal benefit to himself. During the trial in early 1966, it was brought out that Nuckols had had state checks issued improperly to his secretary and girlfriend, Jackie Dillow, as well as to her father. Various other improprieties also came to light. He was found guilty and later went to prison.

The decline and fall of Jack Nuckols upset me. When I was editor in Beckley, I had known him as a capable county commissioner and had endorsed his candidacy editorially when he first ran for State Senate. No one will ever know what happened except Nuckols himself, but shortly into the first of his three Senate terms, word began spreading around Charleston that he was heading for trouble.

Among my acquaintances were two men, each of them astute observers of the legislative process, who kept me apprised of performance ratings on the legislative membership. Both saw flaws in Delegate C. Donald Robertson and Senator Jack Nuckols a few months after each man first took office. Conversely, they saw promise just as quickly in certain other members, such as Delegates Charles H. Haden, of Morgantown, and Ivor F. Bioarsky, of Charleston.

Robertson, later elected attorney general, eventually suffered the same fate as Nuckols. He went to prison. After his service in the House, Haden was appointed state tax commissioner and later became chief judge of the U.S. District Court for Southern West Virginia. Bioarsky, a lawyer/banker, moved up through the ranks of the legislative leadership to become Speaker of the House before his untimely death, a dedicated, honest, and decent man and a wonderful pianist whose talent at the keyboard enlivened many a party and political gathering.

MY DAYS IN JOURNALISM were coming to an end. The recent trip to the hospital had convinced me that I had to make some changes in my life. John Marquis, my physician, had told me I had a medical condition that wasn't going to improve as long as I continued on my present course. The human body, he commented, can accommodate only so much stress. And a stomach that had developed chronic ulcers that hemorrhaged every year with alarming regularity was a strong indication that my body was trying to tell me something. As John put it in his typically blunt fashion, my choices were to slow down or get out; otherwise, he said, he'd find himself attending my funeral within a few years.

It was time for me to look around. I was too young to retire but too old to maintain the pace I had set for myself. With the memory of Knight on my mind, I started a quiet search for a new and less stressful job. But before I left the arena I loved so well, I had one big story left to write.

One afternoon at the close of a House of Delegates session, Delegate Wayne Lanham, of St. Marys, came to me and suggested that I look into a possible problem involving the acquisition of cinders from Monongahela Power Company's Willow Island plant and their resale to the State Road Commission. Lanham, a former State Police officer, said, "I think you'll find it interesting."

It turned out that cinders, a by-product of little use to the power company, had previously been given to the state free of charge for use as a highway abrasive on winter roads. Now, however, the cinders were being purchased by a private source at five cents a ton, mixed with the inexpensive compound calcium chloride, and then sold to the State Road Commission for $5.31 per ton.

Although I exposed the operation in a front-page story, it was so underplayed that Chilton didn't even notice it. In fact, two weeks after it ran in the *Gazette*, he asked Hoffmann to have me look into the mess when he saw something about it in the *Daily Mail*, which had picked up our story.

My travels on the cinder story, although limited somewhat by my need to be on hand for the legislative session, took me to Monongahela Power's Fairmont headquarters; cinder piles in Pleasants, Preston, Taylor, and other upstate counties; and finally to Turtle Creek, Pennsylvania, where the company handling the cinder transactions was based.

The whole thing smelled bad. During my investigation I discovered that Liquor Commissioner Elmore was a silent partner. When I talked with Road Commissioner Sawyers and his chief assistant, Johnkoski, they were less than forthcoming with details about the deal. The Road Commission had already ordered two hundred thousand dollars worth of this formerly free product, but after I broke the story and bird-dogged it into a major exposé, the order was cancelled.

Although we killed off a messy operation with this series of articles, a good highway abrasive was, unfortunately, lost to the state as a result. During my research I had learned that actual cinders, the cast-off refuse from coal-fired locomotives and factory boilers, were no longer available. New burning techniques adopted by power plants and other energy producers had so refined the process that only a greasy residue was left, which was unsuitable for spreading on icy highways. Of all the power plants in West Virginia, only the Willow Island plant still turned out a cinder-like material. But after this story hit the front pages, Willow Island's cinders lay untouched for years.

Sawyers responded to the series by announcing that he planned to adopt a new snow removal method. A salt compound would be mixed with sand or minute rock chips, and snow removal trucks would clear the roads as best they could of snow, right down to the pavement.

Smith's reaction to the series was a thank-you. He called to say he appreciated what I had written. "I have thousands of people under my jurisdiction," he added, "and it's impossible for me to know what all of them are doing here at the Statehouse."

He also put a hold on abrasives purchases and called for an investigation of the entire snow-removal process. After the final report was delivered to him, he directed the state to adopt a more efficient method of acquiring such materials.

AROUND THE TIME the cinder controversy broke, Governor and Mrs. Smith; my wife and I; and our mutual relatives in Beckley, the Tieches, were invited to Puerto Rico as guests of my wife's cousin, Ray Burmeister. Burmeister, a Harvard Business School graduate, had just sold his interest in a hotel in San Juan, the El Conquistador, and had used some of his profits to purchase part of Beef Island in the British Virgins, which he hoped to turn into another playspot for the rich and famous. Our trip was intended to coincide with a visit by the queen of England, who would be in the Caribbean checking on some of her holdings, including the rest of Burmeister's Beef Island. While there, she would be meeting with Burmeister, who was negotiating for access to the island's only airstrip, located on Queen Elizabeth's portion of the island.

Burmeister had planned a leisurely week-long cruise from Puerto Rico to Beef Island for our small group, returning to San Juan for dinner at his home the evening before we were to fly back to the mainland. I intended to use vacation time for the trip, and would be paying all my own expenses. Shortly before we were scheduled to leave, Chilton came up with the suggestion that I listen in on as many conversations as possible while we were away and report back on anything that might seem interesting or unusual. His idea appalled me—spying on my wife's family for the *Gazette*? I cancelled our plane reservations and called my wife to tell her we weren't going to the islands after all. What Chilton thought about his idea afterward I never discovered. Nothing more was ever said. All I can say about this sorry episode is that chinks sometimes appeared in the *Gazette's* vaunted ethical code.

Another controversy that hit the front pages in the summer of 1966 was a charge that improper influence was being used in the awarding of concession contracts at North Bend State Park. News accounts exposed the fact that someone in the Department of Natural Resources with the initials *M. R.* had tried to influence the method of awarding a concessions contract.

Robert P. McDonough had taken over as commissioner a few months earlier, and, at the time of his appointment, Smith was criticized by environmentalists for politicizing a professionally-run department. To complicate matters further, McDonough had made Matthew Reese, a political associate, deputy director. News of the North Bend incident only made matters worse.

When the "M. R." story broke, Reese immediately became suspect. He responded that he didn't think they were his initials, but doubts about the veracity of this explanation spread throughout the state, and eventually Reese resigned. McDonough followed him a few weeks later. T. R. Samsell, who had served as head of the Fish and Game Division, was McDonough's replacement, and David Callaghan, Smith's administrative assistant, moved into Reese's vacant position. Reese later went to Washington, became prominent as a political consultant, and in 1987 sold his consulting business for $35 million.

While this controversy was going on, Hoffmann was away on vacation and I was handling the writing assignment. On his return, Hoffman wrote a glowing column about McDonough, and Chilton followed the next day with an editorial as critical as Hoffmann's had been complimentary. McDonough and Hoffmann had been friends for years, so the air got pretty blue between Hoffmann's desk and mine for the next few days.

My search for a new job eventually took me to Robert E. Maxwell, an Elkins lawyer and former U.S. attorney who had just been appointed chief judge of the U.S. District Court for Northern West Virginia. Maxwell was looking for a new chief clerk to head up his administrative staff. I had first met him at the Democratic National Convention in 1956, and through the years we developed a close friendship.

His reaction to my expression of interest in becoming his clerk and chief administrative officer was favorable, and the matter was later sealed by Senator Jennings Randolph at the Daniel Boone Hotel in Charleston. Randolph called and asked me to join him for a brief meeting.

"Tom," he said, "if you want the clerkship, you can have it. But if you'd rather come to Washington, I can find a better-paying job for you there. It's your choice: Washington or the court."

I knew my wife had liked Washington while she was in school at Arlington Hall. But there were other factors involved in my decision, and I opted for the court appointment, which was one of the best public-service positions open to a non-lawyer in this state.

"I would rather stay in West Virginia," I told the senator.

My health had apparently also become a concern to Chilton. He talked to Hoffmann about it, suggesting that I be shifted into a less stressful position. It would have been a promotion, and I would have been more closely associated with Chilton himself. I told Hoffmann I would like to think about it.

While health was the major impetus, other factors helped push me out of my profession. By this time I had written enough big stories; I had had my share of "scoops." Worst of all, I had become cynical and jaded. I had begun to wonder if there was any integrity in government and the business world. Only the names and dates seemed to change. The corruption and wrongdoing continued. It was time for me to give up and get out. I had begun to question my own objectivity as a journalist.

But the idea of giving up still bothered me. While I hadn't found any overtly corrupt practices in the office of Governor Smith, I was apprehensive. Elmore, a holdover from the Barron administration, had tried to kill the Invest Right story with his visit to Hoffmann's home. Gore had remained in his old position as head of the Purchasing Division after I had disclosed his involvement in the Invest Right scandal. The highway-abrasives series had given Smith an excellent opportunity to tell Sawyers, Johnkoski, and Elmore to start looking for new employment—an opportunity the governor had failed to take. In the case of Elmore, the governor had an even better reason for pushing him out the door.

Back during the previous administration, Governor Barron had sought passage of legislation that would have given him the chance to succeed himself in office. The legislature balked, refusing even to pass the enabling bill that would have put the succession question on the ballot for the voters to consider. Smith was slightly more successful. Succession legislation was approved by the lawmakers. But when it was put before the voters, Smith's effort to get ratification was defeated, and Elmore was among those most forcefully opposing its passage.

In Smith's office a few days after the succession amendment had been voted down, he told me, "I'm going to ask Clarence for his resignation." I offered to write the story, but Smith declined, saying he wanted to wait a couple of weeks. The resignation never took place.

This was a Smith trait. He had difficulty making tough decisions when they involved friends. Had he been willing to move resolutely against Elmore, Sawyers, and Johnkoski when they embarrassed his administration in the cinder scandal, he would not have found himself in an even more embarrassing situation when they were later indicted. He hurt himself badly with his hesitancy. Placing personal friendships ahead of political expediency may be admirable in the private sector, but it's a luxury a governor can rarely afford.

Despite these and other administrative burdens he had inherited on his inauguration, Smith enjoyed smooth sailing during his first year in office. Revenue was no problem. Tax increases during Barron's term, the steady flow of funding from Washington, and the retirement of bond issues for road improvements and veterans' bonuses eased fiscal problems for him. Education became his first priority as governor. He got what he wanted from the legislature—a $32.5 million, three-year school-aid package that was earmarked for a teachers' pay increase, school construction, educational television, and remedial reading.

Smith's second year was less dazzling than the first, although the legislature passed a one-dollar-an-hour minimum-wage bill. Smith also set the stage for the biggest battle against strip-mining ever launched by organizing the Governor's Task Force on Surface Mining and announcing that abuse of the state's scenic beauty had to be stopped.

He was still in the planning stages on long-term programs. They would come together in 1968, but by then, I had moved on to a new challenge.

MISCELLANY ❂ THE JOHNSON CHARM

ON ONE OF MY MANY TRIPS to Washington, Senator Byrd asked if I would like to meet Senator Lyndon Johnson. It was 1960, and I had stopped by Byrd's office on my rounds of the West Virginia delegation.

Johnson, by that time, had risen to the position of majority leader and was so adept at his political craft that there was some question on the capital cocktail circuit as to whether President Eisenhower or Senator Johnson was running the country. It was an election year and, like John F. Kennedy, Johnson was seeking the presidency.

Within a few minutes, Byrd had made arrangements for the two of us to drop by the majority leader's office in the Capitol.

It was really a grand place, tastefully decorated and exuding a warmth seldom found in the offices of the mighty. Most are either overdecorated or so coldly modern that you want to pull up your coat collar against the chill.

Rather than staying seated at his desk while we chatted, Johnson stood and gestured toward some easy chairs. "Tom," he said—we were on a first-name basis from the moment I walked into the room—"let's go over and get comfortable."

The conversation was brief, casual, and directed at my interests rather than his. I was instantly captivated by his style, his charm, his bearing, and his knowledge of West Virginia affairs. The other side of Johnson that has been written about so often, the one that could be boorish and crude, was very much under wraps during our meeting.

Byrd and I were there only a few minutes, but as we left, Senator Johnson put his arm around my shoulders, making me feel ten feet tall.

Walking down the hall moments later and thinking about the meeting, I wasn't sure whether to laugh or kick myself.

"You stupid fool," I told myself. "The man is running for president, and you write politics for the biggest newspaper in West Virginia." I had just been treated to a sample of the larger-than-life Johnson witchcraft.

Chapter 18

"It Wasn't Any Pleasure"

It was one of those tastefully elegant holiday parties shortly before Christmas. The company was pleasant and the conversation stimulating. The food and liquid refreshment were excellent, as one would expect at such an affair. The host, after all, was Clarence Elmore, state liquor commissioner, and among his guests were Governor and Mrs. Smith and former Governor and Mrs. Barron.

As the evening wore on and the celebrants broke up into small groups, I found myself talking with Elmore and Barron. I was nearing the end of my tenure at the *Gazette*. Within a week I would leave for my new job as clerk of the U.S. District Court for Northern West Virginia.

"I have a decision to make shortly after taking over as clerk," I commented, chiefly as a means of keeping the conversation going.

"What's that?" Barron asked.

"The court has money in what is called the registry account in a Wheeling bank," I said. "Judge Maxwell wants it moved closer to our headquarters in Elkins. He feels we can manage it better there."

"How much is it?" Barron inquired, interested.

"It's only about seventy thousand dollars," I said, "but who knows how the account may grow in the future?"

That was an unwittingly prescient statement on my part. The account would grow into the millions within a few years. Barron immediately offered to choose the new depository, make arrangements for the transfer of funds, and pay me five thousand dollars in the process.

"How interesting," I remarked, and that ended the conversation.

For the former governor, then in private practice in Charleston, there was nothing wrong with what he proposed. He was simply an attorney offering his services to a prospective client and offering to pay the client a share of his fee. But for me it would have been an illegal act, deal-making of the type that had long been prohibited at all levels of government.

Nothing more came of the offer except that I thought often of this conversation in the next few weeks, wondering if it was a replay of what was alleged to have been standard operating procedure while Barron was governor.

I WAS REMINDED AGAIN of Barron's offer when, a short time after I became clerk, Woodrow Yokum, a political unknown until that moment, splashed into prominence in the West Virginia press. Federal agents had seized more than three hundred thousand dollars worth of surplus government property hidden on three Randolph County farms and in two storerooms at Beverly, near Elkins. It all traced back to Yokum, a Beverly resident and communications supervisor at the State Road Commission equipment headquarters in Buckhannon.

Included among the wide assortment of items that Yokum was accused of acquiring fraudulently were two Navy assault boats, a five-ton wrecker truck, a bulldozer, a fire truck, three automobiles, one thousand pairs of binoculars, 150 typewriters, two miles of copper wire, dozens of pairs of Army boots. and all of the equipment necessary for a television installation. Yokum's cache had been acquired from an Army munitions plant in Radford, Virginia, and from naval supply depots in Norfolk, Virginia, and Mechanicsburg, Pennsylvania.

Yokum was indicted after the property was rounded up and transferred to the custody of the U.S. Marshal. He was tried in the spring of 1968, with Elkins lawyer Bonn Brown representing him. Although some records considered important by the prosecution disappeared from Statehouse files, he was found guilty and sentenced by Judge Maxwell to four years in prison.

WHILE THE GRAND JURY WAS BUSY examining evidence in the Yokum case, I talked with U.S. Attorney John H. Kamlowsky about taking the Invest Right matter before the grand jury for consideration. Although there was no apparent relationship between Yokum's acquisitions and Invest Right, it nevertheless indicated a strange pattern of related activity during the Barron administration, and I felt it deserved more attention than it had received in state-government circles. The legislature had done nothing with it, despite the fact that it rounded out an investigation so ineptly begun by that body. And it was a given that the Smith administration would do nothing, since its policy-makers had tried to kill the story during the late days of Smith's campaign for governor.

Kamlowsky agreed with my assessment and asked me to turn over my Invest Right notes and background information to federal investigators. Purists would probably contend that, as a journalist, I should not have released this information to the government, but I considered it my own file and one I could dispose of as I saw fit.

When I left the *Gazette* at the end of 1966, I took nothing with me from my office files, all of which were later put into storage and eventually destroyed as standard housekeeping policy at the newspaper. I had kept the Invest Right data at home, however, where I did most of my work on the story, and it stayed there after the series was completed. Thus, I had no qualms about turning it over to the two FBI agents who came to our house in Kanawha City one weekend afternoon.

Before leaving the newspaper, I had been asked by Hoffmann if there was any work I hadn't finished. I typed out some notes on two stories I had been researching and turned them over to him. The first was on the procurement of crushed stone for use in highway resurfacing and maintenance. Once the information was assembled for this story, a scandal bigger than the one surrounding the acquisition of highway abrasives would have resulted—as was proven during the trial of Barron and his associates.

The other story I had been working on involved the distribution of federal Medicare and Medicaid monies to doctors, hospitals, and pharmacies by the State Welfare Department. There was nothing illegal in the distribution. It merely indicated the scope of greed that existed among certain members of the healthcare profession and would have been a follow-up story to the one Bernard Smith had given me while he was welfare commissioner.

None of the *Gazette* staffers manifested an interest in these notes, so releasing my Invest Right file to the FBI seemed to serve a better purpose than leaving it to gather dust in my office desk. As things turned out, Kamlowsky took the information to the grand jury after obtaining his Yokum indictment. This body considered the information briefly, found that there was reasonable cause to pursue the case further, and transferred it to the Southern West Virginia district attorney's office for ongoing action. The reason given for the transfer was that the investigation should be handled in the state capital.

MILTON J. FERGUSON, who lost his own bid for governor in 1956 and later served as one of Smith's campaign strategists during his second run for the governorship, was U.S. attorney for the southern district when the Invest Right case was transferred there for review and continuing investigation. Ferguson was a seasoned federal litigator who had held his present post since July 10, 1965, and had also served as an assistant U.S. attorney in the 1940s.

No one ever knows to any degree of certainty—except the U.S. attorney and the jurors themselves—what goes on in the confines of the grand jury room. All testimony and deliberations are kept secret by law. I was only aware from my contacts in the southern district court that a prolonged series of sessions was underway. It would be a year before a bombshell was released in Huntington.

In what became known throughout West Virginia as the "St. Valentine's Day Massacre," an indictment was returned and delivered to the court on February 14, 1968, against Barron, Gore, Brown, Schroath, Sawyers, and Johnkoski for "conspiracy to carry on bribery activities involving state government." The press dubbed those indicted the "Secret Six."

The voluminous indictment charged that Brown and Schroath in 1961 set up dummy corporations in Ohio and Florida, then told prospective suppliers of goods and services that they could secure contracts for state business by paying money into these corporations.

After the deals were arranged, the indictment continued, Sawyers, Johnkoski, and Gore rigged state bidding procedures to insure that such suppliers would be rewarded with contracts. The rigging operation was accomplished by permitting competitive bids to be considered from nonexistent firms, or firms owned by the same bidder, as well as the drafting of specifications in such a way that only the one firm would be eligible to receive the contract.

Finally, the indictment charged, all payoff money was to be transferred to one of the Florida corporations and, on some future date, was to be divided equally among the defendants. The six conspirators had pledged to one another that they would keep their identities secret.

Smith acted quickly after the indictments were made public by suspending Gore, Sawyers, and Johnkoski. Explaining that he wasn't prejudging anybody, Smith said that the suspension order was in keeping with a previously stated policy of removing any state employee charged with a wrongful act.

Sawyers, who had served as state road commissioner through three administrations, resigned from office. In his letter of resignation he told the governor, "I cannot allow legal action against myself to hinder the continuing development of our road program."

Although Smith announced the suspension of his top officials shortly after the indictments were handed down, he failed to move fast enough to save his own administration from taint. In writing the news story about the grand jury's return, *Gazette* reporter John Morgan said, "Although the origin of the alleged conspiracy coincides with the date Barron was inaugurated governor, on January 16, 1961, the 'overt acts' of those charged reach into the Smith administration."

IN A STATEMENT AFTER THE INDICTMENTS were made public, Justice Department officials said they had studied the "Brown Means Business" series in detail while conducting their investigation. They also said they had made five previous attempts to obtain indictments without success before they began sifting through the information I had assembled for my series of articles.

Barron affirmed this latter statement in a comment the day after the indictments were returned. "On five previous occasions," he said, "they have attempted to obtain indictments against me through grand juries in Miami, Florida, one in Elkins and three times in Charleston . . . Since 1963 my political enemies have attempted to use the Internal Revenue Service and other investigative bodies to discredit my administration as governor of West Virginia."

Barron's "political enemies" accusation was standard hyperbole. To my knowledge, the only people who played a significant role in moving this conspiracy out of the proverbial smoke-filled backroom and into the courtroom, other than the investigating officers, were Ferguson and me, and neither of us could be typecast as political enemies of this group of men. I was a newspaperman pursuing a story, and Ferguson was a public servant administering the affairs of his office.

"It wasn't any pleasure to me," Ferguson, then eighty-one, said in an interview published in 1983 by *Goldenseal* magazine, referring to his office's investigation of Governor Barron and his associates.

I had much the same feeling on the day the indictment was released to the press. At times while I was working on the story I would try to imagine how I would feel, and the celebrating I would do, if I were ever successful in putting it together. There were other times when I agonized over the thought of actually going to press with the story, since several of those involved were men I liked personally and considered friends. By the end, there was no joy in my soul, only a feeling of sadness mixed with a small sense of accomplishment in having managed to see it through to the bitter end.

I had a similar reaction later when one of the special Justice Department strike-force attorneys came to me while I was in Wheeling for a court session and said, "Thanks for your help." I must have looked surprised, since he was then heading up a team that had cracked a racketeering operation in the Northern Panhandle and western Pennsylvania. The case involving the ringleaders was just winding down in our court. This attorney, a man of few words, explained that he had headed an earlier team investigating the Invest Right conspiracy.

"We were about to give up on that operation," he said, "when you provided us with the interlocking corporate structure in your 'Brown Means Business' series. That set us on the right trail. After that we were able to pull the case together."

He said nothing more, smiled, shook my hand, and walked out the door.

Ah, my smoking gun. And I didn't even know it was loaded.

Chapter 19

STORM WARNINGS

THE ADMINISTRATION OF GOVERNOR HULETT SMITH was a period of great promise, grand illusions, some important legislative breakthroughs, and terrible tragedy. After an initial two years spent primarily on planning and achieving some small victories, Smith's final two years provided a study in contrasts.

As Smith liked to say, 1967 was the "Year of Accomplishment." He could make this boast with good reason, since he was successful in gaining passage of one of the most sweeping surface-mine control laws in the country. That same year saw improved air- and stream-pollution controls, liberalized unemployment and workers' benefits, and strengthened human-rights protections in the workplace. Also in 1967 several new tax measures were passed, including a corporate net-income tax, transportation tax, higher business and occupation taxes, and a new tax on professionals.

The new tax measures, some of them farsighted in concept, grew out of a study by Purdue University economist James A. Papke. At the heart of Papke's proposals, however, was a gross-margin tax on value added to products at the point of sale. Although the value-added tax had already been adopted in Western Europe, the 1967 West Virginia legislature was unwilling to make such a sweeping change, and the relative merits of this form of taxation are still being debated today.

Toward the end of the governor's third year in office, storm clouds began to form on the horizon. Ten days before Christmas the Silver Bridge across the Ohio River at Point Pleasant collapsed, killing forty-six people. Liquor Commissioner Elmore was indicted on charges of income tax evasion. Early in 1968 the indictments against Barron and his Invest Right associates were handed down. A wall of water trapped twenty-five miners at Hominy Falls, and four died. In May, a Piedmont Airlines plane crashed at Kanawha Airport, killing thirty-two passengers. A mine at Farmington exploded in November, wiping out another seventy-eight miners, one of the worst mining disasters in state history. One day later, a bomb believed to have been planted by civil rights hotheads went off in the physical education building at Bluefield State College, causing eighty thousand dollars in damage but mercifully resulting in no loss of life.

The Smith administration was experiencing a similar downhill slide. When he suspended Elmore, followed a few months later by Gore, Sawyers, and Johnkoski, Smith advised his remaining top officials that if they weren't comfortable with the goals he had laid out, they were free to tender their resignations. He finally began making tough decisions on a string of holdover problems from the Barron years, but his actions were greeted by his critics in the press as patchwork repair to a tattered fabric.

Smith's "Mr. Clean" image was further tarnished when he was subpoenaed as a witness, first in the Elmore case and later in the Barron trial. His "Administration of Excellence" was also compromised when one witness in the Barron case testified that he had given Smith ten thousand dollars in political contributions. The judge hearing the case ruled it a collateral issue and testimony on it was not required. No records were available at party headquarters to support the claim, and Smith issued a press release saying that he had never received such a contribution.

What religious writer Thomas Merton called a "brute of a year" was not only a West Virginia phenomenon. In 1968, the Navy ship Pueblo was seized by North Korean forces in the western Pacific and the Viet Cong launched the bloody Tet offensive against U.S. forces in Vietnam. Martin Luther King Jr. was assassinated in Memphis, and his murder triggered race riots in more than a hundred cities. Two months after his death, Robert Kennedy was assassinated in Los Angeles. President Johnson told a worldwide television audience that he would not seek another term in office, and his Great Society began to wither. Students at Columbia seized university buildings, and demonstrators were clubbed by police outside the Democratic National Convention in Chicago.

The vision of great expectations, so bright and promising after World War II, began to flicker and fade. The tragedies beyond West Virginia's borders as well as those within the state added to Smith's burdens. President Johnson's decision to retire forced the governor to seek new political alliances in Washington. The mood of unrest and uncertainty in other parts of the country spread into the mountains and contributed to the Democratic Party's loss to Republican Arch A. Moore before 1968 came to a close.

The legislature met twice that year. During the regular session it approved a penny increase in the cigarette tax to finance a teachers' pay raise. At a special session in mid-summer, lawmakers approved a work-incentive program designed to turn welfare recipients into wage earners. But, more importantly, the legislature bent under public pressure and pushed through both houses a bill to create an investigative commission. The indictment of a former governor by a federal grand jury had been too much for most West Virginians to swallow. The voters wanted scalps, and the new commission was given the power to hunt for them.

As Smith's term drew to a close in early 1969, he said in his last message to the legislature that the "heartbeat of West Virginia is strong." He also said, "To those who helped keep the governor humble with their constructive criticism, I offer my humblest thanks."

The outgoing governor would perform one more task after giving this address. A few hours before leaving office, Smith signed orders placing almost two thousand state employees under the umbrella of the Civil Service System, bringing the number of employees given such protection during his term to a total of 5,600. The reason he offered for his late-hour action was this: "These were employees the state could ill afford to lose."

SMITH WAS NEVER LINKED DIRECTLY by any legal documentation to the wrongdoings and indiscretions that took place while he was in office. But he was the state's top executive at the time, and he allowed the problems to continue, at a high cost to both the state and his own political reputation, until he was finally forced to act. If he was guilty of anything, the record states that it was the sin of omission, of neglecting to clean house by dismissing the members of the Barron crowd at the beginning of his own term.

At the peak of the scandals erupting around Smith, a Charleston newsman called me in Elkins to ask me to join him in writing a book about the Barron and Smith years. "This is terrible," he commented. "It's a story that all America should know about." As politely as I knew how, for I felt complimented by the invitation to collaborate on the writing project, I declined. "History has to make its own judgment," I said, "history and future events."

Smith and his staff worked tirelessly to return to the mountains a measure of the pristine beauty that the early settlers found in colonial days. He was successful in getting needed taxes passed for the improvement of education and other underfunded services. He laid the foundation for his successors to implement massive highway improvements by completing most of the necessary planning and gaining ratification of a $350 million road bond issue to fund the work. Smith was also responsible for developing the concept for the Capitol Complex as it exists today. All Moore had to do after he took office was put his officials to work on implementing the planning Smith already had in place and await the day when he could travel around the state cutting ribbons and making speeches.

Despite all the positive aspects of Smith's administration, the legacy of impropriety that he inherited from Barron—and failed to eliminate until it was too late—left him with scars, both political and personal. Ultimately, he fell short of the goals he had set years before as a young man, unseasoned in the political craftsmanship practiced in "wild, wonderful West Virginia."

MISCELLANY ° A RARE OCCURRENCE

Time magazine noted in its January 11, 1988, issue that the collection of events that took place in 1968 was a rare and eerie manifestation. Its editors had to go back to 1811 to find a similar aggregation of extraordinary occurrences, describing it as a "year of wonders."

In that year a double-tailed comet appeared in the sky, rivers overflowed their banks, an earthquake—possibly the worst ever to occur in North America—reversed the flow of the Mississippi River, vast forests toppled over, and tens of thousands of squirrels marched southward to the Ohio River, plunging in and drowning themselves.

Chapter 20

The Party Faithless

AFTER LEAVING OFFICE, Barron opened a law office in downtown Charleston with John E. Davis. A few of the faithful, thinking him still electable, mounted a campaign in the fall of 1967 to run him again for governor, sporting "Wally by Golly" buttons and bumper stickers and taking out full-page ads in the newspapers touting Barron as the man for all season.

Barron hinted in speeches that he might run again. At the same time, he was quietly, almost covertly, exploring the role of kingmaker, searching for a viable candidate to promote for the 1968 election. He knew his days in politics were numbered. The legislature had already refused, midway through Barron's original term in office, to place an amendment on the ballot allowing him to file for a consecutive term, and that had been before the exposure of his involvement in a state purchasing scam. But Barron had spent too many years at the apex of power to give up without a fight.

I became privy to the details of a certain meeting between the former governor and one prospective candidate for the '68 election. This man had both the political credentials and spotless background to stand as a strong contender, had he been willing to accept the terms Barron was offering in exchange for providing support. But he was already well established in the public sector, and the former governor's proposal failed to tempt him.

It is altogether likely that Barron approached others with the same proposition, but at some point he began to realize that he was no longer destined to be a Democratic power broker. According to James A. Haught, the *Gazette*'s investigative reporter at the time, Barron then made a startling 180-degree turn and signed on with Moore, the Republican gubernatorial candidate.

There was precedent for Barron's action. Former Governor Homer Holt had endorsed Republican Underwood for governor in 1956. And John W. Davis, the only West Virginian ever nominated for president by one of the major parties, broke with Franklin D. Roosevelt in 1932. Both Holt and Davis were Democrats.

It took Haught quite a while to put the pieces of the puzzle together. In fact, the story would not appear in print for nearly two years. But when it did, it was a shocker with Machiavellian overtones.

In the late hours of the 1968 campaign, Barron and his associates crossed party lines. They mobilized the ragtag elements of their once powerful political machine and threw them behind Moore. Key support players were Barron's law associate, Davis; former Liquor Commissioner Elmore; and former Road Commissioner Sawyers. Their contacts were Moore's chief strategists, William Loy and Norman Yost.

As elections go, 1968 was a lively one for Democrats and Republicans alike. In the Republican primary, Moore defeated former Governor Underwood by a comfortable margin. In the Democratic primary, State Democratic Chairman James Sprouse went head-to-head with outgoing Attorney General Don Robertson and environmental gadfly Paul Kaufman. It was a close race.

Sprouse had been Smith's choice for state party chairman when he became governor, but he failed to endear himself to the administration's hard-nosed holdovers from the Barron years. Within weeks of Smith's inauguration, Sprouse began distancing himself from members of the inner circle, further alienating them when he refused to be drawn into their schemes. This aloofness almost cost him the primary.

Smith broke with past practice when he declined to endorse a candidate in the primary, choosing instead to wait until it was over and then endorse whoever made it to the final round. And the Barron crowd pulled out all the stops in their efforts to defeat Sprouse.

According to Haught, Barron allegedly offered a bribe to Underwood in an attempt to obtain the former governor's endorsement of Moore. Working with Loy and Yost, Barron and Davis were said to have collected information detrimental to Sprouse and fed it to *The Charleston Daily Mail*. It primarily concerned certain deals presumably made to enrich himself and some of his friends. These stories were so patently at odds with the facts that Sprouse brought a libel suit against the *Mail* and won a judgment of $750,000. On appeal, the State Supreme Court reduced the damages to $350,000.

Underwood confirmed the bribery attempt, saying it was partly responsible "for my silence in the fall of 1968." When he talked to Haught about Barron's offer, Underwood was president of Bethany College and said he was reluctant to embroil himself in politics. The deal, as outlined by Underwood, was for the former governor to endorse Moore. Once he had done so, a high-paying executive position awaited him with West Virginia's largest coal producer, Consolidation Coal Company. "They [Barron and Davis] wanted me to fly to New York with them right away and have the job arranged," Underwood said.

Two things convinced him that Barron and the Moore campaign people had joined forces. First, after the deal was offered to him he began receiving phone calls from various Republicans thanking him for the soon-to-be-announced endorsement; and second, he had told Barron that the only thing that might bring him to endorse Moore would be a personal request from Richard Nixon. The following day, Nixon's campaign manager, John Mitchell, called Underwood and made the request on Nixon's behalf.

Meanwhile, the news stories critical of Sprouse's dealings began to appear in the *Mail*, and rumors started flowing back from the southern counties about Elmore's contacts with Democratic Party workers. In their efforts to elect Moore, Barron operated statewide while Elmore concentrated on the Southern West Virginia precincts and Sawyers worked those around Charleston.

According to state AFL-CIO President Myles Stanley, a Sprouse supporter, "We could see their tracks. They were putting money down in the southern counties through their old organization for Moore. A lot of people told us it was happening. The name Clarence Elmore popped up everywhere as spreading money for Moore."

Another report from a precinct leader in Charleston added to the drama. She said she received a call just before the election from Sawyers asking her to line up behind Moore. "I couldn't believe it was really Burl calling," she said. "At first I thought it was someone else trying to trick me, but then I learned from some friends that it was real."

Both Sawyers and Barron denied helping Moore, but the evidence to the contrary was too strong for their protestations to be convincing.

Despite all the adverse publicity Sprouse was getting, despite the party defections by old-time leaders, despite the soiled baggage of past Democratic administrations that he carried by default and a helicopter accident in which Moore was injured just before the election—which garnered substantial public sympathy for the Republican candidate—Sprouse still lost by only 12,758 votes. Had he not been subjected to "dirty tricks" campaigning by members of his own party, it is altogether possible that Jim Sprouse rather than Arch Moore would have been West Virginia's twenty-eighth governor. He was defeated by only 2.55 votes per precinct.

THERE WERE SOME WHO FELT that the outcome also would have been different had Governor Smith played a more active role in Sprouse's campaign. They forget that, by then, Smith's administration no longer carried the same cachet it had enjoyed in its early days.

By the time of the 1968 election, Smith had blots on his own copybook. Although he had dumped Motor Vehicles Commissioner Nuckols, the scandal that erupted later was a humiliation to his administration. The conviction of his crony Elmore on income tax evasion was another black mark, as was the Invest Right trial.

Finally, Barron's former administrative assistant, Curtis Trent, whom Smith had wanted to retain in his own administration, had been indicted on charges of income tax evasion.

Added to the negative publicity generated by these successive court actions were the problems of growing student unrest, political assassinations, the escalating war in Vietnam, and other tragedies affecting the country's outlook in that election year of 1968. The frustrations were piling up, and the governor was becoming moody and irritable. I found this out for myself on one particular occasion.

I had called Smith from Elkins to ask for his reading on the direction the political winds were blowing in the state, chiefly with regard to the national elections.

While I was still at the *Gazette*, Vice President Hubert Humphrey had asked me to take periodic soundings for him, a practice I continued after leaving Charleston. Humphrey had heard that over the years I had built up a bipartisan network of reliable political contacts. With his sights on the presidency in 1968, he asked that I help keep him informed about the mood of West Virginia's electorate.

When I called Smith on this particular occasion, we talked for a few minutes and that was that. He was pleasant but somewhat distant as we chatted about election trends. A couple of days later I received a phone call from one of Humphrey's top aides.

"What's going on over there?" the aide asked.

"What do you mean?" I countered.

"I just had a call from Governor Smith's office. They're saying you're out of favor in West Virginia, and we would be best advised to have no more contact with you."

I told him about the Invest Right series I had written and how it had led to the conviction of major figures in the Barron and Smith administrations. "There are people here in West Virginia who consider me a leper," I explained.

I had become *persona non grata* not only at the Statehouse. I had picked up the same feeling in the Eastern Panhandle, the southern coalfields, the Monongahela Valley, and elsewhere. More than a few hard-core party loyalists looked not at the root cause of their problems but to somebody they could conveniently finger as a scapegoat.

Humphrey lost the election that year, as did Sprouse. But in the end the Barron crowd lost everything. There can be little doubt that Moore was overjoyed by the defection of these Democrats of little faith. But what did Barron and his associates hope to gain from such an alliance? If Moore won, he would have thousands of Republicans clamoring for jobs, favors, and state business. His first loyalty was to his own party.

If the Barron crowd was hoping for political influence to be brought to bear on the Invest Right case, again they were barking up the wrong tree. Neither a Republican governor nor a Republican president was likely to risk his new administration to help a former Democratic governor and his officials. The Republicans were far more likely to celebrate the potential embarrassment that a criminal trial of those officials might cause the Democratic Party.

Whatever their contributions to Moore's election, Barron and his Democratic disloyalists received nothing of substance from the Republicans. A few months after the election, Barron decided to leave the state that had given him so much and take up a life of leisure in Florida. He could see that the end was at hand.

Sprouse not only survived but prospered. He became a member of the U.S. Court of Appeals, one of the most prestigious positions available to an attorney.

Moore became the first West Virginia governor to succeed himself in office, and in 1989 he completed an unprecedented third term as governor.

Otherwise it was a washout. The political organization that Barron, Elmore, Sawyers, et al, had put together dissolved as the prison doors clanged shut behind them.

MISCELLANY ∘ WEST VIRGINIA'S LOSS

While I was standing in the House of Delegates chamber as a session came to a close, with House members milling around deciding what to do that evening, somebody squeezed my arm. Turning, I found Delegate Brereton Jones standing there.

"I wish you weren't leaving," he said. I had just told my editor that I was leaving the *Gazette* for the federal court, and this had precipitated a public announcement. I told Jones, one of the most promising and intelligent delegates from the Republican side of the House, "I hate to go, but I feel I have no choice. I have to move on."

"I'm thinking about leaving, too," he said, with a note of bitterness in his voice. Explaining that he felt he had done what he could for the state while in the legislature, he added that the system was too rigidly structured for a change of course.

Within days, I left newspapering, and later I read that Jones would not be a candidate for reelection. Still later, I noted in the press that he had gone to Kentucky. "Brery," as I had known him, bought a farm, went into the business of buying and selling horses, made a fortune, and eventually returned to politics—as a Democrat rather than a Republican, which had been a family tradition. His father, Bartow, had been a state senator for some years.

Jones was elected lieutenant governor of Kentucky and, in 1991, was elected governor. His old friend, West Virginia Governor Gaston Caperton, was in attendance at the inauguration. In his seven-minute address at the swearing-in ceremony, Jones made a vintage "Brery" comment. He promised an administration of cooperation and mutual respect.

"There is no limit, absolutely no limit, to what we can accomplish," he said, "with dedication and hard work."

As I read about the Jones inauguration, I couldn't help recalling how West Virginia had lost so many young men of promise like him to other states over the years and been made the poorer in the process.

Part Three

"Nothing except a battle lost can be half so melancholy
as a battle won."

Arthur Wellesley, Duke of Wellington

Chapter 21

THE STRENGTH OF THEIR CONVICTIONS

WHEN WALLY BARRON became West Virginia's twenty-sixth governor, he informed the voters in his inaugural address, "My coworkers and I are possessed with boundless confidence that our goals will be reached and surpassed."

Surpassed they were, but probably not in the fashion he had envisioned. Barron became the first chief executive in the state's history to go to prison, and his merry little band of freebooters went with him. As an IRS agent commented at the time of the convictions, "I've seen all of this before, but never all of it in one place."

The trial of Barron and his friends took place just six months after they were indicted, but not without a spate of creative delaying tactics.

Attorneys for the defense filed for transfer of the trial to another state on the grounds that a "poisonous . . . pervasive . . . saturation of publicity" had destroyed the defendants' chances for an impartial hearing. The transfer was denied, and the trial was scheduled in Charleston. Then, as the date of the trial drew near, an epidemic of health problems beset the ranks of the accused. Barron's lawyer, the ever-dramatic Robert G. Perry, actually collapsed in the courtroom, causing a one-week delay. Just before the trial was to begin on August 12, 1968, word reached Charleston that Brown was in an Elkins hospital suffering from what his physician described as hypertension.

The presiding judge in the case, Robert J. Martin, of Greenville, South Carolina, called for a second opinion and, after reading the report from two doctors assigned this task, refused another postponement. Finally, after the trial had begun, Gore's lawyer developed shingles, and Gore won a marginal edge when he was allowed to step aside until a later date.

The fifteen-day trial opened with a parade of witnesses who testified to the involvement of seventeen different companies with the Ohio-Florida corporate empire and to payoffs totaling more than $166,500. But the most damning pieces of evidence produced by federal investigators were documents signed by the defendants agreeing to evenly apportion the proceeds from the bribery conspiracy among themselves.

The prosecution opened its case by presenting two trust agreements signed by the six defendants pledging to "share equally in all the profits." Agents for the federal government testified that these agreements had been discovered in Schroath's safety deposit box more than four years previously. But according to the government's attorney, this hybrid corporate creation was "nothing but post office boxes."

Other witnesses testified that in their attempts to develop state business, or a larger share of the business they already had, they contacted one or more of the defendants and indicated their willingness to pay a portion of any monies they received into one or more of these dummy corporations. The deals were beneficial to the witnesses or their companies, they added, and fell within what they assumed to be the framework of established bidding procedures.

The typical sequence of events that occurred after such arrangements were made was detailed in testimony from West Virginia, Pennsylvania, and Georgia sales representatives, largely suppliers of paint and crushed stone to the State Road Commission. These witnesses admitted that they had paid anywhere from $1,500 to twenty-nine thousand dollars into the Florida or Ohio corporations for contracts they received from the State Division of Purchases. In every instance, these witnesses maintained that there was nothing wrong with what they had been doing, that they were merely paying "commissions" on sales. Each denied knowledge of any bid rigging and said the payments were made solely for bidding information and "help in getting contracts."

One of these witnesses—M. C. Paterno, of Charleston's Park Tire Company—told the jury that he would have been compelled to hire salesmen if he hadn't entered into an agreement with Schroath, and added that he reported the payments as a business expense on his income tax returns. The contract Paterno had signed with Schroath noted that he was paying for "manifold

services of experienced consultants." Under further questioning, Paterno testified that the only person he had dealt with was Schroath.

Robert L. McClintic, of Frazee Lumber Company, said that his firm sold
3,500 acres of Wetzel County land to the Department of Natural Resources
for the Lewis Wetzel Public Hunting Area for $111,500. He also said he sent
$7,500 to one of the Florida corporations as Brown's fee for assisting in the
sale. Barron, he added, signed the order for the purchase of the land.

The trial also brought out the fact that state bidding procedures required
that contracts be awarded to the lowest bidder of at least three companies
submitting bids. But with the approval of Gore's purchasing director, the bidding rules were sometimes waived by emergency order and the business was
then channeled to the favored firm. At other times specifications were tailored
so that only a single company could meet them and thereby qualify to supply
the work or product needed.

One illustration of the mechanics of the scheme was provided by the testimony of William A. Smith, an Atlanta paint manufacturer. Smith said he had
had difficulty for years trying to sell his product in West Virginia, until 1961
when he engaged in what he said was "consultation with a number of suppliers, and the name of Bonn Brown was suggested to me to contact." A short
time later he met with Brown in the foyer of the governor's office.

"We came to an understanding," Smith added.

In June of that same year, he testified, the first contract for traffic paint
came through, and in November he signed an agreement to pay 14 percent of
the price of the paint into one of the dummy corporations. This was the for-
malization of a verbal agreement, he commented, which had already cost him
$11,475. Within two years of his first meeting with Brown, he estimated that
he had paid kickbacks amounting to twenty-nine thousand dollars.

James J. Arcure, owner of Valley Distributing Company in Fairmont, testified that he had had similar results after meeting with Schroath. Arcure
stated that he was awarded state paint contracts and made $24,370 worth of
payoffs into two of the Florida corporations.

Backdoor dealings with the Purchasing Division also became a lure to
John Ruckman, Wheeling lawyer and Ohio County Democratic Executive

Committee chairman. Ruckman testified that he thought Brown was simply doing him a political favor by helping him obtain a hundred-thousand-dollar order for a client. Involved were twenty steamrollers.

But soon, Ruckman said, "We received . . . an invoice from Atlantic, Inc., a corporation in Florida, for nine thousand dollars . . . Well, we met and wondered who Atlantic was, and thereupon Mr. Brown was contacted and, as I recall, he stated that he was a representative of Atlantic Management Corporation, and that this bill was due and should be paid." Ruckman's client paid the bill.

When he became a middleman for Minnesota Mining and Manufacturing Corporation, Ruckman arranged enough business with Brown for the two of them to split a $2,356 commission. However, Ruckman said he ceased such business dealings after representing 3M. "I realized this just wasn't my line of work," he explained.

The most sensational testimony of all came from Isadore Lashinsky, of Charleston, who was president of Southern Culvert Corporation and several other firms. At first Lashinsky refused to testify on grounds of self-incrimination, but he finally took the stand after being granted immunity by U.S. Attorney General Ramsay Clark.

Lashinsky told the jury that his firm had made sixteen payments totaling more than twenty-five thousand dollars to one of the Florida corporations in return for state purchases of road-building materials. He also said he gave fifty thousand dollars in cash to Johnkoski at the State Road Commission offices in Charleston. Lashinsky said his written agreement with the Florida corporation required him to pay 8 percent of the face value of state contracts into this corporation. Later, he went on, Road Commissioner Sawyers told him to increase the kickback by an extra 5 percent and to pay it in cash to Johnkoski.

On another occasion this same supplier said that Gore advised him that three bids would be necessary in order to obtain a certain contract. Lashinsky said he told Gore he could "take care of that" and had three of his own firms submit bids.

During the second day of his testimony, Lashinsky stunned the court when he testified that he had also given Hulett Smith ten thousand dollars in cash as a "campaign contribution" and continued to make payments after Smith became governor. Payments like these were a practice of his, he noted, until the bribery indictment against the Secret Six was returned, when he was dropped from the state vendor list along with other suppliers mentioned in the indictment.

A wave of denials followed Lashinsky's appearance in court, including one from Smith, who said he received none of the alleged campaign contributions.

AFTER THE PROSECUTION completed its case, the defense attorneys surprised everyone by resting their case without offering any evidence. Instead, they moved for acquittal, arguing that the government had proved no wrongdoing on the part of their clients. The motion was denied.

During final arguments, the prosecution labeled the operation a scheme of "avarice, greed, and kickbacks," and contended that the citizens of West Virginia lost vast sums of money, including a hundred thousand dollars on the "emergency" purchase of centerline paint alone. The defense countered that the Florida enterprise had been a legitimate one to provide "expert service" to companies seeking state business, particularly those trying to cut through bureaucratic red tape.

The jury failed to buy the defense's argument. After two days of deliberation, some of it so heated that it could be heard outside the jury room, this body of twelve men and women returned to the courtroom with a verdict of guilty against Brown, Schroath, Johnkoski, and Sawyers. Barron was set free, and no decision was rendered on Gore. He was no longer a defendant in this particular case, thanks to his attorney's attack of shingles.

Following customary federal procedures, Judge Martin directed the probation service to prepare presentencing reports, and on October 4 he handed down the sentences. Brown and Schroath were each sentenced to four years in prison and fined five thousand dollars. Sawyers and Johnkoski were given terms of two years each and were required to pay five thousand dollars in fines.

In handing down the sentences, the judge stated that there was a "degree of difference in culpability" between the two sets of defendants.

Barron's day in court, however, was not over. After the trial, Ralph Buckalew, who had served as jury foreman, suddenly altered his lifestyle to such an extent that rumors about it found their way back to the newspapers—and to federal investigators. Buckalew quit his job at Union Carbide and resigned from the Dunbar City Council. He then went to work for Koscot Interplanetary Company, a cosmetics firm owned in part by former state Attorney General C. Donald Robertson, and began flashing money around town like one of the last of the big spenders.

Other jurors in the Invest Right case complained of Buckalew's volatile behavior as a juror and his churlish resistance to all efforts to agree to a guilty verdict, particularly for Barron. Balloting, one of the jurors told the *Gazette*, boiled down to an 11–1 deadlock, with Buckalew vowing to keep on voting against everybody else, even if they "remained there until they rotted." Tempers flared in the jury room, and Buckalew was accused by other jurors of having been "bought off."

As it turned out, this had in fact been the case. Almost two years later a new set of indictments was returned against Barron; his wife, Opal; Ralph Buckalew; and Brown by another grand jury charging them with jury tampering. Buckalew promptly pleaded guilty to accepting a twenty-five-thousand-dollar bribe and was sentenced to twenty years in prison by Southern District Court Judge John A. Field Jr.

Barron plea-bargained his wife out of the case—she was the one accused of actually handing over the bribe for Barron and Brown—but was himself given a prison sentence of twenty-five years by Field. Brown, considered a lesser offender, was given five years in addition to the original four-year sentence handed down in the previous case. Barron's sentence was later reduced to twelve years, plus a fifty-thousand-dollar fine.

Finally, on March 28, 1976, almost eight years after the first trial had begun, Gore entered a no-contest plea in an Arlington, Virginia, courtroom before Judge Oren Lewis and was sentenced to ninety days in prison. It was the same sentence Lewis had given in the Sawyers and Johnkoski case after their original convictions had been overturned by the Barron-Buckalew jury-tampering disclosure and the reindictment of the coconspirators.

Schroath had died in 1970 while appealing his conviction and never went to prison.

QUITE A BIT OF DIALOGUE was generated by the severity of the sentence meted out to Barron after the other defendants in the Invest Right case were given relatively light sentences. But in tampering with the jury process, Barron attempted to subvert one of the cornerstones of the American judicial system.

At some point during the development of our present legal system, there came the realization that participatory jurisprudence was required to provide a better guarantee of justice for the average person. Before that time, kings, princes, and noblemen had been the magistrates, and the judgment of innocence or guilt was often determined by the defendant's ability to endure torture.

Introduced into England by the Normans after the Conquest and expanded under Henry II, the jury system is believed to have been an important factor in establishing common law. It spread with the British Empire to regions of Africa, Asia, and the New World. In America, it grew in stature during the twentieth century while losing ground in other countries.

In the past there were certain property and competence requirements for jury service, but true random selection became the policy of the U.S. courts in 1969 after the Supreme Court ruled in *Duncan v. Louisiana* that, for a criminal case involving a sentence of more than six months, a jury trial was a constitutional right. This may not seem a benchmark ruling, but it was intended to address more than a century of southern oppression of African-Americans.

The federal courts promptly went to work on a restructuring of their entire jury process. They threw out the "Key Man" system, better known as the "Old Boy Network," and replaced it with a random selection process in which every citizen, regardless of race, color, creed, or net worth, would be eligible to serve on juries.

Implementation of the new procedure was tedious and time-consuming, but it promised an improved and more even-handed system of representation.

So conscientious were the drafters of the new procedures, so attentive to the spirit of the law, that, when it finally was put to work in federal courts all over America, it became known as the finest and most carefully crafted jury-selection system ever conceived.

When Barron conspired to undermine the jury process, he was dealt with severely for several reasons. Along with the mischief he caused, his crime generated widespread gossip and speculation concerning the possible complicity of court personnel in the tampering operation. But such tampering would have been virtually impossible. As anyone would know who had worked with the system, as I did for nineteen years, it has a series of safeguards built into it to prevent manipulation. Before a juror ever reaches a jury box, his name has been carried through four random selection procedures. If impropriety had occurred, it would have shown up in the records. But the rumors nonetheless built upon themselves and simply added to the gravity of the situation.

In handing down the sentence, Field also considered Barron's position as a former lawyer and officer of the court, sworn to uphold the law and certainly more aware of the importance of the jury process than the average layman. He also took into consideration Barron's past experience administering laws as a mayor, making laws as a state legislator, and enforcing laws as West Virginia's attorney general and, finally, governor.

Barron was given the maximum sentence.

For years after the dust had settled, estimates were bandied about concerning how much the Secret Six realized from their illicit ventures. The figures varied widely.

Governor Moore, at a special legislative session, placed the overall figure at more than $100 million. State Senator William T. Brotherton, cochairman of the State Purchasing Practices and Procedures Commission, said that the Moore estimate (of money both stolen and lost in inflated costs of goods and services procured by the state) was generally accurate. A federal source said, "It wasn't even half that—not even a quarter of it—but it still was a hell of a lot of money." And Barron's attorney, the by-then-disillusioned Perry, put the take at more than $7 million.

No one will ever know how much public money was skimmed off state contracts by this group. As one federal insider said, much of it wound up in secret bank accounts, some in Switzerland. The IRS retrieved what it could of the federal government's share, making the following findings in back taxes and penalties: Barron, $30,321; Brown, $76,000; Sawyers, $17,000; Johnkoski, $14,600; Gore, $14,500; and Schroath, $21,649.

An interesting sidebar to the case was the settlement agreed to by Barron and the IRS. Of the $20,214 sought in back taxes and $10,107 in fraud penalties, the settlement was fifteen thousand dollars. The significance of this settlement was that, by agreeing to it, Barron tacitly admitted that he had profited from the Invest Right conspiracy.

During a lunch break some time later, while he was hearing a case in Fairmont relating to a labor-management dispute, Judge Lewis expressed what he considered the epitaph to the whole sorry affair. He and I talked at some length about the trials and sentencings. Labeling it "white-collar" crime, Lewis said, "The amount of time men like that serve in prison isn't important. They're finished forever if they spend one day behind bars."

BROWN, AFTER SERVING HIS TIME, returned to Elkins and became a member of the management team at a hospital he had helped found in the 1950s. He was also active in civic affairs, his church, and the American Legion. Johnkoski went to work for a Huntington construction company. After suffering failing health for several years, he died at his St. Albans home in the fall of 1988. Sawyers went into virtual retirement in Charleston. Barron, who retired to Florida, returned quietly to West Virginia each summer for a vacation near Pipestem State Park. In Florida he played a lot of golf and became active in church affairs. Gore, who collected more indictments than any of his associates, fared very well. He settled back in Clarksburg after serving his brief prison sentence, re-involving himself in oil- and gas-well drilling and adding to his family's fortune. Always a big player in the stock market while in Charleston, he piled new money on top of old as the years wore on.

Chapter 22

WHY?

WHY DID A MAN with the breeding, education, and leadership abilities of William Wallace Barron allow one of the blackest pages in West Virginia history to be written while he was governor?

Barron's father was a Presbyterian minister and college president. His mother, the descendant of an old and affluent Baltimore family, traced her lineage back to Oliver Hazard Perry, one of America's early naval heroes. During Barron's youth, he never lacked the comforts that money and position can provide.

The first crack in the golden-boy image appeared when his brief marriage to his childhood sweetheart was quickly annulled. After graduating from Washington and Lee University and the West Virginia University College of Law, he became mayor of Elkins but reportedly spent more time drinking than looking after the city's affairs. In the practice of law he was more prone to sit and dream than to work, and he only made a living by serving as land commissioner, commissioner of accounts, and commissioner in chancery, the sinecures of his profession.

In 1950 Barron was elected to a seat in the House of Delegates. It was the beginning of a meteoric rise. In 1953 Governor Marland named him chairman of the Liquor Commission. Three years later Barron entered the race for the attorney general's office and won. Four years after that, in 1960, he ran successfully for governor. In ten years he had gone from the House chamber to the governor's office.

But further cracks appeared during that period. Two years after appointing Barron chairman of the Liquor Commission, Marland fired him. His performance as attorney general was much the same as it had been during his tenure as Elkins's mayor. He was considered long on charm but short on effectiveness and commitment.

During the primary race for governor, he allowed himself to be flown around the state by a known gambler and tried to buy one of his opponents, Orel Skeen, out of the race.

The general election campaign was even worse. Both Barron and his Republican opponent, Harold E. Neely, appeared so uninformed on the issues that the *Gazette* refused to endorse either candidate, saying only that, of the two, Barron's past exposure to public office made him, perhaps, the better choice.

But after the election, he changed remarkably. Taking the oath of office at midnight on January 8, 1961, with the explanation that he wanted to sign into law a penny increase in the consumers' sales tax to raise money to finance a public works program for the poor, Barron was off and running.

When he took the oath again at noon that day during the traditional inaugural ceremony, he launched a remarkable period of public service.

As he told listeners in his inaugural address, "There is a need for improvements in state institutions, roads, education, conservation, and a host of other fields of service to our people. These will be provided as speedily as feasible."

Pointing to poverty as the state's "overriding problem," Barron immediately initiated a series of meetings with the legislative leadership to explore ways of addressing the ills of unemployment.

With the new revenue that rolled in from the tax increases he managed to get through the legislature at the beginning of his administration, Barron was able to maintain sound fiscal balances every year of his term and to significantly reduce unemployment. He was further able to coax out of Washington many millions of dollars in defense contracts. During his term in office, new construction records were set by the Road Commission, strip-mine laws were strengthened, and a retirement system was established for state employees.

IN MANY RESPECTS, Barron served his state with a devotion seldom seen in the holders of that office, and he did it with daring and dedication. But after President Kennedy's assassination, Barron seemed to bank the fires of public commitment. He learned of the shooting on his way back from lunch, shortly after it took place. The next day, when I flew to Washington with a contingent of politicians and press to pay our respects, I could see how badly the governor had been shaken by this tragedy. He was heavy-hearted and quiet during the flight. Now and then he would muse aloud on the impact Kennedy's death would have on West Virginia's future and on the state's dealings with the White House.

Kennedy's death was both a personal and political loss for the governor. As he would later tell John Morgan during his interview for the book *West Virginia Governors*, "I think one thing that people have overlooked is the close relationship between me and John Kennedy. Actually people didn't know, and I never elaborated on it."

In the months following Kennedy's assassination, Barron developed a good working relationship with President Johnson, a relationship strengthened by the governor's efforts on regional development through his position as chairman of the Appalachian Governors' Conference.

But Barron was no longer the inspired leader he had been before Kennedy's death. He was more withdrawn, tending to look backward rather than forward and often choosing to remain at the Mansion instead of going to his office in the Statehouse.

As Barron wound down his term as governor, the old fires were rekindled when he helped mediate strikes at the FMC ordnance plant in South Charleston and Sterling Faucet Company in Morgantown. After Barron moved into the negotiations with his famed persuasive powers, both strikes came to an end. Otherwise, his administrative style became more that of a reclusive caretaker than an active leader.

In his last message to the legislature, he said, "My term is ending, but I am not saying goodbye. I will be available to help my state in every way possible." But he never got the chance. He was too busy answering charges against him in federal court.

IN 1979 BARRON LOOKED BACK reflectively at his nightmare in the courts and prison system. It was "hell and humiliation," he told Morgan.

Barron admitted to tampering with a federal jury, acknowledging that he had participated in a twenty-five-thousand-dollar payoff to the jury foreman and that he had entered into a plea-bargain agreement to remove his wife from the case. But he denied guilt on the conspiracy charges brought against him.

"I was not guilty in that trial," he said, "and I should have gone right through with it knowing that they couldn't have convicted me and made it stand." Yet try as he might, Barron wasn't able to provide a satisfactory answer to the question of why he agreed to pay a bribe if he was innocent of the charges against him.

He also left questions unanswered when admitting that he went to Boca Raton with the Invest Right crowd to look at business opportunities there. "I went down to Florida, and these fellows went with me."

He said the others had joined together in the Invest Right deal without consulting him. "What happened was that the others met, and I was over at the Mansion. And all of them came over and met with me and stated that this was what they felt like we should do."

He said he had heard rumors of dummy corporations on the fringes of government, but he avoided saying whether he had looked into their existence. Furthermore, there were the "share and share alike" agreements Barron and the others signed, which were introduced as evidence at the conspiracy trial. He had no clear-cut answer as to how they might have been executed without his knowledge.

This was the man who had developed a special rapport with two presidents, who had never during his years as governor lost a parliamentary battle with the legislature, and who had kept a tight rein on all facets of his administration throughout his term. Barron's denials strained public credulity. Too much had come out in the press and court records for him to sway the verdict in the court of public opinion.

No jury of his peers was more pitiless anywhere in the state than in the town where Barron was born.

Elkins has historically been a breeding ground for men of political ambition. It has been home to U.S. Senators Stephen B. Elkins, Henry Gassaway Davis, and Jennings Randolph, and Governors H. G. Kump and Barron. Elkins has even honored its notables with lasting memorials. The town itself was named for Senator Elkins. The college was named after Senators Davis and Elkins. A hospital and the Presbyterian Church carry Senator Davis's name. The federal building and an elementary school bear Senator Randolph's name, as did the D&E College library built in the 1960s. Governor Kump's portrait hangs in the Citizens National Bank where he served as president, a bridge is named for him, and Kumbrabow State Forest south of town is a memorial to his efforts on behalf of conservation.

Governor Barron's name was placed on the National Guard Armory in Elkins while he was still in office. It was a thank-you for services rendered, for making possible the construction of the armory, the four-lane highway between Elkins and Beverly, and Canaan Valley resort, one of West Virginia's most beautiful state parks in nearby Tucker County. But after Barron went to prison his name was unceremoniously removed from the armory façade. Not even those citizens who profited from state business while Barron was governor were heard to murmur a protest.

Is it possible that there was more to Invest Right than anyone suspected at the time? Was there another layer beyond the dummy corporations and suppliers' payoffs? Were some of the apparently unrelated activities that took place during the Barron administration actually pieces of a puzzle, clues to a larger picture?

Or is such speculation giving more credit to Barron and the Invest Right crowd than is due?

In his interview with Morgan for *West Virginia Governors*, Barron pointed to his close relationship with Kennedy, a relationship that he said went back to the primary election of 1960. It may have gone back further. Barron began putting together his political organization for the 1960 gubernatorial campaign while he was still attorney general. Kennedy already had his eye on the White House when he made his bid to become Adlai Stevenson's vice presidential running mate at the 1956 Democratic Convention. Although he lost out to Senator Kefauver, Kennedy made a strong impression and became an early favorite for the 1960 Democratic presidential nomination. He spent much of the period between 1956 and 1960 paying his political dues, fund-raising, and giving speeches, visiting dozens of states in the process, including West Virginia. Edward Kennedy visited the state at least as early as the fall of 1959 to begin drumming up support for his brother's primary campaign.

Barron also admitted to providing behind-the-scenes help to Kennedy during the 1960 election despite his pledge to back Humphrey. However, he told Morgan, "We didn't take any money from him [Kennedy]. We just supported him on the precinct level."

But if the Barron campaign was worried that such support "would offend Lyndon Johnson and the Hubert Humphrey people" if word got back to them, as Barron told Morgan, why help Kennedy at all? What did the Kennedy campaign have to offer Barron in exchange for his support?

Whether or not Barron's behind-the-scenes assistance was reciprocated during the campaign, after the election, Kennedy was generous in expressing his gratitude to the state that he credited with giving him his most important primary victory. While Barron was governor, more federal funds were funneled into West Virginia than at any other time during the state's first one hundred years. Many millions of dollars went to defense contracts; money for highways, park development, antipoverty and work-relief programs; funding for the new Green Bank radio astronomy center—the list went on and on. The Barron administration opened the state's first liaison office in Washington, DC. West Virginia prospered.

Invest Right Corporation was established on March 8, 1961, less than two months after Barron's inauguration. Although most of the corporation's officers were West Virginians, one of them was from Boca Raton, Florida. Boca, conveniently, was also the home of Edgar Lawson, a former West Virginia state official who happened to have a drawer full of inactive corporate charters.

Boca was located on Florida's Atlantic coast, forty-five miles above Miami and thirty miles below Palm Beach, where the Kennedy family had a home.

Legal counsel for many of Lawson's corporations was provided by Kenneth I. Van der Hulse of Stewart, Call, and Van der Hulse, the oldest law firm in West Palm Beach.

Other corporations followed the creation of Invest Right. In August 1961 the corporation's officers established First Southeastern Capital Corporation. First Southeastern's authority was broad, extending from manufacturing to the ownership and leasing of airplanes. Dixie Service Center was formed, purportedly, to operate a service station in Boca. Atlantic Management Corporation was authorized to acquire, hold, and manage property. Georgetown Homes Inc. was formed to develop real estate. Three of Invest Right's officers purchased an empty tract of beachfront property.

The assistant treasurer of Atlantic Management was one Joseph R. Evans, reportedly a former Army officer and retired CIA agent.

In April 1961, a group of 1,400 Cuban exiles, recruited and trained by the CIA, staged the ill-fated Bay of Pigs invasion. Nearly 1,200 of them were captured by Castro's forces. Beginning in May 1961, the Kennedy administration unofficially backed attempts to ransom the prisoners. According to Arthur M. Schlesinger Jr. in his book Robert Kennedy and His Times, Castro initially demanded five hundred heavy-duty D-8 Super Caterpillar bulldozers in exchange for the prisoners' release. Concerned that the bulldozers could be used to build missile bases and airfields, the committee negotiating the exchange, headed by former first lady Eleanor Roosevelt, offered farm tractors instead.

Castro then proposed a cash settlement of $28 million, the estimated value of the bulldozers. After New York attorney James B. Donovan, former counsel for the OSS, took over the negotiations, Castro eventually agreed to release the prisoners in exchange for millions of dollars in food, medicine, and machinery. According to Schlesinger, Castro's shopping list was detailed, extensive, and specific, running to ten thousand items. Although the U.S. government objected to some of the items on the list, claiming they had potential military uses, a settlement was eventually hammered out. The prisoners finally returned to the United States in December 1962.

Following the Bay of Pigs debacle, the Kennedy administration continued to support covert activities aimed at the overthrow of the Castro regime. By the fall of 1961, Operation Mongoose, the focal point of these efforts, was taking shape, according to Schlesinger, and continued in one form or another until at least early 1963.

When James Reston publicly revealed the government's "subversive war" against Cuba in his *New York Times* column in April 1963, however, the administration cracked down on the CIA-backed Cuban exile groups that had been sending saboteurs into Cuba "in small, fast boats, setting out from the Bahamian keys, sometimes from Florida itself," according to Schlesinger. The FBI seized caches of dynamite, bomb casings, and other materiel from exile groups in Miami, and a number of Cubans were indicted.

Schlesinger claimed that many of the operations attributed to the Cuban exile groups were actually "planned and conducted under the supervision of the CIA." He also quoted a paratrooper assigned to the CIA who maintained that, even while the FBI was conducting its raids on the Cuban exile camps, "CIA/Miami . . . received orders to 'increase the effectiveness and frequency of hit-and-run raids by exile commando groups.'" The administration's secret war against Cuba continued.

It all came to a crashing halt with the assassination of Kennedy six months later in November 1963. The entire nation went into mourning, and West Virginia's governor seemed to take Kennedy's death especially hard. After spending the state's centennial year acting as a kind of goodwill ambassador and master of ceremonies, delivering patriotic speeches wherever he went, Barron became a recluse, rarely leaving the Mansion even for official business.

Many questions remained unanswered after the trial of Barron and his associates in the Invest Right scheme. Many aspects of the affair seemed peculiar: Why did all the operations of the Invest Right crowd, most of them West Virginians, seem to be centered in Boca Raton, Florida? What were their reasons for creating a corporation that was authorized to own and lease airplanes? Why did they decide to invest in a service station in Boca, a business that would easily justify the purchase of large quantities of fuel with no questions asked? Why did they buy a tract of empty beachfront property?

Such property, of course, probably seemed a good investment, perfect for future development. It also happened to provide handy access to the Atlantic Ocean.

Why was a retired Army officer and former CIA agent involved with these dubious corporate schemes?

Why and how did Woodrow Yokum, a state employee and a resident of a Randolph County town not far from Barron's hometown of Elkins, acquire an unusual assortment of military surplus materiel including the aforementioned fire truck, Navy assault boats, and miles of copper wire? While he would seem to have had little or no personal use for most of the items, and while they would have had limited resale value, much of the collection he assembled would have been quite useful in sabotage operations or to an invasion force.

Was there any connection between the Invest Right affair and Yokum, who was defended at trial by Brown, Barron's former law partner and associate in the Invest Right scheme?

Were any of Yokum's acquisitions included on that detailed shopping list Castro presented to Donovan?

Why and how did records considered important to the federal government's prosecution of the case against Yokum disappear from files at the West Virginia State Capitol?

Might some of the millions of dollars funneled into West Virginia during the Kennedy administration have been intended for other than the publicly stated purpose? Might some of that money have quietly found its way into the acquisition of surplus government property or other activities of Invest Right and its successor corporations, activities undertaken in support of the administration's "secret war" against Castro?

Did Barron, a man known for preaching patriotism, and Brown, an officer of his American Legion post, believe that they were performing a patriotic duty, assisting their government in a backdoor enterprise, once again providing behind-the-scenes support to the Kennedys as they had during the West Virginia primary election?

Was there more to the Invest Right scheme than met the eye?

Or, again, is this giving those involved undue credit for something that was nothing more than petty greed, graft, and corruption?

If the dummy corporations were at least in part a cover and a conduit for clandestine operations undertaken at the behest of the Kennedy administration, the president's assassination in November 1963 would have put an end to those activities and halted the flow of money. With a new president in office, the administration's protection of the enterprise and those involved would likely have ended as well. The Invest Right crowd was on its own. If they truly were involved with the administration's covert operations against Cuba, the government was unlikely to openly acknowledge it. If any problems arose, they would be expected to fall on their swords. It was no wonder Barron appeared so badly shaken by Kennedy's death. The ramifications of such a situation would certainly have contributed to the apparent depression he suffered near the end of his term.

If Invest Right and its sister corporations were ever anything more than a convenient means of laundering suppliers' payoffs, Barron never revealed it. Nor did any of the others involved, although probably not all of them were aware of the full extent of the enterprise, if such were the case. Even at their trial, Barron, Brown, and those indicted with them offered no defense for their actions. But what could they say? What evidence could they present? By August 1968 both Kennedy and his brother, former Attorney General Robert Kennedy, had been killed by assassins' bullets.

Chapter 23

JUDICIAL REMEDY

WEST VIRGINIA'S LAWMAKERS sat up and took notice after Barron and his friends were indicted on Valentine's Day 1968. At the Statehouse, the legislature, and the governor's office, both went to work on corrective measures. Governor Smith, unhappy to find the image of his "Administration of Excellence" soiled by the indictment of three of his top officials, appointed a Citizens Advisory Group to undertake a comprehensive study of purchasing procedures. The legislature, agreeing that substantive changes were needed, made several recommendations to the governor by joint action of its interim study committees during a special session in September 1968.

This was followed by a resolution that authorized the formation of the Purchasing Practices and Procedures Commission. In a meeting at the South Hills home of House Finance Committee Chairman Ivor Bioarsky, the framework for the PPPC was worked out by Bioarsky, House Speaker H. Laban White, and Delegate Carmine Cann, the latter two from Clarksburg. House Minority Leader George Seibert, of Wheeling, was the strongest Republican supporter of the effort, while William T. Brotherton, of Charleston, served as the Senate's point man on behalf of ailing Senate President Howard Carson, who was from Fayetteville.

The PPPC was a unique creation, the first of its kind in the country. Its mission was to end purchasing improprieties and irregularities, and to make skimming operations so offensive a practice that to even be tempted would be akin to mugging your crippled grandmother. Supporters said the new commission, when fully in place, would center its work initially on those businessmen who had made payments to Invest Right and its sister corporations, and would branch out into other areas as time and appropriated funds would permit.

"If there was testimony a businessman bribed somebody to do business with the state, why shouldn't his record be examined?" Brotherton asked in pushing for passage of the new act. "Business people are entitled to know it's not the way of life to buy your way into contracts or by kicking back. The honest businessman should be protected."

The new commission consisted of five members each from the Senate and the House, with Brotherton and Boiarsky serving as cochairmen. Headquarters for the new body were set up in the Statehouse, and a special team of seasoned investigators was recruited. White's choice for top gun was John P. Duiguid. The commission's determination to ferret out crooked practices and thievery was poetically illustrated by the very choice of Duiguid, whose name was pronounced "do good" when spelled either forward or backward. He had served in the Rackets Division at the U.S. Justice Department before joining a prestigious Washington law firm.

According to Boiarsky, sometime after the Duiguid team began its work, the PPPC adopted a "hands-off" policy. Oversight became its only purpose.

"We felt we shouldn't even know what was going on," he explained. "That way, nobody could say it was a political whitewash or a political vendetta."

The commission's charter called for it not only to look into the purchasing mess at the Statehouse but to spread out across the state and determine whether conditions were as bad in the provinces as they were in Charleston. This included federal and local as well as state agencies. Eventually it was determined that the commission was in need of more exacting authority, so on March 11, 1971—coincidentally, my fifty-seventh birthday—the PPPC was made a statutory body. Among those endorsing the legislation was Smith's successor, Governor Moore.

The Justice Department's Law Enforcement Assistance Administration was so impressed with the commission's work that during its first two years of existence, $423,122 in federal money was poured into the commission's operations. This additional funding helped it to expand its investigatory work across the state, improve its intelligence filing system to make it compatible with the system maintained by the Criminal Identification Bureau of the Department of Public Safety, and to begin gathering data on narcotics and organized crime.

One of the commission's stopover points on crime tracking forays around the state was the U.S. District Court for Northern West Virginia. After making arrangements for the meeting, Duiguid and his staff members came to Wheeling where a session of court was in progress. While Duiguid spoke with Judge Maxwell about the court's excellent record on organized crime and narcotics control, two of his assistants spent some time talking with me about my part in the Invest Right investigations and the work I had left unfinished when I moved from the *Gazette* to the court.

THE PPPC WENT ABOUT ITS WORK quietly after setting up shop, methodically collecting information for presentation to grand juries.

Following the return of federal indictments against Barron and his associates in 1968 on charges of bribery and conspiracy, the PPPC sent a report to the legislature that stated, in part:

> . . . *An awareness of the extent to which governmental corruption ran in West Virginia gradually emerged. During the course of the trial that resulted from these indictments, not only were some of the many and varied types of corrupt practices exposed—the rake-offs and kickbacks, the influence peddling, rigged bidding and undercover deals—but also the appalling truth that West Virginia and West Virginians stood virtually helpless in the face of such insidious practices. There was no arm of state government authorized to detect and prosecute these crimes, much less one capable of preventing them. In ever-widening circles it had become a part of the "system" to do business with the state by making deals with and bribing influential officials. Although often considered to be a "victimless" crime, corruption in procurement victimizes all of the citizens of the state . . . through higher taxes. There is virtually no method by which a value can be placed on this loss, but one can safely say that in a democracy, a government dependent upon its citizens, the loss is extreme.*

ON JANUARY 6, 1970, the PPPC went public with the results of their efforts. A Kanawha County grand jury released 107 indictments against thirty-two individuals and eleven corporations on charges of bribery and conspiracy involving state purchasing practices.

Among those indicted were Barron and Gore. Other prominent Democrats caught up in the commission's net were former State Welfare Commissioner W. Bernard Smith (no relation to Governor Smith) who was then a state senator, and J. Howard Myers, Senate clerk, who was a former chairman of the State Democratic Executive Committee and the business community's candidate for governor in 1956.

The grand jury noted in its report that it failed to act on four additional indictments because it ran out of time. Kanawha County Prosecutor Patrick W. Casey commented, "The work is not going to stop," adding that another grand jury would be summoned to hear the other cases.

"We have a great deal of additional information," Duiguid said. "There were only so many days this grand jury could meet and only so much the jury could consider. I think there is a need for additional grand juries."

Casey said he was reluctant to give out details about any of the charges mentioned in the indictments, reasoning that he might accidentally prejudice a defendant's chances for a fair trial. But where Casey was hesitant about discussing the cases, others were not. They filled in details for *Gazette* reporter Don Marsh, who later became editor of the paper.

Generally speaking, it was explained that the 107 indictments did not duplicate evidence already presented at the original trial of Barron and his associates. Some of the indictments were based on actions that had taken place as far back as 1961, while others were alleged to have occurred as recently as 1969. According to Marsh's information, the bulk of the charges were based on conditions and incidents between 1965 and 1969, the period of Smith's stewardship as governor.

Barron, for example, was indicted on the basis of allegations concerning his actions after he left office and began devoting much of his law practice to representing companies and individuals seeking state business. Gore, also cited on various bribery and conspiracy charges, had remained in the Smith administration as a holdover until he was swept up with his friends in the Invest Right indictments and Smith suspended him.

THESE 107 INDICTMENTS lasted only long enough to send another shock wave through the mountains of West Virginia. In a surprise move, the State Supreme Court handed down three decisions that practically wiped out the Duiguid team's first effort at crime control. The only person left with a court battle on his hands was Senator Smith. The court's opinions held the conspiracy law unconstitutional and limited the bribery statute to constitutional and elective officers.

Speaking for the majority in the first case, brought in the appellate court by Myers against Intermediate Court Judge George W. Wood, Justice Thornton Berry said, "There is no question but that there was a common law crime of criminal conspiracy . . . " But, he added, "The Intermediate Court of Kanawha County does not have jurisdiction to proceed with the trial of the petitioner under the six indictments returned by the grand jury . . . by virtue of the fact that all of the indictments are based on an unconstitutional statute."

Justice Harland Calhoun, the lone dissenting voice on the court, said in rebuttal, "It is my view that the court, without any clear duty to do so, but with devastating and far-reaching consequences, invalidated the six felony indictments involved in this case . . . on a technical basis relating merely to the sufficiency of the title of the act of the legislature . . . "

In the other two cases the court split 3–2, with Berry joining Calhoun in opposing the majority viewpoint. The majority opinion, written by Justice Chauncey Browning, held that the bribery statute applied only to constitutional offices and those created by law. The statute's power, the court ruled, did not extend to the many employees of every department of state government who handled millions of dollars worth of purchases. Joining in the majority position in all three cases were Justices Frank C. Haymond and Fred Caplan.

Browning said, "Inasmuch as the petitioner is not an 'executive and ministerial officer of the State of West Virginia,' as alleged in the indictment, and inasmuch as this is a necessary element of the crime purportedly charged, then it logically follows that no crime has been charged in either indictment."

Calhoun said in his dissent, "The court has strayed from fundamental legal principles in relation to the jurisdiction of the trial court, the jurisdiction of this court and the function and scope of prohibition as a judicial remedy."

The *Gazette*, which in earlier years would not as a matter of policy comment on Supreme Court opinions, made its feelings known editorially:

> *One does not need a law degree to understand Judge Harlan Calhoun's incredulity that his colleagues on the State Supreme Court of Appeals would almost blithely dismiss indictments against persons accused of bribery and conspiracy in obtaining state business . . . Calhoun's dissent, buttressed by cases and precedents, are heartening to those laymen who disagree with the court's majority. Calhoun has shown that on purely legalistic grounds arguments exist opposing the ruling . . . Judges of the West Virginia court knew of the larger issues inherent in these cases . . . Yet these are the men who ignored a substantive body of law, common sense and public concern as they marched unerringly to the sweeping technicalities that would benefit only the guilty.*

THE SUPREME COURT HANDED DOWN its decisions in mid-July. Less than a month later Wood bent to the higher court's will and voided most of the indictments, which in effect meant that none of the accused could ever be tried again on these charges. The only person who would go to trial was Senator Smith, who had been accused of accepting a bribe from Ray George, a Charleston office-equipment dealer.

Senator Smith's trial was a major media event when it got underway a few days after the Supreme Court's historic ruling. Although testimony revealed a scheme by George to bribe Finance Commissioner Gore, Purchasing Director Curtis Wilson and Senator Smith, who was alleged to have joined George in putting the deal together, the jury failed to reach a verdict.

The case was rescheduled for trial a few months later but again resulted in a hung jury.

Not until Senator Smith was tried for election fraud a year later, along with four of his Logan County political associates, would he be convicted and sent to prison.

Even Gore's testimony at Senator Smith's bribery trial failed to sway the jury. Gore, along with George and Wilson, admitted to the payment of a fifteen-thousand-dollar bribe on a $150,000 equipment purchase, but the jury was unconvinced. Senator Smith's lawyer centered his client's defense on the immunity granted George and Wilson in exchange for their testimony and on the alleged immunity granted Gore, arguing that this made their testimony suspect. When Gore appeared as a witness in the Senator Smith case, he was still under indictment both in the Invest Right conspiracy and by the Kanawha County grand jury impaneled to hear the information presented by the Duiguid team's investigators. He was an easy target for a sharp lawyer.

But as time proved all too well, Gore was in a no-lose situation regardless of what was revealed during Senator Smith's trial. Despite the number of indictments returned against him in federal and state courts—twenty-two in all—he eventually entered a no-contest plea and was sentenced to only ninety days in federal prison.

IN ITS 1972 REPORT to the legislature, the PPPC addressed the nullifying action of the Supreme Court. "These indictments were but a few of the cases under investigation at the time," the report said, "but the legal consequences of the decision was to render the others non-prosecutable, thereby insulating yet undisclosed subjects at most levels of government employment from prosecution."

The PPPC had also taken its findings relating to alleged irregularities in prison-industry management at the state penitentiary at Moundsville to a Marshall County grand jury. That jury returned no indictments but noted that conditions at the penitentiary were in such disarray that the operation should be either reformed or abolished. This investigation was also wiped out by the Supreme Court's decision.

"One shudders to think of the damage the court's action does to confidence in government," the *Gazette* editorialized. "Already it is almost an article of faith that politicians and their associates are not to be punished for misdeeds in West Virginia."

Browning's son—Chauncey Jr., the state attorney general—moved to action by the high court's crippling of the PPPC's first big investigation, announced in a prepared press statement less than a week later that he would begin procedures to bring suit to recover money lost to the state as a result of bribery and corruption.

Browning said that while criminal prosecution was no longer possible in many cases, the opportunity still existed under the laws to file civil suits and collect damages. "It should be made perfectly clear," he stated, "that, in my opinion, those businessmen, as well as state employees directly connected, are subject to civil liability for any improper, illegal, or fraudulent transactions involving funds belonging to the State of West Virginia."

Shortly after the Supreme Court's action, Moore, who by this time had succeeded Governor Smith, called for a special legislative session. The loopholes in the law uncovered by the rulings needed attention, he said, and he immediately summoned the lawmakers to Charleston to correct the shortcomings.

At the time, Moore himself was under fire from national columnist Jack Anderson for allegedly diverting eighty thousand dollars in political contributions for personal use. Moore denied the charge and said he wanted to underscore his political integrity by tightening the laws that left the door open to official mischief.

The legislation was passed and, according to the PPPC, gave West Virginia the best purchasing procedures in the country. "With proper enforcement of this statute," the PPPC said, "the people of the state will be assured that their officials and employees are working for them, not for themselves."

The operative phrase, of course, was "with proper enforcement."

Despite these damage-control measures—Attorney General Browning's promise of civil suits and the legislature's reform laws—the high court's rulings had effectively halted the effort to clean up the purchasing improprieties of the past. The momentum was lost, and the outcry for reform slowly died down.

Still, some progress was made. The PPPC turned in a praiseworthy performance record during its first two years. It assisted local enforcement agencies in their fight against narcotics and organized crime. It helped the Welfare Department initiate civil action for the recovery of ninety-five thousand dollars in overpayments to a hospital. It also aided the Purchasing Division in pulling together the documentation needed to suspend a law-breaking vendor.

Justice Department investigators carried on the work that the PPPC could not. The PPPC cooperated with federal law-enforcement agencies in putting together cases against former State Attorney General C. Donald Robertson and Treasurer John Kelly.

Robertson pleaded guilty to bribery-conspiracy in the handling of Federal Housing Authority funds; Kelly, to extorting money from bankers and financiers. Trent, Elmore, and Fred Wilmoth (Barron's friend of many years) all went to prison for income tax evasion. Others caught up in the Justice Department's inquiry were Assistant Attorney General Marshall West and a divisional head of the Tax Department, Clarence Tinsley.

But perhaps the most exemplary effect of the PPPC's work was the change of attitude it prompted among those handling the purchase of supplies and services for the state and those doing business with the state. Marsh wrote about this condition in the citation for the *Gazette*'s 1970 "West Virginian of the Year" award, presented that year to Brotherton: "The [107] indictments had the effect of concentrating the minds of both buyers and sellers of state services on the hitherto unsuspected possibility that they might go to jail for stealing—an unheard of concept. Proof is in the pudding—or, in this case, in the purchasing."

He then observed, after reviewing statistical data from state records, that during the years when Barron and Smith held the governorship, the amount of money spent on goods and services and the number of companies providing those goods and services shot sharply upward. After the PPPC was formed, a marked change occurred. "The drop in purchasing was dramatic," he wrote.

"If the figures mean what many people think," Marsh added, "the amount of money that was spent illegally, or needlessly at best, was at least 100 million dollars."

There was also the suspicion, he continued, that during the same period "more than 3,000 dummy companies—businesses existing on paper only, formed exclusively for the purpose of finagling the state out of money" were granted authority under existing purchasing regulations.

In an interview with Marsh, Brotherton talked at some length about how business was done with the state during those years. In the selling of furniture, he said, "it looks as if there was an agreement [among suppliers] to divide the state into regions."

Printers, he went on, would bid on certain types of printing because none of them was large enough to handle major contracts alone. And some suppliers grew so fat during this period, he added, that they shielded their profits by sending them to banks in the Bahamas. "When the Supreme Court threw out the indictments, they hurt us very badly," Brotherton added sadly.

Years later, after serving as Senate president and as chief justice of the State Supreme Court, Brotherton was still embittered by the damage done to the Duiguid team's efforts. He also remained disappointed at the legislature's failure to address another problem he considered important.

Convinced that crime and corruption of the sort that had recently plagued the state was contagious, Senator Brotherton advocated the authorization of the office of statewide prosecutor to serve as a watchdog over illegality in county and local government.

All too many public officials, he said, were "turning their heads" away from crime "which they know exists in many parts of the state." In his opinion, a kind of super-prosecutor was needed, a prosecutor invested with powers that had been removed from the attorney general in the 1930s, powers the county prosecutors were reluctant to use. But Brotherton's proposal found few supporters among his fellow lawmakers.

After the Supreme Court's fateful rulings on the 107 indictments, the *Daily Mail* commented, in discussing the change of attitude regarding state purchasing practices, that "the mass of indictments returned would have thrown a scare into everyone handling the state's money at the Statehouse and elsewhere."

Scare became the operative word in state purchasing oversight. What was originally the Purchasing Practices and Procedures Commission evolved into the Commission on Special Investigations. While the successive body lacked the vigor and dedication of its predecessor, Brotherton believed that the quality of administrative management improved simply as a result of its existence.

MISCELLANY ⚬ "CAN'T WE BE FRIENDS?"

IN THE REORGANIZATION OF THE HOUSE OF DELEGATES after Smith's election as governor, White was in a tight race with Bioarsky for the position of Speaker.

Smith called the two contenders and their supporters together at his home in Beckley to determine whether the apparent deadlock could be broken. Out of that informal gathering came the consensus that would elect White Speaker and make Bioarsky Finance Committee chairman.

White and Boiarsky worked well together, as was later confirmed by their decision to join in creating the PPPC. Another important piece of legislation passed during their tenure called for annual audits of the Highway Department. Previously, there had been no outside review of the many millions of dollars spent on road building and maintenance.

In talking later about that evening at Governor Smith's house when the compromise between Boiarsky and White was hammered out, Boiarsky, a better than average pianist, confessed, "I spent most of my time playing the piano while the others talked in the next room."

Among the songs he played was "Can't We Be Friends?"

Chapter 24

Moore Controversies

Arch Alfred Moore became the third member of the 1952-53 House of Delegates to ascend to the state's highest elective office. As West Virginia's twenty-eighth governor, he followed former delegates Underwood and Barron into the chief executive's suite.

Underwood's path had been direct; he went straight from the House to the governor's office. Barron made his move in stages, by way of the Liquor Commission and attorney general's office. Moore detoured to Washington for six terms as a U.S. congressman before running for governor.

Although Barron, a Democratic governor, supported Moore, a Republican, during his gubernatorial campaign, Moore sought neither the advice nor support of his predecessors after the election. Elected governor the same year that Richard Nixon, also a Republican, became president, Moore was in high clover. The state's economy was sound. He inherited a balanced budget. Barron and Smith had bequeathed him enough road bond authority to continue the highway modernization program they had launched. There was also enough revenue on hand or available through new taxation to improve the state's education system, provide health-care insurance and pay raises for state employees, begin a statewide kindergarten program, increase workers' compensation payments, and fatten unemployment and public-welfare checks. No governor since Patteson had been as well-positioned fiscally to improve governmental services, and no governor in state history had had such unrestrained budgetary power. The Modern Budget Amendment was ratified in the same election that put Moore in the governor's office, shifting budgetary control from the Board of Public Works to the governor.

Yet where Patteson and Barron had both cultivated an atmosphere of collegiality and compromise with the legislature on sensitive and controversial issues, Moore was a hard-liner. He vetoed more legislation than any previous governor. When he couldn't win with a veto, he often took his differences to the Supreme Court. The Statehouse became a legal battleground during Moore's years as governor.

Despite this argumentative atmosphere, two years after Moore took office, lawmakers again passed legislation placing gubernatorial succession on the ballot. Barron had been unsuccessful in even getting the issue through the legislature, while Smith had lost on the succession question in the polling booth, but Moore was able to leap both hurdles in his bid for reelection. During his first term, the legislature also gave him the authority to issue revenue bonds for the construction of a science and culture center—an idea that had been floating around since the early 1960s—passed tax legislation that Moore wanted, and authorized a second medical school at Marshall University and a school of osteopathic medicine at Lewisburg, both ideas supported by the governor. Moore was tough in combat. He sometimes got bruised in a close encounter, but he was resilient and tenacious, and he got things done. He was able to commit more than a billion dollars to highway modernization alone during his first term in office.

MOORE CAME FROM A STAUNCH Republican family with strong political interests. His grandfather on his father's side had been mayor of Moundsville, and his uncle, Everett F. Moore, had been minority leader and a long-serving member of the House of Delegates. Moore himself had been an overachiever from early youth. While growing up in Moundsville he had a paper route, worked as an usher at a movie theater, and, during his last year in high school, worked an eight-hour shift in a local factory. He attended Lafayette College and West Virginia University, and at both institutions he won office in service and social clubs.

During World War II Moore served as a combat soldier in Europe, where he was severely wounded. Shot in the face, he spent a long time recuperating in an Army hospital, trying to regain his ability to speak. Later in political life one of his greatest assets would be his talent for public speaking and his ability to woo an audience with his almost evangelical style. He was one of the best orators ever to serve in West Virginia public office.

This ability paid off handsomely during his 1962 race for First District congressman. Due to a realignment of the congressional districts, Moore found himself pitted against a seasoned public figure, Congressman Cleveland M. Bailey. Bailey's age became an issue during his campaign against the youthful Moore, and the congressman's tendency to fall asleep on the platform during speaking engagements gave Moore additional ammunition. To overcome this handicap, the Democratic leadership brought out the big guns, sending its most notable personalities into the state to campaign for Bailey, among them President Kennedy, Vice President Johnson, and former President Truman. Moore still won by thirty-two thousand votes—quite a coup for a Republican in an overwhelmingly Democratic state—and Bailey never again ran for public office.

My brother Charley often talked about Moore's boundless energy and ambition. He and Arch were good friends during their years at WVU, as were the young ladies each would later marry. Charley, like Moore, saw a lot of action as an infantryman during the war, but Moore came back from the war fired with determination to make his mark on the world. My brother had his own ambitions, but his was a gentler personality. The dynamic Moore seemed bothered by what he perceived as Charley's lack of passion and purpose, and he would try to shift Charley into higher gear with advice and good-natured argument. Despite their differences in personal style, however, both would prove highly successful in their chosen fields.

REVELATIONS OF GOVERNMENT CORRUPTION during the Barron and Smith administrations were of obvious benefit to Moore in his campaign for governor. But as news stories bore out, he had his own skeletons in the closet from his years as an attorney and congressman, and controversy dogged him throughout the campaign.

Stories surfaced concerning a 1967 court hearing during which Moore allegedly testified that his law practice had declined to "zero," although at the time he was listed in a law directory as counsel for seven major corporations. His primary election opponent, former Governor Underwood, raised questions about a four-hundred-thousand-dollar tax cut that he said Moore had obtained for a corporate client. The tax reduction was defended by state Tax Commissioner Thomas Battle, who explained that the corporation in question was not only entitled to the reduction but was due a substantial tax refund as well.

Not long before the primary, a land deal involving Moore became another election issue. According to a news story, in 1967 Moore had purchased property in Marshall and Wetzel counties from three parties who had inherited equal interest in the land. He then sold it to Mobay Chemical Company for a twelve-thousand-dollar profit. The story, citing courthouse records, claimed that one of the heirs, a mentally incompetent person, received seven thousand dollars less than either of the other owners when Moore purchased the property. Moore promptly labeled the story a smear, maintaining that the money had been distributed in a manner approved by the court.

When questions were raised about his income tax returns, Moore produced a statement indicating that his congressional salary for the period in question, 1957–67, had amounted to $98,925 after expenses of $169,075 were deducted; income from his law practice during the same period had netted $85,047, following the deduction of expenses totaling $102,425. Reporters, however, were frustrated by Moore's refusal to release copies of his actual tax returns, a practice common to other politicians.

As the fall campaign heated up, conflicting reports surfaced regarding Moore's actions as executor of an estate that had remained unsettled for six years. In October Moore completed the transfer of assets to the designated heirs, but a Marshall County commissioner of accounts charged that Moore had failed to file the required annual statement of accounts for the estate. The county court chose to table the issue until after the November election.

Moore was a tough campaigner, and in the 1968 primary he whipped Underwood by almost thirty thousand votes. In the general election runoff, he enlisted the support of Barron and his band of disloyalists. Barron's staff helped pull together the information for the news story criticizing Moore's opponent, James Sprouse, which later resulted in a libel suit against *The*

Charleston Daily Mail and a $375,000 court judgment. Moore also characterized Sprouse as "born and bred at the breast of the Statehouse machine." These tactics paid off. Although the Democratic Party held an almost two-to-one margin in voter registration, Moore won the general election by nearly thirteen thousand votes.

SHORTLY AFTER TAKING OFFICE, the new governor faced one of the same problems that had plagued the Meadows, Patteson, and Barron administrations: labor-management strife. One of Moore's first actions was to issue executive orders freezing jobs and purchases and placing state agencies' financial commitments on hold. He told the legislature that he planned to make "appropriate audits of every activity in which state government is involved or in which the tax dollars of our citizens are being and have been spent."

Frustrated by Smith's order placing two thousand employees in five state agencies under the umbrella of civil service, Moore chose to take the issue all the way to the State Supreme Court, which eventually upheld Smith's action. Less than two months after the inauguration, employees of the Highway Department, seeking the right to union representation, walked off the job. After nine days, during which heavy snows made some of the state's roads virtually impassable, Moore fired 2,627 road workers. They took their grievances right into the reception room of the governor's office to make their point, and more than a thousand later massed on the Capitol grounds for a "March on Arch." The demonstrations continued, making state and national headlines, and may have helped prompt Moore's agreement to meet with union representatives. The meeting, however, failed to bring about a resolution. Approximately five hundred strikers eventually drifted back to work, and Moore directed his highway commissioner to hire new employees to fill the gap left by those still on strike.

During his third year in office, a nationwide coal strike erupted across the American landscape. When it continued to drag on with no signs of ending and the West Virginia economy began to suffer, Moore moved into the negotiations. Like Barron and Smith before him, Moore had a great deal of personal charm, and his persuasive powers paid a dividend. Both the UMW and the coal operators gave him credit for playing a major role in settling the strike. That same year, he put the Public Service Commission to work on resolving another strike, this one involving the Charleston Transit Company. The strike came to an end after fifty-four days, but for a while the state operated the city's bus system.

MOORE, ALWAYS A NEWSMAKER in West Virginia, found himself the subject of national news stories midway through his first term when a report appeared in the Charlotte *Observer* charging that the "White House is seriously considering recommendations for income tax prosecution against . . . Moore . . . " The White House press office denied knowledge of any case against the governor. Two months later the story reared its head again when syndicated columnist Jack Anderson elaborated on the subject, tying Moore to the alleged misuse of eighty thousand dollars in campaign contributions. Moore called the column a "fabrication."

After Anderson published a second story on the same subject, the governor labeled him "a muckraking liar" and issued a statement saying, "You are witnessing a deliberately calculated campaign to equate your governor and his administration with the policies of the past." Calling attention to the fact that the State Supreme Court had recently ruled that West Virginia's bribery statutes were badly flawed, he pledged to call a special legislative session to close this escape hatch.

The conspiracy, bribery, and corruption laws were all revised during that special session, but the effort failed to silence Anderson. He wrote that Moore was seeking a tax refund check so he could "wave it around West Virginia as evidence that he had overpaid rather than underpaid his taxes." About a month later the *Daily Mail* said it had been informed that Moore "had an income tax problem of some magnitude." Soon afterward the Associated Press reported that a tax case against Moore "appears headed for rejection by the Justice Department."

The most tragic event of his first term in office was the now-infamous disaster along Buffalo Creek in Logan County. On a rainy night in 1972 an unlicensed waste-water impoundment at a Pittston Company coal mine broke through its dam. Coal-blackened water poured down the mountain, washing away a string of mining towns and leaving a known 125 people dead and four thousand homeless. The legislature appropriated one million dollars in emergency relief funds, and the U.S. Army Corps of Engineers began a massive cleanup effort. In addition to the human misery it created, the Buffalo Creek tragedy became yet another sad and ugly chapter in the history of government mismanagement, although a different governor had succeeded to office by the time the full story came to light.

Moore was busy that year traveling around the state, making speeches and cutting ribbons in preparation for a historic test that loomed on the horizon. He was the first governor since the state's creation who could succeed himself in office, and he wanted to be ready for the challenge. The primary campaign would be no problem. The governor's was the only name on the Republican ballot. His real battle would be in the general election where he would face off against a rising star of the Democratic Party, then-Secretary of State John D. Rockefeller IV.

Rockefeller was a man of vast wealth. He had worked in the state's coalfields as a VISTA volunteer and had served in the West Virginia House of Delegates. His political image was free of the impediments that collect around so many figures in public life. Rockefeller was regarded as a tough foe for Moore, but his name and birthplace created a problem for him. He had been born in New York, and Moore's characterization of him as a carpetbagger hurt him in the West Virginia backcountry. Rockefeller also hurt his own chances when he advocated the abolition of strip-mining in order to protect the environment. Too many West Virginia jobs and too much money depended on strip-mining. By election day it was no contest. Moore beat Rockefeller by 73,355 votes.

FOUR YEARS AS GOVERNOR had failed to mellow Moore. During his second term he continued to exercise his veto power more often than any previous governor. He continued to quarrel with the legislature and rail at the press. He even tried to bend the law by running for a third term. Only the U.S. Supreme

Court was able to make him realize that absolute sovereignty rested not with the governor but with the electorate.

Moore was a mountain original. He not only built more roads than any other governor before him, but he also erected a monument to himself. He chose to interpret both the Constitution and state code in his own distinctive and sometimes fanciful fashion and, when challenged, vociferously argued the rightness of his cause. He seemed to have a compulsive urge to build. The medical school at Marshall University and the osteopathic school in Lewisburg were not the only construction projects he spearheaded. The Cultural Center was also his creation, complete with its prominently displayed bronze bust of Moore. He built so many interstate and corridor roads that he surpassed Patteson's record as the "road buildingest governor in history." This spirited program of road construction was made easier for him by the ratification of a $500 million road bond issue, the biggest in history, shortly after his second term began. Together with the bond authority bequeathed him by the Barron and Smith administrations and the federal money directed to the state by the Republican Nixon administration, Moore had all the funds he needed for highway construction. New revenue sources opened by the legislature also raised the general revenue budget to twice what it had been when Moore first took office.

But the governor also spent an inordinate amount of his second term answering challenges from law enforcement agencies and delivering counterpunches to prying reporters. His decision to deposit $23 million in federal revenue-sharing funds in Charleston and Huntington banks, rather than follow conventional practice by routing the money through the state treasurer's office, set off a storm of protest from members of the legislature. Treasurer John Kelly went as far as the Supreme Court to try to gain control of the money. Although Moore strenuously objected, the court agreed with Kelly.

Reports about Moore's alleged income tax problems reappeared in the *Washington Post*, which wrote that the IRS had recommended criminal prosecution. Moore hired William G. Hundley, the Washington lawyer who represented U.S. Attorney John Mitchell in the Watergate scandal. As the case moved forward, Hundley commented that Moore had "fudged" in his denials about the existence of the case but added that he didn't blame the governor for hedging. That case, he said, "was some turkey . . . [It] should never have been brought." Hundley explained that careless bookkeeping by Moore's campaign staff had led to his difficulties, and that after the case was reviewed by four or five attorneys in the Justice Department, it was dropped.

"I don't believe Moore ever made any settlement," Hundley concluded.

Other problems for the Moore administration were to follow. In a separate case, Moore's labor commissioner, Robert A. McConnell, entered a plea of no contest to a charge of falsifying expense accounts. Kelly, who had opposed Moore's handling of federal funds, pleaded guilty to extortion, mail fraud, and bribery.

Then came the collapse of Diversified Mountaineer Corporation, a four-state savings and loan network with headquarters in Charleston. Moore was indicted on a charge of extorting twenty-five thousand dollars during Diversified's effort to get a state bank charter. Indicted with him was his chief assistant, William Loy. The governor was at the White House when the indictment was made public. In less than two hours he had returned to Charleston, called a press conference, and, apparently on the theory that the best defense is a good offense, announced that he was seeking a third term as governor. He never lacked brass.

Federal prosecutors put together strong evidence against Moore in the DMC case. The president of the company, Theodore Price, said on the witness stand that he had given Moore "a twenty-five-thousand-dollar political contribution to get the bank." Gassaway banker Nolan Hamric testified that he had set up the appointment with Moore on Price's behalf, and he admitted to telling the governor that Price was interested in giving him twenty-five thousand dollars for his 1972 reelection campaign. State Banking Commissioner George B. Jordan quoted the governor as being in sympathy with granting the charter. But the charter was never issued, and after Moore and Loy testified that no such transaction occurred, the jury found them both not guilty.

But this was not the end of the DMC imbroglio. Reporters resorted to court records after they were filed in the clerk's office and found that during a bench conference between the presiding judge and the trial lawyers it was revealed that Moore allegedly had between $180,000 and two hundred thousand dollars sitting in his desk drawer at one particular time in 1972. But the judge ruled that the issue had no relevancy to the DMC case and refused to allow it to be admitted as evidence.

The outcome of the trial revived Moore's hopes of being able to run for a third term, until both the State and U.S. Supreme Courts ruled that the law allowed a governor only two consecutive terms.

In the 1976 general election, Rockefeller, a Democrat, had no difficulty crushing his Republican opponent, former Governor Underwood. Rockefeller won by 242,207 votes, the biggest margin in state history up to that time. Before leaving office to return to his private law practice, Moore took advantage of the same tactic used by Smith in the last hours of his term as governor eight years before, locking more than seven thousand state employees into their jobs under the protection of the Civil Service System. Moore also announced that he had left a surplus of $234 million in the treasury, but later examination of the records indicated that he had grossly inflated his estimate of the money on hand.

ALTHOUGH MOORE'S ADMINISTRATION came to an end in 1977, transgressions that took place during his two terms in the governor's office were still coming to light two years later. In the winter of 1978 federal investigators began a probe of the state liquor industry. One of those indicted as a result of the federal investigation was Moore's liquor commissioner, J. Richard Barber. On August 30, 1979, a federal court jury found Barber guilty of twenty counts of extortion, mail fraud, and racketeering. He was sentenced to three years in prison.

Testimony during the trial brought out that while Barber was commissioner, an office he held from 1970 to 1976, he indulged in what federal authorities considered bribery and extortion to obtain eleven thousand dollars in cash and 1,800 cases of liquor worth about eighty thousand dollars wholesale.

On the witness stand, Barber informed the jury that he had collected contributions for Moore's 1972 campaign for governor and for Moore's assistant, Loy, in his unsuccessful bid for Congress in 1974. There was also testimony that liquor withdrawn from the state warehouse was used by the governor's office, members of the legislature, and high state officials for social and political events, with liquor companies footing the bill. Along with Barber, twenty liquor companies were found guilty of participating in the operation.

Moore was asked more than once to comment on the practice of public officials taking liquor gratis from state inventory. He finally issued a terse statement regarding his own practice of using it for public occasions at the Mansion, saying, "I viewed it purely as a ministerial function."

IN 1978 MOORE MADE A BID for the U.S. Senate seat held by the aging Jennings Randolph, but his old political magic was lacking that day. Randolph retained his seat, beating Moore by 4,717 votes. The final curtain, however, had not yet fallen on Moore's political career.

Chapter 25

A Lifetime Commitment

GOVERNOR JOHN DAVISON ROCKEFELLER IV melded the personal philosophy of
the original John D. with his own in his first inaugural message.

A guiding precept of John the First was that "willful waste makes woeful
want." John the Fourth, who went by his nickname, Jay, adhered to his great-
grandfather's principles, telling the people of West Virginia, "As taxpayers,
you are going to get your money's worth . . . We are going to give you efficient,
carefully planned government—government without frills or fat."

The new governor launched his first effort at eliminating frills shortly
after his inauguration. He went to the legislature and asked for authority to
cancel his predecessor's parting political move, the late-hour executive order
that shifted more than seven thousand employees into civil service. Rockefeller also began a slow and methodical reduction in the number of state workers
through attrition and the elimination of unneeded or overlapping positions.
During his years in office Rockefeller removed five thousand employees from
the bloated bureaucracy that Moore had created.

On the governor's recommendation, the Health and Mental Health departments were merged, the scattered agencies dealing with the state's historical and cultural heritage were brought together under one umbrella, an
office of economic and community development was established, and such
institutions as the women's prison and boys' industrial school were closed as
no longer cost-effective.

THE STATE'S TWENTY-NINTH GOVERNOR was born in New York City three weeks
after the death of the original John D. Rockefeller, then known as the richest

man in the world. A founder of Standard Oil Company, Rockefeller had made much of his wealth in oil, a legacy passed down through the years to a host of heirs, among them his great-grandson Jay.

Jay Rockefeller enjoyed a higher quality of education than probably any other West Virginia governor. After completing his elementary schooling in New York, he was enrolled at Phillips Exeter Academy, an elite private school in New Hampshire. He earned his undergraduate degree from Harvard with additional studies in Chinese at Yale. He also spent several years in Japan studying the language and culture. While majoring in history at Harvard, he had developed a serious interest in the Far East. He was one of the top-ranked students in his class at Tokyo's International Christian University, often devoting fifteen hours a day to his studies. "I really worked at it," Rockefeller recalled later. In a trade-off with the university, he also taught English.

Rockefeller began his public service career in Washington as an unpaid assistant to Peace Corps Director R. Sargent Shriver, brother-in-law of President Kennedy. Shriver had been intrigued by an article Rockefeller had written for *The New York Times Magazine* and offered him a position as his special assistant. Rockefeller spent his first year with the Peace Corps recruiting volunteers to serve overseas and most of the next organizing the content of the Philippines program. During these years he also got to know the Kennedy clan. Of the three brothers, Bobby was his favorite, and they developed a close friendship which lasted until the former attorney general was assassinated in Los Angeles during the 1968 presidential campaign.

With Rockefeller's interest in foreign affairs, it was only natural that he would gravitate to the State Department. Also, he said, he wanted a mainline bureaucratic experience, which he received as desk officer for Indonesian Affairs in State's Far Eastern bureau. In early 1964 he talked to a friend, Charlie Peters, then evaluation director for the Peace Corps, about finding something more closely related to America and its problems.

Peters, a former Charleston lawyer and member of the House of Delegates, advised Rockefeller that if he wanted to see a side of the United States he'd never been exposed to, there was no better place than West Virginia.

Peters said later that he tried to limit his efforts to encouraging Rockefeller rather than pressuring him, but he was determined to recruit Rockefeller for West Virginia, and apparently he was convincing enough. In May of that year, this scion of wealth and privilege spent a week in Charleston, then returned to ride up Cabin Creek and talk with residents there, seeing firsthand problems resembling those in Hong Kong, Tokyo, and New York's Harlem. Soon afterward, Rockefeller decided that West Virginia would be his next destination. It would become his permanent home.

Bobby Kennedy, then U.S. attorney general, had Rockefeller assigned to the Action for Appalachian Youth program, and Rockefeller began his work in the poverty-stricken town of Emmons, south of Charleston. It wasn't easy. Many doors were slammed in his face. But in time, by working with the young people, he developed a rapport with the adults. "The chief reason for lack of initiative is not money," he said after this eye-opening experience. "Welfare checks are the only thing that keep the people going."

Through the joint efforts of Rockefeller and the residents of Emmons, a community center and a thirty-acre park with a softball field were built. "There is a Rockefeller Center in New York with sixty-five stories," he said on the day it was dedicated. "There is one here in Emmons. My heart is with the one at Emmons."

While still working at Emmons he decided to file for the House of Delegates and to break with his family's deep-seated allegiance to the Republican Party. The first Rockefeller in four generations to cross party lines, Jay said he felt compelled to cast his lot with a party that best reflected his personal philosophy.

"Politics is a lifetime commitment," he said. "To have remained a Republican would have been to subordinate my own conclusions and instincts to an undefined feeling of what others think I should be."

Later, at a governors' conference in White Sulphur Springs, I sought out his uncle, then-New York Governor Nelson Rockefeller, who would later serve as Gerald Ford's vice president. I had met Nelson several years before at another governors' conference in Montana and found him to be a very approachable individual. When I asked if he had advised Jay on his political choice,

Nelson said that Jay had talked with him about whether or not he should break with family tradition. Nelson advised his nephew that he wouldn't be making a mistake by joining the opposition party. For a young man of Jay's aspirations and capabilities, he told him, the future looked bright in the Democratic Party.

Jay's bid for a seat in the West Virginia House of Delegates was a cakewalk. He led the field of sixty candidates vying for fourteen seats in the House, and in the general election he was again the leader. His next step was a bid for statewide office. He toyed with the idea of running for treasurer and then settled on secretary of state. Again he won by a wide margin.

During these years of sharpening his skills in West Virginia politics, Rockefeller married Sharon Percy, daughter of the Republican senator from Illinois, Charles Percy. They had their first of four children, Jamie, and bought a three-thousand-acre farm in Pocahontas County.

"There have been only two cases of love at first sight in my life," he said after purchasing the farm. "One was my wife, and one was the land. Land in West Virginia really means something, and it means something very important to me psychologically."

As secretary of state, Rockefeller began setting the stage for a run for governor. Articles about him began appearing in national magazines and newspapers. He appeared on NBC's *Meet the Press*. He established his pre-campaign headquarters on Kanawha Boulevard near the Capitol. In a public address, he attacked what he looked upon as President Nixon's "penchant for mediocrity." And at a press conference he called for the abolition of strip-mining: "I am convinced, reluctantly but strongly, that strip-mining of coal must be prohibited by law."

His abolition law went nowhere in the legislature, and after he filed for governor in 1972 it became a burden which helped defeat him. The chief thrust of his campaign was fifty thousand new jobs for the unemployed, but his position on strip-mining, and the fact that he was a native New Yorker, worked against him. His place of birth was not a relevant issue. Byrd, the most popular political figure in West Virginia, had been born in North Carolina. But Rockefeller's opponent, incumbent Governor Moore, used the most derisive of labels, "carpetbagger," in his critiques of Rockefeller, and it paid off. Moore won reelection.

For the next four years, Rockefeller served as president of West Virginia Wesleyan College, a Methodist Church affiliate, and spent some time reexamining his position on coal mining. "I think we have to have a positive attitude toward coal," he remarked. "Coal can help us become the Saudi Arabia of the U.S. in terms of energy production."

He continued to speak publicly on a broad range of subjects. He was featured in *Time* magazine. He went on a three-week tour of China. He donated $250,000 to Wesleyan for a new physical education building. Then on October 9, 1975, the expected occurred. Rockefeller announced that he would again file for governor. He had no trouble whipping seven other candidates in the Democratic primary, and in the general election he beat former Governor Underwood by the biggest margin in history, an almost two-to-one difference.

At his inauguration in January 1976, which took place in zero-degree weather, Rockefeller told his audience that an economic and industrial renaissance for West Virginia was his first priority. "The Great Depression, the depletion of our assorted natural resources, and the mechanization of the mines each resulted in a loss of jobs and population," he declared. "And in 1960, when John Kennedy put the national spotlight on some of our problems, we became characterized as a poor and almost helpless state; it has been hard to shake that stigma."

The deep freeze that greeted him on his first day in office maintained its grip on the Mountain State for weeks. It was one of the coldest winters in living memory. For the first time in decades, West Virginia's navigable rivers were frozen from shore to shore.

The country was already in the middle of an oil crisis, and the frozen waterways added to the shortage, preventing fuel barges from delivering their cargoes to run the state's power plants. So serious was the problem that Rockefeller asked all citizens to set their thermostats at sixty-four degrees, as had already been directed in state and federal offices. He also limited the use of state cars. Conditions became so critical that many schools were closed and plant shutdowns occurred. Within two weeks Rockefeller estimated that more than seventy-five thousand people had been put out of work and another thirty thousand had been displaced by fuel shortages.

In his first state-of-the-state address to the legislature, Rockefeller called for meaningful retrenchment, zero growth in the budget, and removal of the 3 percent sales tax on food. He also said he wanted the most sweeping secondary-road improvement program in history.

His pledge to reduce the number of state employees was followed by an observation that, in 1967, when he was a member of the House of Delegates, there were thirty-two thousand state employees. By the time of his inauguration, the number had grown to forty-six thousand. "To state it as simply as it can be stated," he added, "the time has come to reverse the trend. It is my plan to reduce the number of employees in state government by several thousand over the next few years."

Twice during his early days in office, Rockefeller cancelled plans his predecessor had put in place. The new governor chose not to apply gold leaf to the Capitol dome and scrapped the planned construction of a new mental health complex. In a state with the economic problems of West Virginia, he said, a gold dome would be a travesty. He also believed it was better to absorb the $2 million already spent on developing the mental health center than to spend another $20 million to $30 million to complete a facility which did not comply with current standards. His only break with the austerity program was to endorse a plan to build a $20 million football stadium at West Virginia University. His explanation for this was that he could see no conflict, since the stadium was to be financed with revenue bonds retired with stadium income.

Much of the character of Rockefeller's eight-year administration was shaped during his first year. He proposed a $10 million program of seed money for economic development. He took the first steps to aid low-income families by gradually eliminating the consumers' sales tax on food, a move that would not reach fruition for three years. He sought and was granted the right to force strip-mine operators to return the land they mined to its original contour. And he began a restructuring of the state's Civil Service System.

Rockefeller's first attempt to reform the flawed Civil Service System was to cancel coverage for the 7,500 employees approved by Moore just before leaving office. He managed to obtain legislative approval for this action. "The days of using the Civil Service System as a political tool have ended," Rockefeller said. "There will be no more rubber stamp actions by the commission and no more secret meetings closed to the press and public."

But the governor struck a sensitive nerve in the legislature with his next step. He took the precipitate action of removing the existing three-member Civil Service Commission and filling the commission with his own appointments. The Senate refused to confirm the governor's candidates, and he had to go back to the drawing board. Rockefeller may have been influenced by the public-administration structure he had been exposed to as a student in Japan, where government service was regarded as an honored calling. Although the centuries-old system had been abolished in 1947 by American occupation forces under General Douglas MacArthur in favor of more modern practices, the cultural tradition of a respected bureaucracy of trained public servants survived. Public administration in Japan requires a high level of education as well as administrative and technical competence.

During Rockefeller's first term as governor, teachers were given pay raises and state monies were appropriated to match available federal road funds. The Eastern Panhandle and the Ohio and Monongahela valleys enjoyed a period of industrial expansion, as did other parts of the state, although to a lesser extent.

But Rockefeller had his share of problems. What would be the longest coal strike in history, 111 days altogether, began during his first term. More than sixty thousand miners walked off the job, a move which affected another forty-three thousand workers in related industries. Before the strike ended, $34 million in state revenue was lost.

At one point, two hundred miners stormed into the governor's office suite, demanding that Rockefeller support them against President Carter, who had ordered an eighty-day cooling-off period under the Taft-Hartley Act. Despite a heated confrontation, Rockefeller refused.

Angry as they were, the miners could not in all honesty label the governor a foe of coal mining. While speaking on one occasion to the West Virginia Surface Mining and Reclamation Association, Rockefeller commented that he had been criticized by the West Virginia Oil and Gas Association for "fighting too hard" for coal.

"I want you to think about that for a minute," he added, "a Rockefeller being accused by an oil industry spokesman of not fighting hard enough for oil and gas . . . and fighting too hard for coal. I just want you to know that I consider that to be the highest compliment paid to me in my entire public career."

As governor, Rockefeller campaigned unceasingly for the marketing of West Virginia coal. He fought for better working conditions for miners and spent long hours developing plans for improving housing in the coalfields. One of his battles on the issue of housing was with Cotiga Development Company, which had vast holdings of mineral-rich lands in Mingo County. Cotiga had agreed to sell eighty-three acres of reclaimed land for the construction of homes for five hundred people wiped out by a recent flood. But Cotiga's asking price for the acreage was so high that the governor went to court to seek eminent domain rights to the land.

"Cotiga has . . . made a mockery of the concept of corporate goodwill," Rockefeller said bitterly. "Cotiga's selfishness and lack of social responsibility are appalling to me as governor."

In 1979 Rockefeller started a program that went beyond housing and into the basics of the state's infrastructure. Entitled the *West Virginia State Development Plan*, nine years in preparation, its purpose was to assess needs and organize ways to encourage orderly growth and development in the state.

In final form, it touched on the root cause of many of the state's problems—more than a century of neglect of everything from water management to sewage disposal. Rockefeller recognized that correcting it would be a costly proposition but one that was essential if West Virginia was to be ready for the challenges of the twenty-first century.

In its prefatory comments, the plan observed that West Virginia was rich in natural resources, that it was geographically well-situated within overnight trucking distance of half the nation's population, and that it had an abundance of trainable people. But it also said that much of what makes a society alluring to outsiders—and to economic development—had either been mismanaged or had suffered from neglect during past periods of development.

The problems cited in the report were sobering. Only 50 percent of the state's population was served by sewer systems. The remainder were served by septic tanks or pit privies, or simply discharged their waste directly into streams. Many water systems in the state faced problems with both quality and quantity. Overall, solid-waste disposal practices were outdated and inadequate. Parks and outdoor recreation facilities were woefully lacking. The isolated and rural nature of the state made firefighting and policing difficult. In smaller towns across the state, even the local streets and sidewalks were substandard. And statewide, book shortages in public libraries amounted to more than one million volumes.

Rockefeller's hope, as he told the public, was that "[through] the use of the Plan and a common investment process, we, as West Virginians, can better marshal our resources to fund those projects and programs that are identified as having the highest needs and best serve the state's orderly growth and development."

The increased focus of the Rockefeller administration on community development was a major breakthrough for the state. More than $400 million in federal, state, and local funds went into 519 projects in four years, much of it spent on water and sewer construction. Additional funding went for improved fire and police protection, and 17,345 housing units were financed through the West Virginia Housing Development Fund.

ROCKEFELLER KEPT HIS INAUGURAL PLEDGE to provide jobs and create an improved industrial climate. Between 1977 and 1981 more than $2 billion was invested in 132 new plants and expansion at 142 existing plants, including Mobay Chemical in New Martinsville, Rockwell International in Morgantown, General Motors in Martinsburg, Volkswagen in South Charleston, and Rockingham Poultry in Moorefield.

Rockefeller also provided hope to the coal industry as chairman of the president's Commission on Coal. When he made his report toward the end of his term, he recommended that coal replace oil and natural gas as the energy source in power plants. President Carter endorsed the idea as a means of helping America become less dependent on oil from foreign countries. Carter further proposed a $10 billion conversion program to Congress. In the U.S. Senate, Majority Leader Byrd, joined by Senator Wendell Ford, of Kentucky, promised the measure would be given high priority.

Although Rockefeller devoted much of his first four years as governor to strengthening West Virginia's economy, he never lost sight of two of the state's most pressing needs: education and roads. Funding for education was increased from 34 percent to 43 percent of the budget, which translated into substantial boosts in pay for teachers and college professors. It was the same with road construction. Nearly ten thousand miles of secondary roads were improved and 390 bridges repaired. A fifty-one-mile stretch of the eighty-six-mile West Virginia Turnpike was targeted for upgrading to four-lane standards, and $200 million in contracts were let for corridor-road construction.

As expected, Rockefeller announced that he would run for a second term, and as the returns began to roll in on election night in November 1980, he said joyfully, "How sweet it is." He had soundly beaten his old Republican rival, Moore, for another term.

As Governor Rockefeller began his second term in office in January 1981, he told his inaugural-day audience, "We enter now a decade of destiny." It was to be a decade, he said, when West Virginia's natural resources would be nationally and internationally recognized, spinning off new business and jobs for its people.

"If in the past," he said proudly, "we have walked together, worked together, and struggled together toward a distant goal, today we can honestly affirm that our goal is clearly in sight."

He had good cause for such optimism. The state had survived the 1979–1980 recession with its economic structure relatively strong. Nearly forty thousand more West Virginians were working in 1981 than had been employed when Rockefeller first took office in 1977.

But Ronald Reagan had taken the oath of office as president on the same day as Rockefeller's second inauguration, and forces were at work that would have a material impact on the economy of West Virginia. Reagan had campaigned on a platform that called for cuts in taxes and spending to stimulate private investment as a means of promoting national growth, which became known as the "trickle down" theory of economics. While it was beneficial to some states like California, Texas, and Virginia, Reagan's program had a negative impact on many states, and West Virginia moved into a prolonged period of recession.

One of the first blows the state suffered at the hands of the Reagan administration was a cutback in funding for the U.S. Department of Energy. This meant a lopping off of funds for the planned Gulf Mineral Resources plant near Morgantown, conceived during the Carter years as a means of making America less dependent on foreign oil.

The Gulf Mineral plant, if built, would have meant hundreds of jobs in the refinery and hundreds more in the mines that would have supplied the six thousand tons of coal needed daily to produce the equivalent in synthetic fuel of twenty thousand barrels of oil. Once the facility was open and running smoothly, it was expected to lead to the construction of other such plants.

The second blow to the state came when the Reagan administration tried to abolish the Appalachian Regional Commission, which had been created when Johnson was president. Through the intervening years, the ARC had pumped billions into West Virginia and other states for highways, waterworks, sewer systems, and community health care. Although Reagan wasn't able to kill the commission, due to powerful resistance in Congress, he left it so crippled that it was able to provide only token help to the states during his years in the White House.

But even before Reagan took office, West Virginia was hurting in another part of its industrial base—manufacturing. Most of the state's steel, glass, and, to a lesser degree, chemical plants had been built between the two world wars and were showing their age. Many of them had never modernized, and the influx of cheaper imports from Europe and Asia was making it less cost-effective to bring them up to date. Some had begun to close their doors. West Virginia had to find other ways to revitalize its economy and continue the community development program which had been started during the Kennedy and Johnson administrations.

Responding to the challenge, Rockefeller came up with a blueprint for self-help which he laid before the 1981 legislature. He asked for and was given authority to extend investment tax credit to existing industries with worn-out facilities, as well as to new and expanding industries, and to allow the West Virginia Economic Development Authority to loan money for equipment purchases, for land, and for building. Bonding authority was increased for housing and water-development authorities, and approval was given for a referendum on a $750 million road bond issue.

The defeat of the bond issue at a special election was a blow to the state's economy no less severe than the Reagan administration's cutback in ARC funds. It cancelled a road-improvement policy that had been in existence since 1920 and resulted in a gradual but steady deterioration of the state's thirty-two-thousand-mile highway system.

SEVERAL MONTHS BEFORE the bond issue referendum, Rockefeller called me at the federal court in Elkins and asked if I would be interested in participating in the effort to pass it. Intrigued by the challenge, I said yes. As a journalist I had always been an observer of the political process, an outsider whose job was to report on what was happening on the inside. This was an opportunity to actively participate in the process and view it from a different perspective.

Heading back to my typewriter, I turned out news stories. I attended strategy meetings in Charleston and organized county support groups. I spoke to civic organizations, debated the issue in county courthouses, and answered questions on radio shows. I helped piece together precinct pressure groups. I went the extra mile because I firmly believed in the purpose of this bipartisan bond issue.

In the beginning, all of us involved in the effort thought we would win. History was on our side. So was the need for improved highways. But while taking part in a debate on the pros and cons of the question in the Tucker County Courthouse at Parsons, I came to the realization that we couldn't win.

My adversary that day wasn't especially convincing. He was a young lawyer from Morgantown with more flair for the dramatic than actual knowledge of the issues we were discussing. I could see that the audience wasn't paying attention to the facts.

The taxpayers sitting there wanted to hear that a new four-lane highway known as Corridor H would be coming through their county if they voted for the bond issue. I couldn't promise that. Corridor H was a billion-dollar project, and there simply wasn't enough money available at the time, or even on the horizon, to build it while continuing to supply the hundreds of needed bridge repairs and two-lane road repavings the bond issue would assure if passed. Everywhere I went during that campaign, the problem was the same. The voters wanted more than they were willing to pay for, and their interest was almost exclusively local.

In the past years when federal and state financing had been more plentiful, Corridor H had been a real hope rather than just a prayer. Taxpayers in the area it was to pass through fought one another over different plans for routing the road. In Elkins some real-estate owners wanted it to be built northward through the Canaan Valley recreational area while others wanted it to go due east to the Mouth of Seneca scenic area. As had happened with the routing of Corridor G around Logan, the area's residents couldn't agree on a location for this major new highway, so the planners in Washington put it on hold.

On election day the bond issue was soundly defeated.

THE STATE'S FISCAL STABILITY was dealt another blow in 1982 when Judge Arthur Recht, of Wheeling, handed down a decision directing that the public-school financing formula in West Virginia was unconstitutional. Recht had been appointed by the State Supreme Court to hear additional evidentiary material after the court had decided in *Pauley v. Bailey* that the school-financing system was in violation of existing law. In his opinion, Recht said that the quality of education in poorer counties was inferior to that in wealthier counties.

Later that summer the Supreme Court ruled in a second case that all property should be appraised at 100 percent of market value, thus eliminating the 60 percent rate fixed by law back in the mid-1950s. Rockefeller called the legislature into special session to consider a constitutional amendment that would reduce the assessment of all classes of property to 60 percent of its value. Under the terms of the amendment, the legislature would have the power to spread the effects of a reappraisal begun in 1973 over a period of years. The amendment passed, and the 1973 reappraisal program went forward.

In a speech to the legislature, Rockefeller said that while the Recht decision had merit, the state could not "afford to provide for all of the judge's recommendations." He also expressed the attitude that the appointment of a special commissioner by the court violated the separation-of-powers doctrine and instructed his tax commissioner to seek a writ of prohibition against the appointment.

After months of maneuvering back and forth, with the State Board of Education naming a special advisory committee to examine the Recht plan, the judge offered a $1.2 billion packet of proposed changes in school financing which was endorsed by the governor. Out of this controversy came an immediate 7.5 percent pay raise for teachers.

The governor next had to deal with the effects of a seventy-two-day coal strike. As it became clear that the negotiators were in a bargaining deadlock, Rockefeller curtailed spending and ordered a 2 percent cutback at all state agencies. Revenues were down $16 million a month. When the strike finally ended, revenues began to pick up, and the governor was able to lift the freeze on spending.

By the end of 1982 the West Virginia economy was hurting more than that of any other state, and the hardships stretched well into 1984. A national recession had begun to take its toll, and the Reagan administration's politics made conditions even worse.

Although the president had hoped with his program to balance the budget and set America on the road to growth, in much of the country, particularly in the industrial midsection and Farm Belt, the opposite was true. The budget deficit doubled in Reagan's first year and by 1984 had climbed to $200 billion. Inflation followed, and American products became less marketable abroad.

In West Virginia, which was a major supplier of coal and chemicals to foreign countries, the impact was harsh. An additional burden was created for the state as Washington continued to cut spending for social programs, education, and community development, which led to further hardships in the state. Some West Virginians were heard to mutter that the state was being penalized for voting for Democratic incumbent Carter in the 1980 presidential election.

The date of March 1, 1982, was a black day in West Virginia's industrial history, one which the people of the Northern Panhandle would long remember. That was the date when the chairman of National Steel Corporation met with Rockefeller in Charleston to inform him that the Weirton steel subsidiary would be made available for transfer to another party or would be closed. Weirton was one of the state's largest employers with eight thousand workers, and its closure would have been a crushing blow to the Panhandle.

Rockefeller, with Senators Byrd and Randolph and economic development leaders from the Panhandle, went to work on a solution. The result was the creation of the largest employee-owned steelmaking operation in the country. But the threatened Weirton closure was, as it turned out, simply the harbinger of other such problems in West Virginia. Wheeling-Pittsburgh Steel and a smaller producer, Huntington's West Virginia Steel, were also victims of foreign competition, as were the manufacturers of glass and clothing products in various parts of the state. Like Weirton, Wheeling-Pitt and the Huntington mill survived, but other manufacturers in the state were forced to close.

Coal-mine employment was a casualty as well during those years. Thanks to Washington's cancellation of the Carter administration's coal-energy policy, the further incursion of foreign steel, and reduced demand for electricity due to the recession, hard times loomed on the horizon. Mine shutdowns and shortened work weeks became the norm.

Coal production had reached 143 million tons in 1970, but by 1983 it had dropped to 115 million tons. Combined efforts by industry leaders and the governor's office to attract new business gradually began to turn the tide, however, and enough major long-term contracts were negotiated to push West Virginia production up to 131 million tons in 1984, the second highest level of output in fourteen years. But while tonnage increased, mine employment did not. Through improved mechanization the mines were able to turn out more coal with fewer workers.

THE ONE INDUSTRY IN WEST VIRGINIA that appeared to be recession-proof during these dismal times was tourism. It had begun to show a growth pattern by the mid-1970s, and by the end of Rockefeller's second term it had become a $1.4 billion moneymaker.

But tourism was only part of the overall economy, and West Virginia was in a prolonged slump. Unemployment figures in some of the southern counties were as high as 25 percent. A full 20 percent of the state's gross marketable product was shipped overseas. The value of the dollar was being pushed upward by high interest rates and the bulging national budget deficit, and West Virginia was suffering disproportionately in comparison to other states.

To meet this growing crisis, Rockefeller slashed spending and asked the legislature for new taxes to maintain an already austere level of state services. He also asked for authority to extend unemployment benefits for the thousands of people who were out of work and proposed the funding of a public works program that would offer the added assistance of retraining. He was granted the entire package.

In an effort to raise additional revenue, in 1984 he endorsed a catch-all bond issue which, if ratified, would have provided money for school, bridge, and highway construction. Other amendments were placed on the ballot that year to create a state lottery, allow prayer in the public schools, exempt intangible property from taxation, and provide home mortgage loans to veterans. All of them passed except the one for roads and schools, including the amendment sanctioning school prayer. The prayer amendment would later be declared unconstitutional.

Despite the difficulties Rockefeller faced during his second four years in office and the bleakest economic conditions since the Depression years of the 1930s, the governor was able to maintain essential services while keeping the books balanced. He also managed to see that approximately two thousand miles of roads were resurfaced, 780 bridges upgraded, and the remainder of the turnpike put under contract for expansion to four lanes. Adult literacy gained ground during this period, and programs for the elderly were expanded. And in spite of a billion-dollar cutback in federal grants-in-aid, funding for community infrastructure shot upward.

Throughout his years in public office, Rockefeller carried two burdens that were part of his inheritance. In many parts of West Virginia, particularly in the high mountains, he was still regarded as the "city slicker" from New York. This situation generated a distrust and increased electoral resistance.

Conversely, he was expected to be a miracle worker in delivering new industry. Because he was a Rockefeller, West Virginians believed their governor could simply walk into the boardrooms of corporations large and small and demand commitments for new factories wherever they were needed. While he was successful at bringing in some new industry and saving some existing plants, it was never enough for those who envisioned West Virginia as another California.

When Rockefeller came to Elkins during his 1984 campaign for the U.S. Senate seat then occupied by Randolph, we talked about his years as governor. We were standing on Railroad Avenue in Elkins, looking at the tracks of the old Western Maryland Railway which were soon to be removed.

"My first four years were good years," Rockefeller said, in what sounded like an apology to his constituency. "These second four years have been difficult, and we haven't been able to do what we expected in the beginning. But we're going to do better. West Virginia is a good state. It has an exciting future."

Rockefeller defeated Morgantown publisher John Raese in the Senate race, a victory which did not come cheaply. His first bid for the Senate, which many observers of the American democratic process believed was a calculated step toward the presidency, cost more than $12 million, according to *Forbes* magazine's 1988 report on "The Richest People in America."

But while Rockefeller flirted with the idea of running for President in 1992 and was mentioned as a possible running mate for Bill Clinton in that election, he remained what he had worked so hard to become: an advocate for West Virginia and its people. He continued his efforts to make coal a more marketable energy source and to enlarge the national focus on the problems of the underprivileged, especially children of the poor and the many millions of citizens unable to afford medical insurance.

Rockefeller would also have the distinction of being one of only two West Virginia chief executives to move directly from the governor's office to the U.S. Senate. The only other governor to manage that feat was the state's first, Arthur I. Boreman.

Chapter 26

THIRD TIME AROUND

AFTER THE UNCHARACTERISTIC EQUANIMITY of the Rockefeller years, the world of West Virginia politics was about to get boisterous again: Arch Moore was back.

He was more restrained in his third inaugural speech than he had been in his first two. When he took the oath of office on January 14, 1985, as the first chief executive in the state's history to be elected to three four-year terms, he warned his audience that a "revolution in thought" would be necessary if the state was to climb out of its "winter of discontent." Moore promised to "excite the minds of all West Virginians with the prospect that a new and better West Virginia is indeed possible." He said he would be tough-minded, innovative, and creative in restoring the state to its former vitality.

In comments to the press later in the day, Rockefeller, who was scheduled to take the oath of office in Washington the following week as a United States senator, said, "It's going to be a tough period ahead." He recalled that federal aid to the state had been cut by a billion dollars during the previous four years, and he saw little prospect of an increase in aid from such federal agencies as the Appalachian Regional Commission, the Economic Development Administration, and the Farmers Home Administration, which had been so helpful in the past.

Moore's reversal in attitude, his new solemnity, was further emphasized in an interview with *The Charleston Daily Mail* prior to the inauguration. "I am approaching my third term," he said, "with cautious optimism. Some feel we had a great eight years before . . . My problem is to match those eight years."

He talked of commitment. "If I have to fight to get through my programs, fight I will." Expressing the hope that disharmony with the legislature could be avoided this time around, he added, "We want to turn this state around, and it won't be done overnight."

Moore maintained an uncharacteristically low profile for the first month after his inauguration while he pieced together his new program. Then, on February 14, in his budget message, he proposed putting the state in the electric-power business, taking it out of the liquor business, and building a pipeline system. "In solving our economic problems," he declared, "we must undertake a broad program to again make our state attractive for jobs and investment. We are today our own worst enemy in this regard."

His plan, as outlined to the legislature, called for the state to build two coal-fired power plants and a distribution system from the gas fields to industrial centers. It was a notable departure from the conservative policy adopted earlier by the Reagan administration, but Moore, a Republican like Reagan, said that desperate times required desperate measures.

"We have to understand that we West Virginians are going to solve our own problems without waiting for someone else to do it for us," he said. "We shall be the masters of our own fate."

This move from old-style Republicanism to socialization of industry was given qualified endorsement by influential members of the press, particularly the traditionally conservative Ogden newspaper chain. The Ogden papers commented that if the idea was feasible, it deserved more than casual consideration by the legislature. But Moore's plan went nowhere. United Press International reported late in the session, "These ideas died on the day they were proposed."

IN A MAJOR MOVE to make West Virginia more attractive to out-of-state industry, the legislature began a concerted effort to replace the business and occupation (B&O) tax with a series of other taxes. This proposal was the result of a study undertaken during the Rockefeller years, one the former governor had endorsed in his last legislative message before leaving office. Although Moore had advocated doing away with the inheritance tax in his budget message, he cautioned against taking the same action on the B&O tax, West Virginia's major source of income.

The B&O tax had originally been passed in 1921 as a means of meeting the public service demands of the post-World War I period. In the depths of the Depression in 1933, the B&O rates were increased to offset the loss of revenue from the Tax Limitation Amendment.

In succeeding years there had been periodic efforts to eliminate the tax, which the proponents of change argued was oppressive to business and industry because it was a tax on gross income rather than on the profits of doing business. But many of the industrial giants took a dim view of repealing the B&O tax, arguing that there was no assurance that what they might get as a substitute would be an improvement. As one industry spokesman said, "We know what our taxes are today, and we can factor them into our overall cost structure. If the B&O tax is repealed, we don't know what we will be getting, and years might pass before West Virginia has everything straightened out."

Former Governor Smith, during whose administration one of the finest tax studies ever authorized by the state was undertaken, also warned against repeal of the B&O tax. Moore's tax commissioner took the same position. But as the 1985 session drew to a close, the legislative leaders pressured Moore into siding with those advocating repeal of the tax. They had a precedent to back up their arguments. In the last year of Rockefeller's tenure as governor, revisions had been made guaranteeing a 25 percent reduction in B&O taxes, at the rate of 5 percent per year over a period of five years. This reduction mainly addressed the problems of small businesses. But lawmakers had the ammunition they needed to persuade Moore to support the proposed changes, and the new tax package was passed.

The advocates of change had been over-zealous in their efforts to set in motion an industrial renaissance through tax relief. The repeal of the B&O tax led to a shortfall in revenue, which remained a problem throughout the rest of Moore's term.

At the end of the session, members of the Senate and House leadership commented publicly that Moore had gotten what he wanted from the lawmakers. Legislation was passed creating a regional jail system, the departments of Energy and Commerce were authorized, and teachers and public employees were given pay raises. In the legislature's opinion, a new atmosphere of goodwill had been established with the governor's office, in contrast to the tempestuous relationship between the two branches of governments during Moore's previous administration. But in their enthusiasm they lost sight of the fact that Moore had been pressured into supporting a major tax revision he did not subscribe to, and that his innovative electrical- and gas-distribution ventures had been tossed on the legislative scrap heap.

As stated several months later by the National Conference of State Legislatures, the extent of the tax reduction was $67 million. West Virginia had joined a national trend to cut taxes. Altogether, the legislative conference estimated, a billion dollars in tax reductions had been approved in 1985 by various states.

The proposal to put West Virginia into the electrical-generation business was not a pie-in-the-sky scheme. Moore had talked at length with New Hampshire governor John Sununu—later administrative assistant to President George Bush—about creating a new energy base for the New England states, which were largely dependent on an aging oil-fired system.

The benefits, as outlined by the two governors, were that New England would get cheaper power, West Virginia would be able to put 3,500 miners back to work producing coal for the power plants, and the acid rain problem in the northern states would be lessened.

Seventeen states joined in a study of the proposition. Among those most interested in it were Pennsylvania, Ohio, Kentucky, and Illinois, which had a surplus of power they were willing to sell outside their borders.

But the cost of the power plants was estimated at around $2 billion, and a transmission system from West Virginia to New England would have cost another $900 million or so. The governor of Vermont said that cheaper electrical power might be available in Canada and that gaining federal approval for the transmission system could prove a stumbling block. The Associated Press, writing about the plan, wondered how a state like West Virginia that couldn't "afford to build schools, roads and hospitals" could afford to finance the new system. In 1986 Moore again sent the proposal to the legislature and again it went nowhere.

ANOTHER ISSUE OF PRESSING IMPORTANCE at this time was property tax equalization. Local tax associations opposing change were being formed, editorials
on both sides of the issue were appearing in newspapers, and taxpayers were
voicing their concern over the idea of making changes in the assessment process. In Logan County, a judge had ruled that property values were not being
determined uniformly statewide. The Supreme Court had agreed in 1982 and
ruled that property should be assessed at true and actual value.

The court's ruling was related to an electoral mandate of 1932 which had
set limits on property taxes. Before that time, county assessors had been free
to determine values by personal whim and political motivation, and all too
many assessors from counties rich in coal, oil, gas, and timber had bent under the pressure from big landowners when making assessments. The market
crash of 1929 emphasized with scandalous clarity how widespread the tax-
ing inequities had become. In many counties, land that abounded in natural
resources was valued at fifty cents an acre while that of the small farmer or
urban homeowner was valued at much higher rates. Conditions became so
serious after the market crash that thousands of property owners lost their
holdings at auctions on the courthouse steps.

Tax limitation, which had been sanctioned by amendment in 1932, was
precisely that. It set limits only on tax rates. It did not put limits on property
valuations. So the large out-of-state landowners continued paying dime-store
taxes while the small property owner paid taxes on assessed values closer to
actual worth. This practice of manipulating assessed values went on unchallenged until the mid-1950s, when experts in the field of property valuation
were retained to assist the state with the development of a new several-step
assessment procedure.

Although the 1950s were a benchmark period in property tax assessment,
assessors were adept at serving their own interests before those of their constituencies and gradually slipped back into the old ways. This condition finally
began to be addressed in the 1980s after the State Supreme Court sided with
the Logan County judge's ruling and determined that all property in West
Virginia was to be assessed—under a long-ignored constitutional clause—at
true and actual value.

Cries rose up across the state from property owners who said they could not afford to pay taxes based on true and actual value. They took their complaints to their legislators and Governor Rockefeller and, as a solution, the Property Tax Limitation Amendment was placed on the 1982 election ballot. It called for assessment at 60 percent of value, the same rate that had been determined as realistic in the 1950s. Needless to say, the amendment was ratified. Reevaluation of all property was called for by 1985, with a ten-year phase-in at the new values.

The same procedure for fixing value that had been used previously was already on line. The firm of Cole, Layer, and Trumble was contracted to work on the new statewide reappraisal. After the reevaluation work was completed, copies relating to each of the fifty-five counties were distributed. This set off another wave of complaints as individuals and corporate landowners looked at their assessment schedules. It was altogether possible that reassessment mistakes had been made. But rather than go through the process of making adjustments, assessors and lawmakers joined in what to them was the more politic ploy of simply delaying implementation. Protest groups, some linked to large property owners, were organized as a further delaying tactic. It soon became evident that there was no real support for the reassessment program in the legislature or the governor's office.

Legislation was passed delaying implementation first until 1986, then until 1987 if the new assessments were certified as substantially correct by the tax commissioner. Ultimately, Moore's tax commissioner, Michael Caryl, declined to put his certification stamp on the reevaluation program, and the public mandate of 1982 remained an ignored stepchild throughout the remainder of Moore's term. This venture into tax equity, which had cost the state $35.5 million, was no more a reality when Moore left office than it had been on the day the Logan judge made his fateful ruling.

WHATEVER HOPE FOR HARMONY that had existed at the beginning of Moore's third term disappeared in the second year when the governor and the legislative leadership began budget negotiations for the coming fiscal year. The governor set the stage for a clash of wills in his State of the State Address when he said that any political opposition to his proposed budget would "plunge the state and its citizens into a political morass from which there is no hope of escape."

After his finance committee had had an opportunity to study it, Senate President Dan Tonkovich responded that Moore's budget, which the Governor had said was "balanced on a razor's edge," was actually $104 million higher than the amount of revenue anticipated. Tonkovich also recalled that Moore had said he would drive the budget deeper into debt to educate the legislature about deficit financing. Tonkovich called this comment irresponsible and asked the governor for a new sense of cooperation in working out differences. Moore's response was, "I think we now have the legislature's attention."

Moore and the legislature came churlishly to terms during an extension of the session, and a budget was passed which called for no increase in taxes. They also agreed to a $500 million bond issue for road improvement, to be repaid with a penny increase in the sales tax, but the bond issue was later defeated at the polls. After the vote, Tonkovich remarked that the voters had spoken, and there was no need to move ahead on road improvements.

The following year was a replay of the preceding year. Moore, still agitated that the B&O tax had been repealed and was due to expire at the end of that fiscal year in June, proposed a $1.6 billion budget which included $100 million in extended B&O taxes. In his budget message, he said the legislature had "marched itself into a hole" with the repeal of the B&O tax. The legislature countered with a budget of its own totaling $1.56 billion. Labeling it "devastating," Moore vetoed it.

This set off a prolonged period of gamesmanship between the governor and the legislature. At one point, Tonkovich even proposed that Moore be impeached, an action made more interesting by the fact that, as Senate president, Tonkovich was the next constitutional officer in the line of succession.

House Speaker Chuck Chambers sought relief through legal action in the Supreme Court, but the court refused to hear the case, saying the budgetary impasse was a quarrel the legislature and governor should resolve themselves. The infighting became so polarized that a Morgantown senator, Buffy Warner, made himself a hostage of the situation by holing up in the Senate chamber and telling his fellow members that he would remain there until they came to terms on a new budget. Finally, after yet another veto, an agreement was reached. By then, the 1987 session had become the second longest in history, exceeded only by the 1863 session when West Virginia was granted statehood.

All through this budgetary conflict, the state remained in fiscal crisis. Except for one period of a few months, the governor refused to reduce spending—a practice implemented by past governors in similar situations—and informed his department heads that they should continue to operate their departments as they had previously.

Conditions became so serious that money for routine bill-paying almost disappeared. A backlog of state income tax refunds went unpaid. Funds owed for medical services were withheld, forcing some hospitals to reduce services. Pharmacies were unable to fill prescriptions for welfare customers. The Board of Regents cautioned that it might be forced to close the colleges and universities for a brief period. Auditor Glenn Gainer and Treasurer A. James Manchin issued public statements about the problem, but Moore said the whole condition was "manufactured."

As the legislature convened for the 1988 session, Moore's last full year in office, the House and Senate were still in disagreement over the best way to cope with the continuing fiscal shortages. Chambers suggested new taxes, while Tonkovich, who had announced his candidacy for governor, claimed that no new taxes were needed. Moore submitted an unbalanced budget for the coming fiscal year, with no recommendations as to how the state's financial problems could be solved. He asked for $100 million in borrowing authority to help him finish out his term.

As the session wore on, the governor was given the right to borrow $50 million, but a budget agreement would not be worked out until midsummer. After the governor vetoed the first budget, the legislature was convened in special session three times. Moore continued to use the unusual tactic of submitting only partial budgets.

Near the end of the fiscal year, he announced that a surplus existed in the treasury, but House Finance Committee Chairman George Farley countered that West Virginia was in debt by more than $200 million, which included thirty thousand unpaid income tax refunds amounting to $24 million. With typical Moore aplomb, the governor then informed the press that $25 million could be made available to build a new stadium at Marshall University.

The Marshall stadium was only one of many ideas Moore proposed without offering a precise means of financing them. He wanted, for example, to turn Weston State Hospital into a prison and build a new mental hospital at nearby Jane Lew. He wanted to spend several million dollars on improvements at Spencer and Huntington hospitals. He wanted to consolidate government services in new state office buildings at various locations around West Virginia. And despite the critical state of fiscal affairs, he pushed ahead with his plan to apply gold leaf to the Capitol dome, a project he had started during his first term in office but which his successor had later cancelled due to the expense.

Throughout Moore's third term, the economic recession continued. There were a few pluses, however. Wheeling-Pittsburgh Steel moved its headquarters from Pittsburgh back to Wheeling, and AT&T opened a credit management center in Charleston. With the help of a state loan, the closed Volkswagen plant in South Charleston was reopened by Park Corporation of Cleveland. CSX announced the consolidation of its locomotive repair operations in Huntington. Bruce Hardwoods began building a new plant in Elkins. CSX, however, later reduced its Huntington workforce, and a number of glass plants in the state closed, including the largest—Anchor Hocking—at Clarksburg. The Quaker State Refinery at St. Marys also shut down.

Like Weirton Steel before it, the Quaker State management had announced that their struggling oil refinery at St. Marys was for sale. If no buyer could be found, the refinery would be closed at the end of the year and 160 workers would be laid off. In order to keep the plant open, the Governor's Office of Community and Industrial Development arranged for Morgantown businessman Charles Lazell to purchase the refinery with the help of a low-interest state loan of $5.5 million.

Lazell had no experience in the oil-refining business. One of his other companies had just climbed out of five years of bankruptcy. He was unable to apply his managerial experience in coal sales and auto repair to his new business, Mid-Atlantic Fuels Inc., and within a year the refinery was closed down. When it finally ceased operations, it had debts of $12 million, $4.7 million of which was owed to the state.

One type of project in the industrial-development field that Moore advocated tirelessly during his third term was the construction of small minemouth electric power plants. Late in his last year he announced that plants would be built in McDowell, Raleigh, Nicholas, and Kanawha counties. Two other such power projects had already been announced for Marion and Grant counties. All were planned to reclaim cast-off coal from gob piles and slate dumps as their primary energy source. "We've got contracts to sell the power," Moore said, and named the buyer as Virginia Power Company.

After Moore left office, however, it was discovered that there were contracts to sell power from only two plants because of transmission problems at the others.

Late in Moore's term, the last segment of the interstate highway system in West Virginia, the section of I-64 between Beckley and Lewisburg, was finally opened. The interstate system, a creation of the Eisenhower administration, was a long time coming to the Mountain State, and billions of dollars were spent building it.

A few weeks before the I-64 ribbon-cutting ceremony, Highway Commissioner William Ritchie criticized the legislature for refusing to consider increasing the gasoline tax to pay for highway improvements. The road system was in a serious state of disrepair, and Ritchie wanted to give it some of the attention that had been lacking since West Virginia began building multiple-lane roads. When the Highway Department first began gearing up for the interstate program in the 1950s, Ritchie's predecessor, Burl Sawyers, had expressed concern that other parts of the system—primary, secondary, and farm-to-market roads—would suffer if a financing plan was not developed to maintain them while the interstates were being built. Sawyers's warning was ignored, and years later Ritchie found himself with the almost impossible task of trying to find the funds to maintain the major highways while keeping the rest of the road network from falling apart. And unlike the earlier years of the century, by this time the state was no longer tied together by any form of public transportation—railroads, airlines, or buses.

Moore entered the 1988 election campaign as a reluctant candidate, in my opinion. I had been to the Mansion around the time he announced that he would seek another term, and during a long dinner conversation, I had found him to be a different person from the man I had known in the past. The intensity and vitality that had been his hallmark were gone. The energy that had carried this Republican stalwart to victory after victory in an overwhelmingly Democratic state was still evident, but his missionary zeal had been muted.

This type of malady seems to be a hazard of the political world. In 1966, when Randolph had just won reelection to another term in the U.S. Senate, he invited me to meet him for a chat. He wanted to let me know that he planned to never again run for the Senate. He gave no reasons for wanting to step aside, and, as it turned out, much of his public career was still ahead of him. But at the time, I was convinced that Randolph, like Moore later, was suffering from political fatigue.

Both Moore and Randolph had by that time reached the pinnacle of their careers as public servants. Randolph was a respected and influential member of the highest lawmaking body in the land. Moore had served in the state legislature, in the U.S. Congress, and longer as governor than any other West Virginian in the state's history. The thrill of pursuing the goal was gone, and the inevitable pressures of their respective positions had begun to take their toll. There were no more mountains left for either man to scale, no more flags to plant on the crest. Disenchantment had set in. Running twice more as Randolph did, and running for an unprecedented fourth term as Moore was doing, became less a matter of personal choice than an obligation to their staff members, friends, and political associates. Both men had become prisoners of their party, and the only winners in another race would be those of the party faithful who wanted to keep their candidates in office merely to serve their own special interests.

In the polls, Moore moved into the general election campaign behind the Democratic nominee, Gaston Caperton, a businessman who had never before run for political office. By Labor Day the governor could see that his situation was serious, so much so that he informed the State Chamber of Commerce that he would be present for a debate with his opponent at The Greenbrier, whether Caperton appeared or not. Caperton, a longtime member of the chamber, had said that he would attend the meeting but had no plans to face off against Moore. Standard operating procedure in election campaigns is for the trailing candidate to challenge his opponent to debate, and Moore relished the idea of debating Caperton whenever and wherever possible.

But they actually debated only once, in mid-October on statewide television. Moore, an experienced and eloquent public speaker, pulled out all the stops and succeeded in upstaging Caperton. But Caperton's political innocence proved more of an asset than a handicap. As they watched the two men discuss the issues, many viewers remembered the unfulfilled promises Moore had made in the past, his endless battles with the legislature, his repeated assertions that all was well fiscally when millions of dollars in unpaid bills were stacked up around the Statehouse. They chose to put their faith in the untested Caperton rather than in the promises so glibly spun out by Moore.

Moore's flights of fiscal fancy did not end with the debate. During a campaign swing through Monongalia County he said that a medical research park was coming to West Virginia which would generate forty thousand new jobs and possibly be located in Morgantown. In Clarksburg he said the same thing, implying that the medical park would be located in Harrison County. He told his audiences that he would be more cooperative with the legislature if elected to a fourth term, expecting them to believe that he would suddenly change his ways after twelve years as governor. He traveled all over the state promising new water plants, bleachers for football fields, street-paving projects, sewer lines, and so forth, when in actuality there was not enough money on hand to cover the state's current expenses, let alone fulfill promises of additional expenditures.

As it turned out, the governor became yet another political casualty of what Thomas H. Huxley called "[that] mysterious independent variable of political calculation, Public Opinion." Moore had extended his credibility to the breaking point, and the voters had had enough. They wanted a new face, a candidate who offered the prospect of change from West Virginia's politics-as-usual. Voter willingness to alter course had already begun to express itself in the primary election. Cast aside was John Raese, former Republican Party chairman. Among Democrats, Tonkovich, former House Speaker Clyde See, State Senator Mario Palumbo, and Gus Douglass, who for twenty-four years had served as agriculture commissioner, were snubbed by the electorate. In Caperton, the voters had a candidate who had never been elected to public office and who made few campaign promises. They found him a refreshing change.

On inauguration day, Moore had difficulty remaining in Charleston for Caperton's inaugural ceremony. He broke with tradition by leaving for his home in Glen Dale even before the new governor delivered his inaugural address. Later, he said he would return to the practice of law.

It was Moore's last hurrah.

Chapter 27

Three Words Again

ON DECEMBER 12, 1988, one month after Gaston Caperton had been elected West Virginia's new governor, Fanny Seiler reported in the *Gazette* that a surplus of nearly $53.4 million had been mysteriously lost from the state's Consolidated Investment Fund.

The state treasurer's office had had problems before. In 1875 the House of Delegates impeached Treasurer John Burdett on charges of accepting kickbacks from a Charleston bank in exchange for keeping at least forty thousand dollars in state funds in that bank. One hundred years later, in 1975, State Treasurer John Kelly pleaded guilty to extortion and went to prison. He admitted to receiving payoffs for maintaining state funds in various banks around the state. At that time the FBI reported that there was no formal policy for investing state monies and, on average, between $70 million and $170 million sat idle in non-interest-bearing accounts in banks at all times.

State planners decided that reforms were in order. Kelly's successor, Larrie Bailey, began a program that, in time, evolved into what was known as the Consolidated Investment Fund. As envisioned, the fund was intended to be a clearinghouse for state investments, with the treasurer's office handling transactions for other state agencies. Under the terms of the new statute, county and local governing bodies were extended this service as well. The State Board of Investments, composed of the governor, auditor, and treasurer, served as the administering body for the fund.

As a means of maintaining solvency, the legislature placed restrictions on the types of securities the board could invest in. The fund was not to engage in stock market speculation or similar risk-prone ventures. But as often happens with the best-laid plans, something went awry. What had been a vision of unending streams of money turned into a nightmare of hellish proportions.

The discovery of the missing $53.4 million was made by the legislative auditor. Precisely when the losses occurred, however, was not known. Associate Treasurer Arnold Margolin, who had assumed his position with Treasurer A. James Manchin in 1985, said the losses took place—without his knowledge—between August 1984 and December 1986.

Another team of auditors from the accounting firm of Touche Ross and Company, of Pittsburgh, had also been examining the treasurer's records and was expected to disclose even larger losses in its report due out in a few weeks. Manchin confirmed this fact the day after Seiler's report on the missing funds appeared in the *Gazette*, admitting that as much as $150 million might be a more accurate figure. The state investment pool was then valued at $1.7 billion. As finally reported by Touche Ross, the actual losses amounted to $279.1 million.

Manchin, the constitutionally designated custodian of state monies, refused to accept responsibility for the missing funds. He pointed the finger at Margolin. Under Margolin the fund had generated income at a rate of almost 14 percent during 1986, which, according to the treasurer, was the best yield in the country. Manchin had declared Margolin a financial wizard in press reports and speeches. But after the story broke, the treasurer took a different stance, and as the pressure mounted, Margolin was made the official scapegoat.

"I never knew what was going on there," Manchin said. "I just trusted my expert." Margolin, he added, should have maintained closer oversight of his investments director, Kathy Lester.

Margolin, who had served as a top financial assistant to Governor Rockefeller before moving to the treasurer's office at the beginning of Moore's third term, was vacationing in Florida when the investment scandal first broke. He had accepted the position of administrative assistant to incoming Governor Caperton and was scheduled to assume his new duties upon his return to Charleston. When Margolin got back home, he too refused to accept responsibility for the losses. He also tendered his resignation to Caperton.

In a full-page interview with members of the *Gazette* staff, Margolin said it was a mystery to him why the various auditing firms had not uncovered the losses earlier. "We're the only program in state government to my knowledge where the audit is all the time. The legislative auditor, as a practical matter, has offices within our office."

During the period of time when the shortages occurred, Margolin noted, five independent audits of state treasury records were conducted. "Why the internal auditors did not discover this is very perplexing and indeed concerns me," he said. He further stated that although he was given daily reports of activities taking place in the investment office, they were not accurate, a problem he discovered upon going personally to files in the Statehouse basement.

It was on such inaccurate data that he based his judgments, he told the *Gazette*, regarding the amounts of interest to be paid to public agencies on money the agencies had on deposit in the fund.

Lester, the former investments director, had resigned her position with the treasurer's office in late 1987 and was living in Michigan. When she returned to Charleston to consult an attorney, she talked with the press about the missing funds. As she explained it, Manchin, Margolin, Assistant Charles Capet, and other state employees had known of the fund's losses for some time. Also, she said, Margolin signed transmittals which were summaries of purchases and initialed deposits. Whenever he wasn't available, his assistant, Jerry Simpson, performed these tasks.

"I haven't done anything wrong," she added.

Investment clerk Mary Jane Lopez corroborated Lester's story. She said she gave Margolin daily reports showing the losses, and she grew so frightened that she warned Capet of the situation. Margolin contradicted both Lester and Lopez. He denied learning about the fund's shaky condition until later, but he said Manchin and Capet had both been advised about what was going on some months before and withheld information. Meanwhile, Capet acknowledged that Lester and Lopez had put out warnings in early 1987 but that Margolin had shrugged them off.

"Who's lying?" the *Gazette* asked editorially. "Who's telling the truth? God only knows. Federal, state and county investigators are sorely needed to dig out the facts and determine whether crimes were committed. Even with probes, perhaps it will be impossible to learn precisely what happened."

By early January 1989, four investigative agencies had responded to the call for an inquiry into the investment mess. The U.S. Attorney's office, FBI, Legislative Commission on Special Investigations, and county prosecutor all announced that they would try to determine whether there had been unlawful activity in the management of the Consolidated Investment Fund. Senate President Larry Tucker suggested that the U.S. Securities and Exchange Commission be invited in as a participant.

Tucker, a Summersville banker, was on target with his idea. *The Huntington Herald-Dispatch* had just revealed that three investment firms had been paid a total of $335,000 to advise the State Board of Investments while the fund was losing more than a quarter of a billion dollars.

These payments for investment advice were separate from the commissions paid to brokerage houses, which handled about seven thousand transactions totaling $80.58 billion and continued to earn commissions in 1987 while the losses were mounting. The amounts of commissions were not reflected in state records since they were part of the bid price. The treasurer's office paid an additional forty-two thousand dollars a year to Charleston National Bank for advice on managing the state police pension fund and the judges' retirement fund.

Manchin's office collected a fee equal to three-fourths of 1 percent of the earnings from the fund's investors to pay administrative costs, and the Huntington newspaper uncovered some bizarre uses of these monies. Manchin paid forty-five members of his staff from the account, but only eleven of them were directly involved in work for the investment board.

The *Gazette*, after also examining the records that disclosed these expenditures, concluded that while certain employees supposedly were assigned to the task of encouraging local governing bodies to place their reserves in the investment fund, they were actually political field workers who spent their time building Manchin's support base in the courthouses and city halls across the state.

The Herald-Dispatch listed other creative ways Manchin found to spend the fee receipts.

According to the paper, he chartered a plane to hand-deliver a check to a Roanoke, Virginia, bank. He used the fees to pay for photos of himself for distribution to voters and bought a car. He flew banners bearing his name over Mountaineer Field in Morgantown during football games. And he flew to New York with Margolin to discuss a $200 million stock purchase with Chase Manhattan Bank officials. As it turned out, the state lost $27 million on the Chase Manhattan deal.

Commenting on the many purchases and sales of securities in 1987, Jack Hall, state securities chief, said, "It strikes me that there were an excessive amount of trades." State Republican Party Chairman Edgar Heiskell, of Morgantown, suggested that the fund might have been "churned," a brokerage term used to describe massive transactions that produced no profits for the client but made large profits for the brokers.

Moore, who served as chairman of the Consolidated Investment Fund, broke his silence on the missing money scandal just before leaving office in January 1989. He confirmed that an audit showed the state lost $279.1 million during a two-year period. The treasurer's office, he went on, paid out $30.4 million more in interest to participating agencies than it made on investments during 1986. "The audit will tell you," he added, "that they kept two sets of books and they never reconciled them."

The audit he referred to had been prepared by the accounting firms of Touche Ross and Suttle, Stalnaker, and Schoen. The bulk of the losses occurred during April, May, and June of 1987, when interest rates rose as the value of the state's holdings took a nosedive. By March 1987, treasury officials had built up a surplus of around $54 million in investment earnings, but the surplus was wiped out by June and approximately $224 million more was lost.

"Putting the two of them together, they lost $279 million," Moore said.

He explained that Manchin had an incentive to keep interest rates up to encourage local governments to place their savings in the state fund, since the treasurer's office received a commission on interest earned. "It was only natu-

ral to create a climate that would induce money into the consolidated fund,"
Moore added. The use of the commissions by Manchin, which amounted to
more than $1 million dollars, was not monitored by either the Board of Invest-
ments or the legislature, he said. "They were essentially a fund out of which
the treasurer's office could do whatever Manchin wanted to do, and he did."

A few days after Moore addressed the problem, the Elkins *Inter-Mountain* editorialized:

> *An independent audit of the state's Consolidated Investment Fund reveals
> some 'unusual' practices . . . Consider: In 1987 alone, the fund traded more
> than $80 billion. The fund borrowed an astounding $31 billion to help pay for
> its heavy trading. The fund traded as much as $2.7 billion in one day. Two sets
> of books were kept. There was no correlation whatever between what the fund
> paid in interest and what it actually made . . . The audit does not answer one
> important question: Who authorized, who approved all these unbelievable
> activities?*

Soon after the losses were exposed, the U.S. Attorney for Southern West
Virginia subpoenaed records from the treasurer's office and summoned the
main players in the fund's operation before a grand jury. Among them were
Moore, Manchin, Margolin, and State Auditor Glen Gainer. The time had
come to determine whether federal laws had been broken.

Regardless of the outcome of the U.S. Attorney's investigation, it was apparent that Manchin had risen beyond his level of competence, as was revealed a short time later in his own testimony before a legislative committee.
His spectacular mediocrity as an administrator and his cavalier attitude toward the masses of money entrusted to his care were documented. Not only
did his testimony confirm a serious loss of state funds, it helped explain why
West Virginia's once fine reputation for prudent management of its fiscal affairs had been so badly damaged.

Manchin, a Farmington native, had entered government service as a
member of the House of Delegates in 1949. He was later appointed state

director of the Farmers Home Administration by President Kennedy, then served as state director of the Environmental Action program, which primarily removed junked cars from state roadsides. He was elected Secretary of State in 1976 and again in 1980, and treasurer in 1984. From the very beginning of his years in public service, he was a consummate politician. While Secretary of State and Treasurer, he toured the state making speeches, appearing at fairs and festivals, and dispensing self-promotional certificates, plaques, and flags, all at the taxpayers' expense. An accomplished hill-country speaker with an evangelical style of delivery and a fondness for melodrama, he built a large following among voters in both political parties.

When Manchin appeared before the legislative committee, he refused to take responsibility for the problems in the treasurer's office, trying instead to shift the blame to other parties. But he made so many conflicting statements that he only wrapped himself up more tightly inside the tangled web of loose money management. He had advised his friends in certain courthouses and city halls to withdraw their deposits from the state fund, prompting a run similar to those made on banks in the Depression years of the 1930s. The fund lost $528 million in this manner during 1988 alone. He was unable to provide a clear and precise answer as to why his aides had engaged in the highly speculative and prohibited practice of futures buying. All he would say when asked about such activity was that fund management was a duty he had not assumed personally upon taking office. What he believed his obligations as treasurer to be he never defined. So troubled were members of the House of Delegates by Manchin's testimony and his disavowal of any responsibility or accountability that they started a movement to impeach him, with Republican Marc Harmon, of Grant County, as point man.

Harman's impeachment resolution was referred routinely to the judiciary committee where a hearing was arranged. There was intense pressure from the membership to make it an in-depth inquiry. The first witness called before the committee, Michael Sizemore, set the tone for the hearing when he stated that a cover-up had been ordered from some place to screen the heavy losses in the fund. In his opinion, an unknown party or parties had intentionally falsified the critical state of investments.

Witness after witness told of creative bookkeeping practices designed to prevent auditors and the public from discovering the deteriorating state of the fund. Among those testifying to the dual system was Dorothy Gillespie, who had been demoted from her position as data processing director and afterward resigned. According to Gillespie, losses were hidden from the public but not from the staff. "It was like working on Wall Street, and the bottom fell out," she told the committee. When questioned about Treasurer Manchin's knowledge of the fund's precarious condition, she said, "I don't see how he could not have known."

Margolin told the committee that Manchin, at the start of his reelection campaign, asked him to solicit political contributions from members of the investment community. "I told him it would not be appropriate or ethical to ask these people for money since we were doing business with them," Margolin said.

He also told the committee that his assistant, Lester, had gotten threatening phone calls advising her not to appear in Charleston to testify about conditions in the treasurer's office. She had been warned that if she said anything hostile or detrimental to Manchin, there might be an accident to one or both of her children. The same phone warning was delivered to members of the House of Delegates before they were scheduled to vote on the impeachment resolution.

Gainer, appearing before the committee as a member of the investment board, said that the root cause of the fund's losses traced back to early 1985 when Manchin and Moore agreed on a change in investment regulations. It was like giving Manchin "a blank check," he added. Gainer said that he had succeeded in late 1984 in having restrictions imposed to allow investment only in ninety-day securities, to require that all sales be approved by the board, and to ban speculative investing. A short time later this procedure was discarded by a two-to-one vote.

Gainer said he had originally sought the changes because he was worried about Manchin's management style. "He did a lot of ribbon-cutting and passed out a lot of certificates," the auditor explained. "He spent a lot of time in ceremonial duties, and that is not conducive for the type of administration the Board of Investments demands."

Gainer also said he was disturbed by the way members of the investment staff handled millions of dollars in trades by telephone with Wall Street brokers. "You would think they were talking about ten dollars instead of $10 million," he said. The majority of the trades were executed by Lester, Gainer continued. "What was amazing to me . . . is when you listened to her making the calls. She was asking the brokers what she should be doing today, buying or selling."

Moore told the committee he saw signs of trouble in fund investments in 1987 but did not know the full range of losses until late in 1988. "Had we had an idea anything was wrong," he commented, "we certainly would have had the treasurer on the carpet in a moment."

The first indication of problems appeared when the New York bond firm of Salomon Brothers sent a letter to the treasurer's office warning that the state's investments were at risk due to an unstable situation in the bond market. The second sign came a month later when the State Housing Development Fund withdrew $235 million from the investment fund. At this time, Moore said, he called an emergency meeting of the investment board, where he and Gainer insisted that Manchin reduce interest rates being paid to agencies with money on deposit.

"There was some resistance to that suggestion [from Manchin]," the governor said, "but the only way you could rebuild value was to quit giving away all the money in the store."

Moore was asked to comment on whether he considered Manchin intelligent and articulate. "Articulate, certainly," he responded, "as long as you're talking about God, country, and family. I'm not going to comment on his intelligence. I think you're going too far."

Manchin had spent days in the House chamber trying with his own down-home style of persuasion to bring the impeachment proceedings to a halt. Unsuccessful in this strategy, he turned to histrionics when he reached the witness stand. "What you're talking about now is a person's life, a man's career," he whined. "You're talking now about the death penalty." In six hours of testimony, he said he didn't recognize the storm signals Moore had talked about. "In retrospect, many of us must share the responsibility," he said, nam-ing—among others responsible for the losses—Moore, Gainer, and the legis-lative auditor for not discovering the problem.

In his attempt to shift a portion of the blame to others, Manchin told the committee, "I have a style that I delegate authority, which is not uncom-mon." He also mentioned his lack of financial expertise. "I was not elected as a financial authority," he remarked. "Rather, the people elected me as an administrator." He said that he was not familiar with the investment board's regulations, did not have much knowledge of investment terms, and knew little about financial reports prepared by his office. "A lot of these reports look alike," he added.

Toward the end of his testimony, Manchin said removal from office would be more than a simple firing. "It's tantamount to giving a sentence of death, stripping the dignity from a man who has served the state long and well," he complained.

The committee was not impressed with his emotional plea. It recom-mended impeachment to the full House.

The House of Delegates, with one member not present, debated the Manchin charges for seven hours on March 30, 1989. Much of the debate centered on whether to impeach the treasurer or impose the lighter punish-ment of censure.

By a vote of 65–34 the members chose to impeach him on seventeen counts of incompetence, neglect of duty, and maladministration of his office. They also voted to censure Gainer but refused to consider any action against Moore since by then he was no longer in office.

Delegate Harman set the tone when he said, "There is only one person to blame . . . and that person is A. James Manchin. If he didn't know about the losses, he should have. You're setting a standard for years to come for public officials in this state. For too long we've had public officials with no standards. We've been victims of political corruption in my party and your party."

Following the House vote, the impeachment proceeding shifted to the Senate, which set the trial for midsummer. Supreme Court Chief Justice William T. Brotherton was invited to preside. Conviction by the Senate would have prevented Manchin from ever again holding public office and would also have stripped him of his right to collect his state pension of approximately twenty-five thousand dollars a year.

Manchin dallied for weeks over whether to resign or go to trial, hinting by turns that he would take early retirement or that he planned to stay and fight. Then, on West Virginia Day, June 20, 1989, he threw a party in his office during which he announced that he would step down. "I cannot in good conscience ask the people of the State of West Virginia to bear the cost and the emotional process of the trial," he said. He set his retirement date as July 9, the day before the Senate was scheduled to convene for the impeachment trial.

On July 7, a Friday and his last day in office—he had scheduled speaking appearances around the state on Saturday and Sunday—Manchin staged another party, at which he said, "I'll never grow tired of celebrating with West Virginians." The name of his possible successor came into speculative discussion during that affair, and Manchin was asked if he had any advice for him. The treasurer replied, "Don't invest."

Two days later Caperton named State Senator Thomas E. Loehr, a New Martinsville Democrat, as Manchin's replacement. Loehr, a lawyer and certified public accountant, went to work on July 10 with the comment that he planned only to serve out the remainder of Manchin's term.

On the same day that Loehr assumed his new duties, the State Senate's proceedings against Manchin were halted with the concurrence of the House of Delegates. The special legislative session lasted only a few minutes. Manchin was present as the Senate brought this political embarrassment to an end.

"Meanwhile," wrote *Gazette* reporter Patty Vandergrift, "a report outlining evidence that the House would have presented at trial was submitted but was not released publicly." A day later the report was leaked to the press, and it disclosed that James Lees, special prosecutor for the House Judiciary Committee, had stated that Manchin engaged in a practice of fraudulently apportioning money to local governments which they hadn't earned. Manchin, Lees said, also was responsible for his office staff's speculative trading practices, which were contrary to investment guidelines.

"My conclusion," Lees commented, "is that Mr. Manchin would have had to be blind, deaf, and dumb not to have been aware in April 1987 of precisely what was transpiring within the Consolidated Investment Fund."

Losses to the fund were never precisely determined prior to Manchin's resignation from office. Lees, in his report, calculated them at $344 million, a sharp increase over the estimate provided by state and private auditing organizations. This higher figure was reached by factoring in overpayments made by the treasurer's office to local governments for earnings not realized and by runs on the fund after the losses were reported publicly in 1987, panicking county and municipal agencies and causing them to quickly remove their deposits.

State officials decided in the fall of 1989 to try to recover a portion of the losses by bringing suit against the New York investment firms that had served as advisors to the treasury during the ill-fated investment spree. One of those firms, County NatWest, chose to settle out of court rather than continue the litigation. "Our government securities unit was not responsible for the state board's losses," a NatWest spokesman said. "Nonetheless, this settlement is cheaper than litigation."

The settlement amounted to $2 million on losses alleged by the state to have totaled $10.3 million. A few weeks later, three more Wall Street firms decided to settle rather than continue the court actions.

While they acknowledged no wrongdoing, Shearson Lehman Hutton, Citibank, and Merrill Lynch settled with the state for nearly $2 million. Other defendants brought countersuits, and this tangle of litigation filed in two different states was expected to remain in the courts for years before final judgments could be handed down.

Then early in 1991 Salomon Brothers broke ranks and settled with the state for $15 million. In 1992 Morgan Stanley and Company, one of the firms that had chosen to take the matter to court, lost after a five-week trial in Kanawha Circuit Court. The jury awarded the state a $4.9 million judgment after finding Morgan Stanley guilty of "constructive fraud."

As another way of recovering losses, the Consolidated Investment Fund's operating officers considered making an attempt to collect on $7.7 million in performance bonds held on the members of the Board of Investments who were in office at the time the losses occurred, as well as its top management team and two members of the treasury staff: Margolin and Lester.

This action, if taken, would have addressed the accountability of those who were in charge when the fund plunged over a precipice. However, it would, in a sense, have meant that the state had to proceed fiscally against itself.

The $7.7 million would be collected by seeking forfeiture of the Board of Investments' $5 million bond, three $250,000 bonds held in the names of Moore, Manchin, and Gainer, and two million-dollar general liability bonds held in the names of Margolin and Lester. "We would end up sharing a part of the cost," said the investment board's director, Robert Corey, "because there is a large deductible."

The performance bonds were issued by CNA Insurance Company, but the state's liability insurance coverage carried a $5 million deductible on claims, which would ultimately lead simply to another shifting of bond payments from one state agency to another. As Corey explained, collecting on the bonds would be a questionable exercise because the state would have to prove what the losses were and whether the bonded parties had failed the legalistic test of faithful performance in their management practices. Court action could result, which, like that against the New York investment houses, might go on for years.

As a third means of recouping lost monies, late in 1989 the treasury bought $6 million in bonds. "We're not exactly getting rid of the losses," said a treasury officer, "but this is a method of correcting our books." Those bonds were expected to be worth $20.7 million upon maturity fifteen years later.

Midway through the 1990 legislative session, it was decided that none of the local governing bodies—counties, municipalities, and boards of education—would be held accountable for any of the money improperly paid to them in interest while Manchin was in office. A bill was sent to Caperton excusing them from payment of approximately $125 million. The governor said he liked what the lawmakers had done and signed the bill into law.

A few weeks later, the man Manchin had described as a financial wizard, Margolin, was indicted on nineteen counts of violating federal securities and exchange laws and seven counts of lying to a grand jury. "I plead innocent to all charges in the indictment," Margolin said in an appearance before U.S. District Court Judge John T. Copenhaver.

But Margolin changed his mind four months later. He entered a guilty plea to two counts of violating the law and admitted to having issued statements to agencies with money in the investment fund informing them that they were earning income when in actuality they were not.

When this former political consultant to Governor Rockefeller and financial advisor to Governor Moore appeared in court, he did not equivocate.

"Were you aware of the magnitude of the losses?" Copenhaver asked.

"Yes, I was, Your Honor," Margolin responded.

In handing down the sentence, Copenhaver told Margolin, "You are a kind and gentle soul . . . but the enormity of what occurred cannot go unpunished." Margolin was sentenced to a year in prison and fined ten thousand dollars.

The scope of the losses from the investment fund fiasco, both actual and in unrealized interest, were outlined to the House Finance Committee in spring 1990 by Manchin's successor, Loehr. It was a bitter pill the state had to swallow. According to Loehr, over the next fifteen to twenty years, the state stood to suffer an erosion of funds amounting to one billion dollars.

Part Four

"The tragedy is not that things are broken.
The tragedy is that they are not mended again."

Alan Stewart Paton

"Those who do not remember the past
are condemned to repeat it."

George Santayana,

The Life of Reason, *1905*

Chapter 28

CAPERTON'S INHERITANCE

WEST VIRGINIA'S THIRTIETH GOVERNOR, Gaston Caperton, took office under economic and political stresses similar to those faced by Kump in 1933. The state was almost bankrupt. Unemployment soared above the national average. Families were leaving the mountains in large numbers, hoping to find a better life elsewhere.

The legacy the Moore administration left to the next governor included a mountain of debt, much of it documented in unpaid bills kept in cardboard boxes scattered around the governor's suite. Among other debts were thousands of unpaid tax refunds. The Human Services and Veterans Affairs departments owed the IRS $160,000 in back taxes. Other agencies and offices failed to meet their tax deadlines in 1987 and 1988, including the governor's office. As a result, more than a half million dollars in penalties was levied against the state in fiscal year 1988–1989.

"These are unnecessary charges," Caperton said about the IRS penalties, "resulting from delayed paperwork and bureaucratic inaction which I will not tolerate."

Caperton inherited another debt from his predecessor, this one dating back to Moore's first term in office. Following the Buffalo Creek disaster in 1972, Moore's finance commissioner, John Gates, had agreed to pay the U.S. Army Corps of Engineers for emergency work the Corps had performed at the disaster site. Three days before Moore left office at the end of his second term in 1977, the outgoing governor accepted a $1 million dollar settlement offer from Pittston Coal Company and absolved Pittston from any further liability as part of the settlement agreement.

Later, during Moore's third term as governor, it became known that West Virginia still owed the Corps of Engineers for the disaster cleanup; the bill totaled $3.7 million. Because of Moore's settlement with Pittston, the state could no longer collect anything from the coal company responsible for the illegal dam that had burst, leaving 125 people dead and four thousand more homeless. By the time Moore left office in January 1989, the state's debt to the Corps had mounted to $9.4 million in cleanup costs and interest charges.

The amount of debt uncovered by the new Caperton administration was so extensive—almost half a billion dollars—that the $400 million package of new and higher taxes proposed by Caperton would not be sufficient to bring the budget back into balance. Strict economies would also be required, amounting to almost $100 million. The state's fiscal condition was so serious that two and a half years would elapse before West Virginia would be able to achieve a cash surplus in the general revenue budget.

But the full extent of Caperton's inheritance from his predecessor was just coming to light. For months federal and state investigators had been delving into public and private records. Caperton had been in office less than six months when state officials began falling like dominoes.

The resignation and early retirement of Manchin in the summer of 1989 was followed by the resignation of State Attorney General Charlie Brown. Brown and his ex-wife were embroiled in a child custody dispute at the time, in the course of which Brown made certain statements in public records relating to the dispute that were not only a political embarrassment to him but which nearly turned the child custody proceeding into a grand jury probe.

At issue in the custody battle was Brown's alleged liaison with a former employee in his office. The only newspaper references to the case were based primarily on gossip because of tight restraints on news releases imposed by both Brown and county prosecutor Bill Forbes. In fact, the whole affair was pretty well contained behind the stone walls of the Kanawha County Courthouse—until someone leaked it to the *Gazette*.

The result was a multimillion-dollar libel suit against the *Gazette* filed by Brown's former employee, Brenda Simon. The newspaper had alleged that Simon asked Brown for money in exchange for her silence about her pregnancy in 1986. Simon denied that she received any money and called the story "dastardly, malicious, and false." The thirty-five-year-old woman, by then living in Columbus, Ohio, said that her husband had fathered the child, which died in infancy. She produced a death certificate to support her statement.

Simon had worked in Brown's 1984 campaign for attorney general and, after the election, became a secretary in his office. She remained there through 1986. The press reported that notes filed in the child custody case between Brown and his former wife claimed that Brown was going to pay Simon fifty thousand dollars to keep quiet about the relationship. When asked whether his client had been personally involved with Brown, Simon's attorney, Monty Preiser, responded, "That's not important as far as I know."

Brown also denied the information contained in the news stories, although he was then under investigation by the Kanawha County prosecutor on charges of false swearing in the custody suit. Brown complained to the press that the investigation had been prompted by a "vindictive ex-wife." Nevertheless, Forbes said he would take the matter to the grand jury the following week.

Instead, Brown resigned as attorney general and the grand jury probe was halted. Simon's libel suit against the *Gazette* was dropped, and Simon herself was indicted on charges of extortion, later dismissed. When Forbes was asked if the issue of possible sexual harassment of an employee by her employer had been addressed in the grand jury investigation, he failed to reply to the inquiry.

In an effort to restore credibility to the attorney general's office, Caperton named a five-member committee of lawyers headed by Brotherton, chief justice of the State Supreme Court, to provide him with a list of replacement nominees. From that list, Caperton selected Charleston attorney Roger W. Tompkins as Brown's successor. Tompkins had served four terms in the House of Delegates, two of them as majority leader. He was a graduate of West Virginia University and the Yale University law school, and had been a Rhodes Scholar. When accepting the appointment, Tompkins said, "I'm here to run a law firm and a very sizeable law firm. I want to see it run well. I want to see it have some discipline and professionalism."

Tompkins chose to serve only until the next election. He was succeeded by former State Senator Palumbo, a Charleston attorney, who announced that he intended to ask the next legislature for statewide powers to prosecute corrupt officeholders.

Scandal next struck what members proudly referred to as their "august body," the State Senate. In a matter of months two members, who had both served as Senate president, pleaded guilty to crimes against the state, and a majority leader pleaded guilty to tax evasion. Tonkovich was brought down after serving two terms as president and then losing in his 1988 bid for governor. His successor as Senate president, Larry Tucker, served only eight months in that post before he too was convicted.

Tonkovich admitted to extorting money from parties who wanted to establish casino gambling in West Virginia. Tucker admitted to accepting a bribe from officers of Tri-State Greyhound Park near Charleston. Tonkovich was indicted for allegedly trading his influence for fifteen thousand dollars; Tucker, for ten thousand. Both of them informed the U.S. attorney that they had returned or attempted to return the money to the parties offering it, but this was an action after the fact and they were both hauled into U.S. District Court in Charleston for what can be broadly described as abuse of their legislative trust.

Two weeks before, Si Boettner, of Charleston, who had served as Senate majority leader, had pleaded guilty to tax evasion. In the plea agreement, Boettner offered to cooperate with the government as an unindicted coconspirator in the investigation of Tonkovich and the gambling casino proposal. Tucker was listed as a defense witness in the case.

Tonkovich, Tucker, and Boettner were all old hands in the legislature. Tucker was the first to arrive, elected to the House in 1970. Tonkovich was elected in 1972, Boettner in 1974. Tonkovich and Boettner each served as Senate majority leader, Tucker as chairman of the powerful judiciary committee.

A potential witness in both the Boettner and Tucker cases was Sam D'Annunzio, a Clarksburg banker, beer distributor, and lobbyist for the West

Virginia Beer Wholesalers Association. Records indicated that D'Annunzio had paid some of Boettner's campaign debts after he had run unsuccessfully for attorney general against Charlie Brown in 1984. D'Annunzio was also alleged to be the money source for Tucker's ten-thousand-dollar trade-off of support on the dog-track legislation. But by the time the Tonkovich trial began, D'Annunzio was no longer available to testify. He had committed suicide late in 1988.

In a surprise move at his trial, after government attorneys finished presenting their part of the case, Tonkovich caved in and pleaded guilty to extorting five thousand dollars from persons seeking to pass the casino gambling legislation. Tucker and Boettner had entered guilty pleas without going to trial. They also resigned from the Senate.

There were consequences to pay for more than just this trio of high-ranking officials. The federal government's sweep through the West Virginia Capitol also netted Tonkovich's administrative assistant, Robert Cain, who was indicted on charges of tax evasion; and Robert McCormick, a former House member from Logan, convicted in an unrelated tax-evasion case linking him to foreign-born doctors and their difficulties with state licensing tests. The McCormick case, however, was later set aside by the U.S. Supreme Court.

A few days before Christmas 1989, Copenhaver handed down sentences in the Tonkovich, Tucker, and Boettner cases.

Tonkovich was sentenced to five years in prison and fined ten thousand dollars. Tucker was sentenced to six months in prison followed by 250 days of community service and fined twenty thousand dollars. Boettner was placed on five years' probation and directed to perform two hundred days of community service.

In sentencing Tonkovich, Copenhaver said, "You come before the court now as one who has corrupted this state's highest legislative office, being the second highest-ranking office in state government. Your misconduct, along with others, has quaked the very foundation of our public institutions and has left the citizens of the state shaken in their confidence and trust of the legislative process."

After the sentencing, U.S. Attorney Michael Carey sent a warning to others in state government. "This series of prosecutions, guilty pleas, and convictions show there are consequences to pay when public officials take advantage of their office for private gain." Ironically, Tucker and Tonkovich had both been members of the Legislative Commission on Special Investigations, which had been created in the 1970s as a result of the Invest Right scandal.

For nearly three decades, West Virginia had been unable to shake off the debilitating burden of corruption, thievery, and the institutionalization of wrongdoing in every branch of government. The state's flawed reputation was documented frequently in the early 1990s, but none of it was related to the new governor's management practices. On the contrary, Caperton was never once accused of engaging in the sort of indiscretions indulged in by at least two other governors. In fact, one of Caperton's first acts after taking office was to submit to the legislature a bill proposing the creation of an ethics commission, which passed with little opposition.

Regardless of Caperton's efforts, however, the state's bad press continued. *Financial World* rated West Virginia dead last among the fifty states in fiscal management. *Business Week* magazine and *The New York Times* commented disparagingly on the state's government and the extent of government corruption. But these news stories were only the tip of the iceberg. The press services, *USA Today*, and the television networks all spread the word about the dark side of West Virginia politics. A member of the production staff for a well-known television news program described politics in West Virginia as a "contact sport."

Don Marsh, editor of the *Gazette*, called West Virginia "a Third World country, a Third World state." "Why does disaster keep befalling us?" he asked in his column. "We're bankrupt. If we were a business, we'd be in Chapter 11."

Speaking to *The Washington Post*, Caperton's press secretary compared state politics to "the stock car races. Most people say they are going to see who wins, but in their heart of hearts, they want to see who crashes."

And it never seemed to end. During Easter week in 1990, Carey announced from his office in Charleston that Tucker, who at the time was still in prison on other charges, had been indicted on tax evasion and perjury charges. The indictment alleged that he conspired to impede the IRS and failed to report seventy-five thousand dollars on his 1983 tax return. The perjury charge was related to Tucker's purported false statements to a grand jury and others made during his sentencing in September 1989 in the dog-track extortion case.

Then Carey dropped a bombshell. He announced that Moore had agreed to plead guilty to a five-count indictment charging him with extortion, obstruction of justice, mail fraud, and tax evasion. Moore's famous Teflon coating had finally failed him.

Chapter 29

ONCE TOO OFTEN

ALGERNON SIDNEY, in his 1698 *Discourses on Government*, noted, "Liars have good memories." Moore had long been known for his own remarkable memory, but at the age of sixty-six, it apparently failed him.

Moore had a reputation for turning fact into fiction throughout his public career. As a congressman running for governor, he was quoted as saying, under oath, that his law practice had decreased to "zero." At the time that he made the statement, however, he was listed in a national lawyers directory as Moundsville-area counsel for seven major corporations.

Underwood recalled his experience in running against Moore for governor in the 1968 primary. "He saw things from his perspective almost exclusively," Underwood said. "What he thought happened, happened . . . In television debates he would make statements that were not true, and I had to use my time to correct them."

And the *Gazette*'s John Morgan, who covered the governor's office during the Smith administration and Moore's first two terms, summed up Moore's propensity for mendacity in his usual understated manner. "There sometimes existed an over-statement and credibility gap between the governor and the press," Morgan said in his book, *West Virginia Governors*.

Signs of trouble had begun appearing during Moore's first year as governor in 1969. In a conversation with one of the best holdovers from the Smith administration, Natural Resources Commissioner Pete Samsell, I learned that conditions were not as they seemed on the surface.

"How are things going?" I asked Samsell one day.

"Not very well," he answered. "I'm required to clear everything—down to the purchase of a box of pencils—with Moore's office."

Translation from Statehouse language: I was being given the distinct impression that the same sort of fix was on that had existed during the Barron and Smith years. In a conversation with Hoffmann several weeks later, I told him about Samsell's complaint. Hoffmann, a knowledgeable critic of Moore, said, "Arch makes Wally Barron look like an altar boy."

When confronted by federal investigators on April 12, 1990, and presented with documented proof of his misdeeds, Moore broke down and agreed to plead guilty to indictments charging him with various corrupt practices.

The indictments covered the period from 1984—when Moore's campaign manager, Huntington attorney Thomas L. Craig, was secretly handed a ski cap by the governor containing a hundred thousand dollars to be used in getting Moore reelected to 1990, when Moore lied under oath to federal officials.

Among other wrongdoings allegedly committed by Moore was the 1985 extortion of $573,000 from coal operator H. Paul Kizer, of Beckley, in exchange for the governor's influence in obtaining a $2 million refund for Kizer's company from the state's black-lung fund.

Moore was also charged with tax evasion in the receipt of fifty thousand dollars from Island Creek Coal Company, ten thousand dollars from D'Annunzio, and $2,500 from Robert Gilliam, a former Logan County school board member. Rounding out the indictment was Moore's attempt to obstruct justice by lying under oath and trying to persuade his 1988 campaign manager, John Leaberry, to lie for him.

According to the indictment, Leaberry, a former top official in the Moore administration, wore a listening device while meeting with Moore in a Parkersburg parking lot to discuss what Leaberry would say to the grand jury. The deal with Kizer was apparently struck in much the same way. Kizer told federal investigators that he and Moore made their arrangements at night behind the Charleston municipal incinerator.

At a press conference, called after Moore admitted to these charges in a signed plea agreement, John Campbell, a U.S. Justice Department public integrity prosecutor, commented, "It is extraordinary that a former governor of a state be indicted for offenses of this magnitude and unprecedented that he plead guilty."

The plea agreement was out of character for Moore, a complete reversal of his standard method of dealing with crises, and it baffled both his political friends and foes.

Moore was famous for his coolness under fire, his ability to brazen it out and bounce back from adversity. The public had expected him to fight the government's accusations, as he had twice in the past when faced with charges of income tax evasion and later with a charge of accepting a payoff of twenty-five thousand dollars from a savings and loan company president. He had come through these bouts unbowed, if not entirely unscathed, and it was generally expected that he would once again demand his day in court.

But Moore's surprising about-face—from a born scrapper who always relished fighting the odds to a man who surrendered quietly without a struggle—was short-lived. After several weeks' reflection on his impending fate, he informed the court that he would like to withdraw his guilty plea. His admission of guilt could have meant a maximum penalty of thirty-six years in prison and a fine of $1.25 million.

In the period between Moore's admission of guilt and his petition to withdraw the confession, a major Charleston stockholder in Tri-State Greyhound Park, Bill Ellis, was tried on charges of racketeering, conspiracy, aiding and abetting extortion, and obstruction of justice.

The charges related in part to his participation in payoffs to such state officials as Tucker. The jury found him guilty, and he was later fined fifty thousand dollars and sentenced to seven years in prison. However, the prosecution failed in its effort to link Ellis to an alleged hundred-thousand-dollar payoff to Moore. Ellis admitted on the witness stand to having met with Moore to discuss legislation that would have favored the dog track, but said he paid Moore nothing.

Also brought down by federal prosecutors were Jerry Bradbury, the State Tax Department's chief compliance officer under Moore, and Patricia Bradley, a member of the House of Delegates from Hancock County. Bradbury pleaded guilty to lying before a federal grand jury about his role in collecting cash for campaign purposes during Moore's 1988 reelection campaign. Court papers noted that the money collected was "distributed for the purpose of illegally influencing voters in 'controlled precincts' in certain counties in southern West Virginia."

Bradley was charged with failing to report for tax purposes $375.87 she had received from a lobbyist, which she used for a vacation at Hilton Head, South Carolina. She had served on a conference committee appointed to mediate differences between Senate and House versions of the bill allowing a $1.4 million benefit to Tri-State Greyhound Park. Court papers revealed that Bradley took the trip to Hilton Head after helping achieve a compromise on the Tri-State legislation. She later placed herself at the mercy of the court by entering a guilty plea.

In seeking to withdraw his own guilty plea, Moore argued through his attorney, William G. Hundley, that he had been pressured to enter the plea or face additional charges as well. Government attorneys countered that Moore had known for some time what the charges were before he appeared in court. They also argued that the judge had asked Moore at the time if he understood the charges and if he was entering his plea voluntarily. Moore had responded in the affirmative to both questions.

The judge hearing the Moore case was Walter Hoffman of the Eastern Virginia Federal District Court, who was brought to Charleston to handle the case. All federal judges in West Virginia had recused themselves from the assignment, and Hoffman, a senior judge, was asked to serve. His last appearance in this state had been to hear the case against Mike Roark, former Charleston mayor and Kanawha County prosecutor who was found guilty of charges relating to the possession of illegal drugs.

Hoffman listened patiently for three hours to opposing attorneys before rendering his judgment. Assistant U.S. Attorney Joseph Savage said:

"For nearly four decades Arch A. Moore was a dominant figure on the West Virginia and, occasionally, national political scene. And while untold thousands of words have been written to describe Arch Moore, this court today must fashion a sentence most appropriate for the one word that best describes him.

"Let there be no mistake—Arch Moore is a criminal. No governor or other public official of that responsibility has ever been convicted of election fraud of this scope. Moore capitalized on a tradition of corruption in the electoral system—raising money illegally, buying votes, and then lying about it."

Hundley said in response, "He is a man who not only served his country in World War II; he almost gave his life. He was wounded, left for dead, decorated. The fine people of West Virginia elected him three times to the highest office in the state."

Hundley also commented on what he described as "underground campaigning" in West Virginia. "The underground campaign was going on in West Virginia when Jack Kennedy was running for president and I was working for him."

After hearing the opposing arguments, Hoffman handed down a sentence of five years and ten months, plus a fine of $170,000. Moore was later directed to report to a federal correctional facility in Alabama. Ever the showman, the former governor was attired in a blue suit, white shirt, and red tie for his sentencing hearing.

Hoffman also denied a request by the state attorney general's office to require Moore to repay more than $4 million which the state had allegedly lost as a result of Moore's illegal activities. Hoffman advised that a lawsuit filed in a court of proper jurisdiction could determine the validity of the state's claim, a suggestion followed by the filing of a civil suit in the court where he was sitting. The state pension fund had already taken action to disallow payment of Moore's pension of approximately twenty thousand dollars a year, and the West Virginia State Bar had begun proceedings to disbar him from the further practice of law.

A few days after the sentencing, U.S. Attorney Carey discussed Moore's guilty plea. "It's clear the chief executive of West Virginia set the tone for corruption," he said. "Those who knew him said he had been a crook for years, and public officials seemed to believe that everyone was doing it, including the governor, so why not them." Carey made this statement after releasing a list of sixty-nine county, state, and federal officials who had been prosecuted by his office between 1984 and 1990. He also praised the press for their role in the successes his office had achieved.

One of the standout newsroom warriors in those years was Williamson *Daily News* editor Walter J. Warden, who had carried on an unrestrained crusade against coalfield corruption in Mingo County and eastern Kentucky.

In summing up Moore's fall from grace editorially, the *Daily News* wrote, "Arch Alfred Moore, Jr., a criminal who robbed West Virginia at will during his career in politics, received a prison sentence of five years and ten months and was fined $170,000 on five federal corruption charges. In actual jail time, the three-term former governor faces about 2½ years in prison before he is eligible for parole. If that's any kind of justice at all, it's rich man's justice."

The Beckley *Register Herald* declared, "From our perspective, justice has been done. Moore has been exposed for his corruption, and punishment has been handed down. Whether the fine and sentence were 'enough' to suit the situation is arguable—and no doubt will be argued for many years to come."

Oce Smith, longtime House of Delegates sergeant-at-arms, political columnist, and a friend of Moore's for many years, wrote in the Fairmont *Times-West Virginian*, "In the final chapter of this long-played human drama, a once invincible personal political empire was proven to be only a fragile house of cards . . . which came crashing to the ground under the weight of its own phenomenal greed, and the eventual scrutiny of the American people."

And *The Charleston Daily Mail* offered perhaps the definitive verdict: "He has shamed his wife and children. He has betrayed all those who admire his intelligence and believed his protestations of innocence. He has humiliated the state he loves."

Still to come was the disposition of the case against Leaberry, a major role-player in the government's effort to send Moore to prison. The U.S. attorney's office had recruited Leaberry to help obtain evidence against his boss by wearing a listening device while talking to Moore. Leaberry was charged with filing a false income tax return and chose not to go to trial. After admitting his guilt, he was fined ten thousand dollars and placed on three years probation. At the sentencing, Carey said, "Mr. Leaberry's assistance to the government was critical in the conviction of Governor Moore."

As 1990 drew to a close, Tucker appeared in federal court for the second time in a year, charged with lying to a grand jury and obstruction of justice. In closing arguments to the jury, the federal prosecutor said Tucker had entered into a criminal conspiracy to evade taxes by arranging for the money he had earned from two nursing home companies, a sum of $125,000, to be deposited into a grocery store bank account. Although Tucker faced the possibility of ten years in prison and a fine of five hundred thousand dollars, Judge Charles Haden chose to sentence Tucker to thirty-seven months in prison and fined him forty-five thousand dollars.

Fallout from the government's investigation of Moore also struck down Craig. He was accused of lying to a federal grand jury about the handling of the hundred thousand dollars that Moore had allegedly handed over to him in a ski cap during the 1984 election campaign. In June 1991 Craig admitted to having distributed the money and apologized to the State Bar's legal ethics committee for "having embarrassed our profession by my conduct." The committee recommended to the Supreme Court that Craig's license to practice law be revoked for a period of two years. That same summer, Moore's name again hit the front pages when he filed a motion from prison to withdraw his guilty plea, saying that his decision to plead guilty had been made "with great haste and without benefit of having time to reflect." The motion went all the way to the U.S. Supreme Court, where it was rejected.

Moore was later transferred to a correctional center in Kentucky where he remained until his release in May of 1993 after serving two years and eight months of his nearly six-year sentence. He was allowed to return to his home in Glen Dale to spend 120 days under home confinement before becoming a free man.

West Virginia voters can be loyal to a fault. In a 1990 poll taken after he had admitted his guilt to various crimes, former Governor Moore received a higher popularity rating than sitting Governor Caperton. Typical of public sentiment following Moore's release from prison were the remarks of Glen Dale Mayor David Kuth. Speaking of Moore's years in public office, Kuth said, "I think everybody felt Arch Moore did good for his state and the Northern Panhandle . . . There's a lot of people who would vote for him today. I've heard it more in the last two weeks since he's been home."

Shortly after being appointed executive director of Caperton's new Ethics Commission, attorney-businessman Richard Alker, of Clarksburg, took a few minutes to talk with a newspaper reporter. As spokesman for the new standards in government, Alker discussed office arrangements for the commission and the members of the media. There would be "uncomfortable chairs [provided] for the press," he observed.

Having met and worked with Alker some years before when he served as law clerk to Judge Robert E. Maxwell, I could only believe that his remark about press seating was made in jest. But it had a serious ring nonetheless, echoing as it did the sentiments of many others at the highest levels of government toward the press.

When Moore's guilty plea and subsequent revelations about his wrongdoings made headlines around the state, the media also came in for its share of blame. Had the press been more vigorous in its coverage, the criticism went, thievery in the Statehouse could have been brought under control a long time ago. But as few readers—and most politicians—realize, there are a number of factors governing newspaper publishing in general and investigative writing in particular which conspire to limit coverage. Some newspapers feel their responsibility goes no further than "police beat" reporting and "tea time" coverage, with a generous offering of sports and comics thrown in. That is their privilege under the First Amendment to the Constitution. Other papers have the desire to take on a broader mandate but lack the financial resources needed to enter the fray. They simply cannot afford to pay the frightfully high costs of retaining attorneys with the necessary expertise in newspaper law, or to endanger the future of their newspapers with the threat of a large libel award by a jury that believes all newspapers have deep pockets.

Most of the investigative reporting in West Virginia during the second half of the twentieth century was done by the newspapers in Charleston, the seat of state government. Those papers were well established, financially secure, and able to absorb the cost of the reportorial staffs—and potential litigation—

needed for such a mission. It was a mission they regarded as their journalistic responsibility, a civic and moral obligation, as Knight expressed to me when he first approached me about going to work for him at the *Gazette*.

"There's a lot of mischief going on up there at the Statehouse," Knight said. "We're not keeping an eye on it like we should, and I need somebody who will dig it out the way you've been doing in Beckley. How about joining us as Hoffmann's and my associate?"

Needless to say, I accepted Knight's offer, convinced that if I was ever to have the chance to practice the sort of journalism I had dreamed about for years, I had to start while I was still young enough to handle the rigors of an investigative writing assignment. And it is without a doubt a rigorous job, taking unexpected tolls on a reporter and leading to disillusionment, disappointment, and the growth of personal cynicism. The greed and corruption among politicians, the sheer pettiness and predictability, are enough to weary even the most dedicated journalist.

The cavalier attitude of our public servants toward the principles of integrity and responsibility was expressed by the complaints of various legislators in the fall of 1991. Members of the legislature claimed that the ethics law they had passed two years earlier was too rigid. They were being denied, the legislators grumbled, the opportunity to accept hotel bonus points in Charleston, choice tickets to university football games, white-water rafting trips, and similar freebies. Being denied any honoraria totaling more than twenty dollars, as permitted by law, they argued, put them at a disadvantage in administering the affairs of office.

Certain questionable perks continued unabated, however. More than a few legislators continued to have the Senate and House clerks fix parking tickets for them. Officials in the executive as well as legislative branch were accepting the loan of paintings and artwork from the Division of Culture and History for display in their offices and then allowing the art to mysteriously "disappear."

Slack management practices became such a concern to Caperton that he sent a letter to Lee Feinberg, chairman of the State Ethics Commission, calling for a tightening of the ethics law by encouraging employees to come forward when they had valid complaints against their superiors.

"I am particularly disturbed," Caperton wrote to Feinberg, "at the perception that a state employee who files an ethics complaint against a superior can be subjected to retribution, including dismissal."

Although the governor did not go into detail, it was believed that he was making reference to a West Virginia Parkways worker who had been fired after complaining that his boss had used government cars for personal jaunts. Caperton had ordered an investigation into reports that top officials with the Parkways Authority were using public vehicles for hunting trips and other outings.

"I will . . . take decisive action against any state manager," Caperton warned, "who is shown to have fired or otherwise taken any action against an employee for the filing . . . of an ethics complaint."

The investigation by Caperton led to the resignation of the head of the Parkways Authority and the reinstatement of the whistle-blower.

Ethics, as the evidence shows, is a popular subject for advocacy along the campaign trail and in legislative chambers, but as an actual working philosophy, it finds few friends in the corridors and backrooms of the Capitol.

"THE PRINTING-PRESS," SAID J. M. BARRIE, "is either the greatest blessing or the greatest curse of modern times."

While it has roots in English common law, the power of the press and its protection under the law is a uniquely American institution. Few of us give more than passing thought to the fact that our press and judiciary both occupy singular positions in the American system, both deliberately set apart and specifically addressed by the U.S. Constitution. Neither has the power to legislate or execute. Neither has an army or a constabulary to enforce its editorial opinions or courtroom judgments. But these fragile creations are a civilizing force with power and prestige accorded them by this nation's rule of law. Both are intended to act as a check on the abuse of power by those in positions of authority. The judiciary is constitutionally established as a separate branch of government. The press, enshrined as independent of all other parts of our system by the First Amendment, is the only institution specifically and permanently protected under the Constitution.

Ideally, the press, through the responsible exercise of its freedom, is expected to expose and condemn violations of law. Ideally, the courts, through the responsible and unhampered conduct of their business, are expected to promote justice. This is their function.

All things considered, the courts are the agencies by which freedom is protected. "The history of liberty," wrote U.S. Supreme Court Justice William O. Douglas, "is the history of due process."

The press, on the other hand, is the chief instrument for informing the governed about the activities of the governors. Its mandate is, in the words of H. L. Mencken, to "comfort the afflicted and afflict the comfortable."

And the responsibility of the press to afflict the comfortable never ends. The press was intended by the Founding Fathers to serve as part of the established system of checks and balances that help to protect and preserve our form of government. The sentiment voiced by Irish patriot John Philpot Curran is as applicable today as it was two centuries ago: "The condition upon which God hath given liberty to man is eternal vigilance."

And vigilance is the first duty of the press.

Afterword

"Oʜ, Dᴀᴅᴅʏ, what's going to happen to West Virginia now?" Margo asked, a heavy note of sadness in her voice.

W. E. "Ned" Chilton, publisher of *The Charleston Gazette*, had just died of a heart attack as he walked off a squash-ball court in Washington, DC.

Many tributes were heaped on Chilton after his sudden death at the age of sixty-five, but nothing quite summed up his goodness and decency, his unwavering commitment to the state that he loved, as much as this question from a young woman who had been a keen observer of journalism and politics from a unique perspective since early childhood.

Chilton was the last of a special breed of journalistic gadflies, muckrakers, and idealists. His passionate crusading for civil rights, his unrelenting war against dishonesty and conflict of interest in government, and his unflagging promotion of community support for the unfortunate made him valuable beyond measure to his state.

I was privileged to be associated with Chilton. I was also privileged to be associated with several other men of similar ilk during my career in newspapering. These men walked a perilous and lonely path every day of their professional lives, giving their best to a stressful and demanding profession.

Raiford Watkins, Associated Press bureau chief in West Virginia and editor of *The Raleigh Register*, died at the age of thirty-seven of a heart attack.

Frank A. Knight, editor of the *Gazette*, died at forty-eight of a cerebral hemorrhage.

Charlie Hodel, publisher of the *Register* and president of Beckley Newspaper Corporation, lived to the ripe old age of eighty-four but spent the last decade of his life in a coma following a massive stroke.

Harry G. Hoffmann, successor to Knight as *Gazette* editor, died—like Chilton—at sixty-five from a heart attack. Hoffmann did it with style. He slumped over his typewriter and went to the Great Beyond while writing a political column.

But as the poet admonished, they did not go gentle into that good night. They were all tough but honorable men, all crusaders, all fighters for causes. But in their efforts to expose the thievery, corruption, greed, and hypocrisy around them they took on a profound burden. Newspapering is a harsh task-master and exacts a heavy toll.

When I think of these five men, with whom I was associated both person-ally and professionally for so many years, and of their efforts to make their state a better place for their own and future generations, I am reminded of the words of Etienne de Grellet:

> *I expect to pass this way but once;*
> *and any good therefore that I can do,*
> *or any kindness that I can show to any fellow creature,*
> *let me do it now.*
> *Let me not defer or neglect it,*
> *for I shall not pass this way again.*

Index